TWO SISTERS

TWO SISTERS

A Journey of Survival Through Auschwitz

LIVIA SZABO KRANCBERG

LIBRARY of the HOLOCAUST
Washington, D.C.

Printed in the United States of America
ISBN: 978-1882326-12-9
Library of Congress Control Number: 2015946013

Library of the Holocaust Foundation
PO Box 1651
Silver Spring, Maryland 20915
202-241-1538
www.LibraryoftheHolocaust.org

To Shelly, Beth and Amy Rose

ACKNOWLEDGEMENTS

My daughters, Shelly Lewis and Beth Krancberg encouraged me to write my memoirs. Shelly brought out the playwright in me and Beth put me in touch with my life-calling. Yes, my life-calling. She suggested that I impart my experiences in the concentration camps with students of various schools: middle schools, high schools, colleges and universities.

My granddaughter Amy Rose is my pride and joy and my future.

I want to acknowledge my sister Toby Fogel as well as my nieces, Susan Szabo, Barbara Reisner, Marty Crane, Maxine Guthearts, Gail Weiss and my nephews, Julius Kahn, Michael Kahn, Howard Szabo, Ron Szabo and Sandy Szabo.

I am thrilled to now have Jay Silver as a member of my family.

Josie LaFrancis and her entire family are the most kind-hearted people. They made a commitment to raise the money to make my memoir a reality. If we'd have more of their kind, it would be a beautiful world to live in.

Josie's daughter, Maddie LaFrancis might be young but she's already ten feet tall in my eyes. She has reached humanity at its core.

I want to thank Florence Heinze for her early editing. Doug Hefflin, a teacher of Modern World History at La Costa

Canyon High School in Carlsbad, California took care of my endless computer glitches and arranged my annual speaking engagements at his school. Maggie Reilly from Wangenheim Middle School, Emily Jimimez from Rancho Del Ray Middle School, Angela Smith from Santana High School and the school administration of Olympian High School also arranged numerous assemblies of hundreds of students. I spoke about my sister Rose and my experiences in Auschwitz, Ravensbruck and Neustadt-Gleve Concentration Camps. I never failed to talk about hate, diversity and compassion as well.

If I could name one person, indispensable to the completion of my book, that would be Iris Clauss. Who else but a friend like her would tolerate my endless needs for her help.

I have written four plays, three of which were produced and staged at the Community Actors Theater in San Diego, California. They are, "Rendezvous with Fate," "A Match Made in Heaven," and "The Pact." Floyd Alexander, my friend and colleague introduced me to the talented and inspiring director, Jennie Hamilton. My fourth play, "We Should Not Accept That Children Are Still Hungry" is looking for a home.

I want to tell Peter and Andrea Newman how much I cherish their friendship and acknowledge Bret Card and Lou Rose as true friends for years and years. I continue to admire and respect my ninety-six-year old friend Beatrice Heller for her alertness, excellent memory and sharp mind.

Jewish Family Service in San Diego answered our first cries for help as my husband and I moved from Passaic, New Jersey to San Diego in 1997. They put us on the "S.O.S. Program" for Holocaust survivors. As recipients of this program, we were independent; we stayed in our own apartment; and we lived the present to our fullest. I want to thank Hedy Dalin, Director of Care Management and Lori Panzer, S.O.S. Care Manager. They have not forsaken me to this day.

There couldn't have been chosen a more qualified person

than Mary Fawell for the position of Director of Leichtag Family Assisted Living Residence at Seacrest Village Encinitas California, a "one of a kind" retirement establishment where I now reside. She's "everyone and everything."

About Rabbi Patti. I don't read or understand Hebrew, but the way Rabbi Patti enunciates the words from the Prayer Book on Sabbath in our Synagogue, I get the full picture. And when we gather in groups with Rabbi Patti in the lead, I swallow her every word of wisdom.

I want to thank Jeremy Kay, Executive Director of the Library of the Holocaust, for publishing my memoir so that as many people as possible can read my story.

When my late husband, Sigmund Krancberg published his book, *A Soviet Postmortem*, I said to myself, why not write a companion book to my husband's brilliant work? My head began filling up with voices, one outsmarting the other.

"She cannot write a companion book, she's not a Sovietologist like her husband is."

"Yes, yes" chimed in another voice "Hey, who says she has to be a Sovietologist, she could write her life story as long as her memory still serves her." And my life story it is.

A HOPEFUL WORLD

To be born into an era of hopeful world harmony only to become a victim twenty-five years later of the mass annihilation of European Jews by Adolph Hitler is the tragic irony of my life. However, because of my brave and strong sister Rose, I am here today to tell my story.

I was born October 13, 1919, the same year that the Paris Peace Conference, The Treaty of Versailles and the League of Nations marked the end of World War I. An international policy of maintaining world peace was shaped that intended to prevent the horrors of another grand scale world war from ever happening again. World War I was supposed to be "The War to End All Wars." The year 1919 was also the year that the German Workers' Party was founded and a young unknown corporal in the German army named Adolph Hitler became a member. This short-lived group eventually dissolved only to resurface again as the National Socialists, or Nazi party of Germany.

Everyone has stories to tell. Some tragic, some happy, some outstanding, some serious, some even silly. Here are *my* stories, shuffled like a deck of cards, and dealt out onto the magic table called the mind.

When people meet for the first time, they usually offer their names. So I'll begin by giving you some of mine. *Libelah* (a diminutive of *Libe*), *Libushka* (a diminutive of *Libush), Lillika* (a diminutive of *Lilly*), *Livi* (a diminutive of *Livia*). When I lived in New Jersey, a librarian friend named me "ChapStick!" The first time we met, I wasn't wearing my colored chap stick. I had gray hair and ghastly looking lips. As my husband introduced me to her, I covered my mouth with my hands. From then on, whenever she saw my husband, she'd say, "Give my regards to ChapStick." Sometimes, having *so* many names is a burden. Just call me Livia!

My Native Village Petrova

I'm almost half a world and nearly a century away from Petrova, but I've never felt closer. Petrova will always occupy the biggest space in my heart's geography. I was born among seven other children; my sisters Molly, Rose and Toby, and brothers Vigdor, Yosef, Chayim and Yitzchak. There were three others, but they died in infancy, We were raised by parents who loved us with everything they were, had and knew.

Petrova borders four villages. To the north, it borders Bistra. To the south, it borders Leordina. To the east, it borders Ruscova, and to the west, it borders Crasna, which is separated from Petrova by the river, Raul Viseu.

Petrova is part of Maramures County, Romania. It sits on a plateau, surrounded by mile after mile of corn, wheat, pumpkin, and potato fields. Golden and green during the spring and summer, these fields lie neglected and barren during the late fall and winter. Beyond the petticoat lace of the fields are stretches of lush, green pasture where cows, goats and geese graze, nibble and scramble.

We had 600 inhabitants in Petrova of which 250 were Jews. Our main street never ended. To the north, it led to Bistra. To the south, it went all the way to Leordina. The rich Jews' homes with gardens, orchards and stores faced the main street, a symbol of status. Side alleys off the main street were where the poor people lived. Rich peasants and their properties also faced the main street. The Orthodox Church, the post office, the village pharmacy, the synagogue, the rabbi's house, the mikveh, the Jewish ritual bath, the registry office, (the *primcria*), the elementary school, and the train station made the neighborhood complete. Petrova was divided by a shallow creek with such clear water you could almost count every pebble lying on the bottom of it. All the way from Leordina to the south and the creek to the north, we had a mixed neighborhood where Jews and rich peasants lived side-by-side. The Orthodox Church, the post office and the village pharmacy made the neighborhood complete.

The center of Petrova stretched from the creek to the north. It contained stores, the store owner's homes, the synagogue, the rabbi's house and the *mikveh,* the Jewish ritual bath. Toward the edge of that center sat another mixed neighborhood with its special features: the registry office (the *primaria*), the elementary school, and the train station.

Nearly all of the adult Jews in Petrova were deeply religious, going to the synagogue every morning and every evening as well as on Sabbath and holidays. The older men, including my father, would return to the synagogue immediately after supper. Some wanted to listen to the Talmudists' (students of the Torah) debates; others tried to pit their own knowledge against these scholars.

The Jewish community of Petrova took good care of its poor. It had a *Chevra Kadisha,* a Jewish burial society that paid the burial expenses for the poor. It also had *Hochnuset Kalah,* a charitable organization that provided dowries and wedding expenses for orphans, poor brides and poor grooms. Lastly, the community funded Talmud Torah, a parochial school that served the orphans and the children of the poor free of charge. During the winter, when there was knee-deep snow and the poor children had no warm clothes or transportation, the community would hire "Strong Men" who would go to the poor people's homes and put the school-age children on their back, cover them with blankets, and deliver them to school. And when school was over, bring them back home.

My Paternal Grandfather Moishe and Grandmother Yita

My paternal grandparents lived in a spacious five-room house just down the street from us. Three of their rooms overlooked the street, while the other two offered a pleasant view of their vegetable garden as well as their neighbor's magnificent estate. Alongside the rooms facing the street there were two sets of stairs with big, heavy wooden steps.

Grandfather Moishe dealt in cattle for slaughter. He was a handsome, corpulent man who wore a long, white beard below his healthy-looking pink cheeks. I was about six when I saw my grandfather sitting on the front wooden steps, warming his swollen feet in the sun. When he rolled his pants to his knees, his legs looked almost like two bluish-grayish barrels. I began praying, "God is good, God is great. Please God make my grandfather's feet look like my brother Vigdor's feet, nice and strong, Amen." When Grandfather asked me what I was mumbling, I said, "I asked God to make your feet look like my brother Vigdor's feet." He stroked my cheeks and I was in seventh heaven! Grandma Yita was a slender, petite, rosy-cheeked woman. She was ten years older than Grandfather Moishe. Rumor had it he was her second husband.

In my memory, it's always a warm summer afternoon and Grandma Yita is sitting alone in the shade across the street from her house. She always looked alone, so, so alone! One day, as I kept her company, she said, "I hear you are the smartest kid in your school." I lowered my head. "I'm very proud of you," she continued.

"I wish I were pretty instead of smart!" I burst out.

"But you *are* pretty," Grandma Yita assured me.

"Yeah? Then why was I given the part of a witch in the school play?" I resentfully said.

Grandma caressed my face. "You see, dear . . . they gave the part to you because it was a hard part to memorize; they thought you could do it," she said.

Well, I did not see what Grandma Yita saw. I saw school children pointing fingers at me saying, "Here goes the witch!" And so I declined the part. Suddenly, Grandma Yita became restless. "What's the matter, Grandma?" I asked. She gave me no answer. I looked around and saw Aunt Golda staring at us.

My grandparents were prisoners in their own home. Long before I was born, they had transferred their house, their properties, and all they owned to their youngest son, Shmuel, his wife, Golda and their son Fishel. Now my grandparents lived in a corner of their own kitchen. They had side-by-side twin beds with just enough space between them to get in and out of bed. My family stopped speaking with Golda and her family because of the way she treated my grandparents.

When I wanted to see my grandparents in their home, Aunt Golda would say, "They're sleeping now; try next time." When I tried next time, she'd say, "They're resting now; they're about to fall asleep." I was convinced that my grandparents were afraid of Golda.

I would have given anything if I could have reached back in time to convince my grandparents not to transfer everything they had to Uncle Shmuel and Aunt Golda. If only they hadn't done that, I could have gone to their home whenever they felt like having company. I could have followed their daily activities. I could have looked forward to a hug or even a peck on my cheek. I could have sat at their table and cupped my face in my hands as my eyes followed Grandma's every move. My parents might have celebrated holidays together or some Sabbaths together, talking freely, learning from their wisdom. I might even have gotten in their way, earning a welcome reprimand.

After World War II, I learned that Mother, Father and my siblings also lived with my grandparents Moishe and Yita at the time that their youngest son Shmuel, his wife Golda and their son Fishel lived there.

At some point, Golda charmed the old people to transfer their entire fortune to her husband, herself and her son. What about my father, their oldest son and his family? my grandparents took care of him as well. They purchased for him some property from a peasant. On the property there were two buildings. A small building facing the street consisted of two rooms. A giant building in the deep of the backyard consisted of 5 unfinished rooms. In the small building the peasant presumably housed his family of eleven children and his numerous icons. We never found out what the peasant housed in the giant building with the 5 unfinished rooms.

My Maternal Grandparents Mechel and Batya

I never met my maternal grandparents. We had no financial means to travel to Szasz Regen to visit them. Grandfather Mechel was a well-known lumber businessman who lived with his wife Batya and his family in Slatinsky Doly, Czechoslovakia. When he retired, he and his wife moved to Szasz Regen, a town in Transylvania. Most of his adult children followed him.

Father

I loved my father. To me he was a long-bearded, red lipped giant, although he was of medium build. When I was very young, my father's skullcap fascinated me. Every time he took his fedora off, I'd expect to see his skullcap slipping down the back of his head, or maybe slipping halfway down his forehead the way other men's skullcaps scooted around. No, my father's skullcap was abidingly in the middle of his head as if it were stuck in place. Even more captivating to me than his skullcap was his Sabbath attire. He wore a black silk caftan with a fringed rope belt around his waist.

On his head sat a streimel which looked like a soft, flat pillbox hat with beaver tails sewn on all around the base of the hat. In a brisk wind, the beaver tails separated, spinning like a pinwheel.

My father was a businessman dealing in precious fur rawhide. He would buy fox, mink and rabbit skins directly from the trappers in Crasna and then sell the skins to my Great-Uncle Gershon Schwartz, a well-to-do wholesaler in Sighet, a town two hours away by train from Petrova. Father seldom returned from Sighet without a gift for my mother, his beloved wife, Rochelah.

The fur business was seasonal, winter only. The rest of the year, Father negotiated grain and lumber deals, earning a commission. From time to time, he'd get together with other dealers. Together, they would lease a three mile stretch of orchards with plums, pears and apples from an absentee landowner. In the late fall, special workers would remove the fruit from the trees one by one—bruised fruit was not accepted. The fruit was then loaded into transport cars. Trains with fruit-loaded cars were then shipped all over the country and sold for profit.

Father was easygoing with his daughters, calling us *Lamelah,* "Little Lamb." Maybe addressing each daughter by the same pet name was easier than trying to remember which daughter he might be speaking to.

He was strict with his sons and often scolded them, "Why don't I ever rip *my* pants? Show me a rip in *my* pants! Just look!" he'd point to each part of his pants.

At those times, I felt like saying, "That's not fair, Father! Your pants aren't ripped because you don't climb trees or fences like your sons do." But Father was so imposing, that no smart word left my mouth. Sometimes he'd punish the boys with a curfew or even a two-finger tap on their forehead. The root cause of these curfews and finger tapping was always the same.

One of my brothers would become defiant, saying, "No way! I will not stand like a dummy when a peasant punk calls me a

'Christ killer' or a 'dirty Jew!' I know the other Jewish boys pretend nothing's happening. They're scared, I'm not!"

Once I asked Father how he'd feel if someone ran after him, calling him a *"dirty Jew!"*

"Lamelah," he said, "In my youth, the peasants my age treated me the exact same way their children are treating your brothers. But I pretended they were talking to the wind, hoping that someday they would stop."

"But Father!" I said, "It's been thirty years since you were a boy! They haven't stopped."

"They've stopped, alright."

"Then why are your sons getting in trouble, if they've stopped the name-calling?"

"Lamelah, the peasants my age have stopped. Don't you see?"

"So? It's okay for the older peasants to teach their sons contempt for the Jews, as long as they, themselves, aren't acting-out what they're teaching?"

"If both the old and the young acted out their hatred of the Jews, would we be here? It will stop some day, Lamelah. The peasants need us. We hire them to do certain jobs; we give them business, and we sell to them on credit when they ask for it. What would they do without us?"

Livia's Parents: Betzalel and Rochel

"Father? Just last Easter the young, hate-filled peasants broke our windows on their way out from church while we hid in the orchard."

"Lamelah! Believe me, some day this nonsense will stop."

"You call this nonsense?"

"What else is it?"

When his son, Chayim, my older brother, was beaten to a pulp on the school premises because he told his school mates that Jesus was a Jew, Father said, "Lamelah, Chayim will get better and the hatred will stop some day."

My father wanted to believe that humans were inherently humane and civilized toward each other and that this way of life would someday prevail. He could not have foreseen the catastrophe that would befall the Jews of Europe fifteen years later, and the annihilation of six million innocent Jews, including his beloved wife, Rochelah, his son Chayim and his grandson Shullie.

The Sabbath Queen: Mother

At the age of five and six I was obsessed with Mother's lighting of the Sabbath candles. Every Friday, just before sunset, I'd stop whatever I was doing and ask my sister Rose, seven-years my senior, to wash me and dress me into something festive. Then I'd tiptoe into a corner in the all-purpose room, waiting for Mother to light the Sabbath candles.

The ceremony entranced me. Mother was always dressed in her finest, with a beautiful silk scarf tied under her chin. My eyes followed every motion she made. She'd swing her hands over the lighted candles three times, move them to her eyes and then intone the blessing in a soft, almost hypnotic murmur.

During her prayer I'd cover my own eyes, imitating her. Everyday reality stopped and otherworldly magic reigned. Mother became a fairy tale queen, shining and glittering as only a five-year-old child could imagine her. Now the otherworldly queen was blessing the Sabbath candles, her dainty, jewel-laden fingers moving in an alluring breast stroke over the candles. She was ready to cover her eyes when, in my imagination, the flames began dancing as if at her command. They'd be whipped high one instant, the next moment, they'd shrink and quiver like stars twinkling in a clear night sky.

Just as I supposed I'd never have to wake up from my trance, I'd hear Mother whispering, "I'm waiting!" When I opened my eyes, the enchanting scene had disappeared, but my mother's hands were reaching out for me. I ran toward her. She lifted me in her arms, kissing my cheeks saying, "Gut Shabbos!" (Good Sabbath!)

One Friday, as Mother kissed me after lighting the Sabbath candles, I saw her eyes were filled with tears. I felt troubled so I went to look for Rose. I found her in the girl's bedroom getting ready for the Sabbath. I began rushing toward her, my arms open. I wanted to embrace her, lean on her, tell her about my concerns for mother, but I could not go through with such demonstration and stopped. From an early age, I would not hug or kiss my sister. This kind of display of affection I reserved for Mother solely.

Rose asked me to explain my behavior. "I only hug Mother and you're not Mother!" I said defiantly, as if she was trying to force me to embrace her. Rose lifted me, put me in her lap and asked me what it was that upset me. I told her I saw Mother crying at the lighting of the Sabbath candles.

She hesitated for a moment then said, "Mother isn't feeling well, she must've asked God for a cure."

"Will Mother die?" I said, scared out of my wits. "I don't want her to die! My friend, Elie, said that people can give years to each other. I want to give lots of my years to Mother, please, please, Rose!"

Next I heard, "Your friend is wrong. People cannot give years to one another. Besides, Mother has no need for your years. She will live to be 120."

"Is 120 a lot? I want her to live a lot, a lot!"

"Yes, 120 is a very good number."

I still insisted I wanted to help Mother.

Rose looked at me. Then as if something entered her mind she said,"You could help Mother! You could stop telling your problems to her. Some of them might aggravate her, and aggravation is bad for her condition."

"How could I guess what would aggravate Mother?" I gave Rose an inquisitive look.

"I'll tell you what. For now, you come with your problems to me. I'll sort them out. Some day, when you'll have it all figured out, you'll take your problems directly to Mother."

I sighed in relief. I draped my hands around my sister's neck and rested my head on her chest. I stayed like that for a long time. While resting on her chest, Rose explained to me, the best way she could, about mind boggling things. About siblings' love for one another, about children's love for their parents and about love among strangers. I even found out that Mother and Father kissed! From that day on Rose and I became inseparable. That day I began the very long journey from emotional childhood to emotional maturity

The Village Jokester

If anything was in abundance in our family, it was all sorts of food. Still, I was physically underdeveloped. I was scrawny and barely noticeable. My frailty drew the attention of our village jokester. He'd make fun of me on a regular basis. He'd threaten to put me in his pocket, or thread me through a needle, or use his magic wand and make me disappear if I didn't fatten up. The jokester started a chain reaction. Mean-spirited children began to tease me as well. They went as far as telling me that my parents bought me from the Gypsies.

I was six-years-old and still made a stop-over with my problems and questions to Rose. Then the unexpected happened: Rose gave me permission to go with my troubles to Mother. I sheepishly approached my mother and told her about the village jokester, the way he made fun of me. She lifted me and put me in her lap.

Just as I hoped I'd never have to get off of her lap, I heard, "Listen, my dear, you might be small and scrawny, but your mind makes up for it. You have more up here (she'd point to my head) than all the people who are teasing you put together!" In time, the idea that I was smarter than lots of people put together took root. As soon as I started school, I began pushing my mind and have never stopped since.

Mother, the Mikveh and I

A ritual *mikveh* is a pool connected to a body of natural water, like a spring or river. Although it can be used by men, it is primarily used by a woman, who is considered ritually impure during her menstrual period as well as seven days following it. She may not resume sexual relations with her husband until she has immersed herself in a mikveh. As a result, ritual mikvehs are always part of public bathing facilities. If you've never seen a mikveh, I'll take you with me to the one in my village, Petrova.

It was the day before *Shavuot,* a spring holiday. I was around seven-years-old. The sun was slanting off toward the west and the air felt a little brisk. I hop-scotched alongside my mother who was on her way to the mikveh. Mother bought a ticket near the entrance door of the mikveh. She then opened the door and we entered into a small undressing room. There were wooden benches all along the walls and the floor was concrete. Mother put her big bag with things on a corner bench just as the bath-house door opened. Two towel-wrapped women entered, trailing clouds of steam after them. Right then the outside door opened. Three women stepped into the room followed by a whirlpool of cool air. "Please! Shut the door already! I'm in a hurry. I got to get dressed," moaned a towel-wrapped woman. One of the newcomers closed the door, turned around and noticed me. "Rochel, I left my daughter Suralah at home; she's such a pain when I bring her with me," she addressed Mother.

I directed my attention to the towel-wrapped women who had just entered from the bathhouse. I couldn't stop starring at them. I expected their towels to come off any minute and feast my eyes! I never saw my mother or my sister Rose or any other woman naked.

"Rochel, watch your daughter!" cried out one of the toweled women. Mother looked at me and said, "Libelah, turn toward me; I need to get you ready for your bath." By the time I faced Mother, she was already undressed and wrapped in a towel. Missed my chance! She placed herself in front of me, shielding the women from my curious stare.

The next room we entered appeared so gigantic that I couldn't see the walls. The higher level windows were steamed up and seemed to be floating far above us. A short, heavy woman who stood at the door signaled us to stop. Three middle-aged women with a ballet-like grace emptied their buckets of hot water onto the concrete floor to keep it warm. Great clouds of steam rose toward the almost invisible ceiling, merging with the steam waiting for company. I was mesmerized by the scene when Mother's voice broke my trance, "Let's go!" She took my hand in hers.

As I followed Mother across the warm, wet floor, I asked where all the water was going.

"In there," she pointed to a drain snaking the room's perimeter. On the other side of the drain, a row of wooden tubs reached as far as I could see. A strong male peasant operated both a hot and a cold water pump.

"Look Mother; a man works at the pumps!"

"We need a strong person to operate the pumps. Besides, he's blind."

"How can a blind person see?"

"He works with his touch." Later, I realized he actually wasn't blind. Before I could open my mouth to put forth another question,

I got deafened by the shouts of some attendants. "Ivan, I need warm water! Quick! I need cold water! No, no! Ivan! I asked for warm water!" I pitied the man. I thought these women purposely tried to mix him up or keep his eyes on the pumps.

A tall, lean woman named Rifka approached us. "Did you make your choice Rochel?" Mother pointed at a tub and asked her to get it ready for us. She opened her tiny evening bag and dropped something into Rifka's pocket. The evening bag looked familiar. It had arrived in one of the packages my oldest sister Molly sent us from America. Since no one ever took a handbag to the synagogue on Sabbath or dressed up for the evening, Mother used her little evening bag to carry coins to the mikveh.

"Mother, I saw you giving something to Rifka, was it your ticket?"

"No. It was a tip. She's going to wash my back, cut my nails and help me wash you." I began crying. "If *you* don't wash me, no one else will!"

To stop people's stare—I was the only child there—Mother said, "Come, come, I'll wash you myself!" I stopped crying. Mother removed the towel from around me, put it on the tub's headboard and lowered me into the tub. She bent down, washed my hair with saddle soap and the rest of me with a sweet-smelling soap. She then took a small towel, folded it and put it on the bottom of the tub for me to kneel on. "Turn around, please." I did. Surprisingly, I liked my new place. The water level reached my chest, and best of all, I could watch the room in front of me with all the ongoing activities.

While busy watching the traffic in the room, Mother snuck into the tub behind me. The water suddenly rose to my neck. "I'm drowning!" I screamed. Just then, I heard a splash. Mother stood up. Miraculously, the water level fell to my chest "May I face you?" I asked Mother. "Not yet. I have to wash myself, first."

After a short while and some water-pouring noises, Mother said

I could turn around. She was immersed in water to her shoulders, her hands covering her breasts.

Disappointed, I began with questions. "Why was the water having tantrums? Why did it go from my chest to my neck, back to my chest, down to my waist, and then, back to my chest when you got into the tub?"

A long explanation followed. "When I immersed myself into the tub, the water level went up to your neck. You screamed, so I stood up. The water level then went back to your chest, just where it had been. But I didn't come here to stand in the tub. So I asked Rifka to take a few pails of water away from the inside of the tub. When she did so, the water level went down to your waist. As I set down in the tub, the water level was back to your chest."

Looking back, Mother had explained to me Archimedes' Law: "The proportion of the liquid displaced equals that of the matter submerged."

Rifka must have been keeping an eye on us, for as soon as Mother finished talking to me, she was right beside us with a small penknife. "Rifka will cut my fingernails and toenails," said Mother, "she's had a lot of practice."

I might have screamed had I not remembered seeing my father cutting his nails with a penknife. Rose had always cut *my* nails with small scissors. Nevertheless, I closed my eyes. When I opened them again, Rifka was holding two buckets of water. "Mother, why more water?" I asked.

"To rinse the soap off of my body. Please turn around."

"Mother? Can't I see the rinsing? Please!"

"No, Dear." After a minute or so, I heard Mother's voice again. "It's now time for your rinsing. Please stand up and don't turn around." I wasn't pleased, but I stood up. She began pouring warm water over my shoulders from a bucket. I liked the feeling of the water running down my body. When I asked for more rinsing, Mother said, "Maybe next time. Rifka has to help me immerse myself into the mikveh."

"Aren't we in the mikveh right now?"

"No. For some reason, people call the whole building 'the mikveh'. But the real mikveh is there." Mother pointed to a solidly built wooden cubical in the center of the room. "That wooden enclosure protects a small, deep, concrete finished pool of water. This time of the month, I have to immerse myself in that water."

"How do you get in there?"

"There's an opening on one side."

Wrapped in towels we headed toward the real mikveh. I stood at the entrance while Mother and Rifka walked down the steps. Just then, someone shouted, "Rifka! Rifka! Come quick!"

Rifka ran up the staircase, giving Mother's towel to me to hold and disappeared. When Mother returned from her immersion to the platform, she must have been surprised to see Rifka was gone. She began walking up the stairs just as Rifka returned and ran down them, grabbing the towel out of my hands. Not knowing who was pulling the towel, I kept holding on to it and got myself dragged down some of the steps right into my mother's naked arms. I saw my mother naked after all.

I went with Mother to the bathhouse almost every week. We enjoyed talking with each other as we scrubbed ourselves clean. I would tell Mother what I learned in school and how much I admired my teachers.

When I was twelve and ready to go away to high school in Sighet, Mother began ordering separate tubs for each of us, explaining I'd have to get used to bathing alone. In my memories, those bathhouse visits were indescribably beautiful and precious.

Rose

As I'm walking down the long, bumpy road that's been my life, I see *this* place *that* place, *anothe*r place. Yet my mind keeps turning to my childhood home in Petrova, the place Rose and I bonded emotionally from the time I was six-years-old.

Rose was beautiful in every way someone could be beautiful.

Her physical beauty matched that of her inner beauty. Her complexion was ivory; her eyes shone deep amber brown; her hair reflected light of warm chestnut browns. Her features were well proportioned, her nose was small and her teeth were perfect pearls.

Rose was completely devoted to Mother who suffered from an under active thyroid condition. She helped her raise our large family. From an early age, I realized Rose was interested in learning—she barely made three grades. I shared everything I learned in elementary school with her but I never gave her homework. This practice became the basis of my tutoring skills in high school.

I am still alive. Rose died in Jerusalem in 1984. I spent many, many sleepless nights trying to convince myself Rose was dead. I tried to heal the open wound her death caused, but my sliced-up-flesh would neither heal nor shrink. So I took refuge in memories.

Rose Takes Me to the Water Mill in Crasna

Our neighboring village, Crasna, a mountain-hidden village, was home to about 300 Ukrainian speaking trappers and shepherds. To get to the their homes and their grazing lands, you had to walk in the narrow, winding and treacherous roads between the mountains. You never knew when a loose rock might cripple you or a mudslide might bury you alive. The mountains poking their rugged heads right into the sky fascinated me. The Pop Ivan's tallest peak was covered with snow all year round and towered over the rest of them.

I remember my first trip to Crasna on a midsummer's day. Our family had just finished lunch and my brothers, Yitzchak and Chayim had quietly disappeared through the door. I was expecting to join my friends in our backyard when Rose said, "Libelah, I'll take you to the water mill in Crasna."

Rose, only fifteen-years old, hoisted a burlap bag of corn kernels to her shoulder and took my left hand into hers. We walked through the orchard behind our home and some fields I'd never seen before. After about fifteen minutes of trotting in these fields, Rose and I reached the bridge that connected Petrova to Crasna.

On the other side of the bridge, Rose pointed to a white-painted, red-roofed mansion, "The Perl girls live there," she said. I was surprised and excited. These mysterious three sisters were very pretty women in their late twenties who dressed as if they were sophisticated city women. Whenever they'd come to Petrova, they'd parade all along Main Street. I thought they wanted people to admire them and maybe envy them. I, at all times, was wondering what it would take me to be as pretty as they were when I grew up. Maybe if I learned to paint my face just like they did?

To the right of the bridge, there was a raised area with rectangular stone slabs standing at regular intervals. "What's that?" I pointed to the flat rocks.

"The Jewish Cemetery."

"And what's that over there?"

"The mill."

I saw what looked like a two-room cottage built next to a waterfall pouring itself over a giant wheel. We were very close to the hut. The miller must have heard our voices. He opened the door. I might have jumped into the pond if Rose hadn't been holding my hand. He looked like a fairy-tale monster! He was covered with flour from head to toe. Even his eyelids looked encrusted with it. I was trying to decide whether he could see us when he spoke to Rose, "Just wait here. You don't want to bring that kid into the mill. Give me your sack."

With freshly milled cornmeal we walked down to the river. It was so wide, I could barely see the other side. I decided it was running too fast, someone ought to arrange to slow it down. Maybe just thinking about all that water made me thirsty? I told Rose about it. "I'll take you to the mansion and ask for water," Rose said. This could be my chance to see the Perl sisters without any paint on their faces, I thought.

We got to the mansion and stopped on a porch. The sound

of our shoes told the Perls they had company. Someone peered through a curtained window, a key turned in a lock, and there was Mrs. Perl standing in the doorway, a surprised look on her face.

"Could my little sister have a glass of water, please? She's thirsty."

"Of course. Wait here, I'll be right back."

Missed my chance! A minute or so later, Mrs. Perl returned with a glass of water on a tray. "Here, little girl," she handed me the water, a friendly smile on her face. I decided she was as beautiful as her daughters even though she had no paint on her face.

The Incident in the Brush

We were about to cross the bridge to return home. A lot of brush was growing around the bridge. In the undergrowth, a young girl was shrieking for help as a very large man, wearing no trousers, was riding on top of her.

Rose swiftly covered my eyes with her free hand, leading me across the bridge. When we arrived safely on the other side, she took her hand away from my eyes. I knew something was terribly wrong. Every time I tried to say something, Rose lifted her index finger saying, *"Shhhhhh!"*

After that disturbing incident, I never wanted to go back to Crasna again. The screams of the girl in the brush beside the bridge still haunt my dreams to this day. Years later, when Rose knew I'd understand, she admitted we'd seen a young girl being raped. She had done nothing about it because the rapist was the son of the Chief of Gendarmes in Petrova, a mean-spirited man with a reputation for being ruthless and vengeful.

I wondered why Rose, who always helped people in trouble, did nothing in this situation. Her explanation was essentially, self-preservation. Had she interfered, the Chief of the Gendarmes' son could have invented a false story that may have landed Rose in jail, maybe for the rest of her life. Courts were non-existent in Petrova.

Our Geese

My family raised geese, ducks, and chickens for eggs and food. When I was very young, I believed the world was one endless chain of God's miracles: from the sunrise to the sunset, to the occasional dark foreboding sky, to the summer's heat, to the winter's cold, to the mountains, to the rivers, to the exact homing instinct of our geese.

One whole summer, just before sunset, I'd wait for our geese at the entrance to our yard as they returned from pasture. I watched in awe as hundreds of geese were returning from pasture, parading down the street, my eyes blinded by the bright, snow-white blanket of glorious geese. You could figure out the number of the geese families by the ganders' heads with their long majestic necks standing above the crowd. I expected our geese to forget where they lived and wander into some neighbor's yard. After all, geese weren't human! Yet our geese always returned home.

Every afternoon a commotion in a flock of geese would break out right in front of our house. I heard piercing honks and saw flapping wings and geese trying to rise into the air as if to say, "Folks, please step aside, please; don't give us a hard time; we're home; we'll see you tomorrow!" Less than a minute later, our geese waddled into our yard. The first in the parade was the huge, proud gander, its neck outstretched, honking. If I could guess geese talk, I'd say it said, "We made it again! We're home safe and sound!"

Next, the plump honking mother goose who followed the leader said, "Home sweet home! Home sweet home!" None of the young had anything to say.

At the end of the summer, without any explanation, three of our geese just disappeared. *Poof*! I wondered whether they were playing hide-and-seek with me. Maybe those geese enjoyed games as much as humans do? "Rose, three of our geese are missing! They must've followed the wrong gander!" I panicked.

"They did not follow the wrong gander. They are home; I'll

have to fatten them up for the fall holidays." I had no perception of what Rose was talking about; but I took her word. About four weeks before the fall holidays, I was playing in the backyard with friends when we heard noises of distress coming from a goose.

"The noises are coming from your house," said one of my friends. I wondered who could've chased the goose into the house. A cat or some evil creature? I tiptoed into the house. Rose was sitting on the floor with a struggling, protesting belly-up goose in her lap. She was pressing the sides of the goose's mouth with one hand while pouring a handful of corn kernels into its beak with the other hand. "Rose! What are you doing? You're killing the goose!"

Rose looked up in surprise as her hand slid down the poor goose's beak. The goose vehemently shook its head, scattering corn kernels left and right. "I'm fattening the geese; we need lots of fat for the fall holidays," she explained.

I left the room a most disappointed six-year-old. As I lay in bed that night, I debated with myself. Shall I hate my sister for making the goose suffer? How could I hate her? She shields my mother from my problems and spares Mother from aggravation. The last thing I wanted to do is aggravate my mother.

Playing Soldier

No one in Petrova had heard of window screens. I remember when I was about eight, flies invited themselves into our home during the summer and early autumn. If you grew up in homes with window screens, you probably don't know about using rags to chase flies out of rooms.

Every Saturday, just after lunch, Chayim, ten, Yitzchak, six and I, eight, played soldier. Rose was our captain. We'd open the windows and the door, line ourselves up for a frontal attack and face the flying foe. My assignment was the platform over our oven. The ceiling was so close to the platform that I had to kneel to be able to use my hands. At a signal from Rose, we'd begin fanning flies off the walls and ceiling of our all-purpose room. After a few unsuccessful tries at going back to their posts, the flies always gave up. We took full advantage of their disarray. We lifted our rags above our heads, swinging them in circles, advancing slowly toward the open windows as Chayim negotiated with them: "Hey flies! Listen up! Be good! Cooperate! We're not trying to kill you! We just want you to leave the room!" Sometimes he'd get so interested in one single fly; he'd forget the others and let the rest escape. "No! No! Stupid fly! Come back! It won't help you!" With time, he learned never to break rank, and never to chase after one or even two fugitives.

Once, a swinging rag brushed against Chayim's open eyes. We were so absorbed in our mission that we hadn't even noticed the accident. Like the hero he was, he continued swinging his rag with his eyes closed. However, he wandered off from his appointed spot and bumped into the table. Rose caught him and brought him back to his place in the now-broken line. When he left his post a second time, Rose became suspicious, checked him out and canceled the job.

When our operations went as scheduled, three to four offensives were enough to rid the room of most of the flies. The few we did miss met their doom on the flypapers that were always hanging from the ceiling.

Rose, the Inspector General and I

It was winter; I was about eleven-years-old. The night before, Mother told me that my tonsils looked red and swollen and that I would have to stay in bed until I recovered. I did feel achy, feverish and even a little dull-sighted. But how could I stay in bed? Tomorrow was the day the Inspector General was coming to our school! I was fixated on my blind devotion to my teacher, Margit. An inner voice insisted, "Livia, you must be in the classroom tomorrow; you must help your teacher; she'll need you to answer the Inspector General's questions. She'll need you to make her look good concerning her teaching!"

Next morning, I sensed someone standing beside my bed. I felt hands smooth my feather comforter. I felt fingers caress my face and my forehead, and I felt lips press against my cheeks to check my temperature. I heard soft footsteps move away from my bed. Yet Rose was still sleeping beside me. My mother had been there!

Rose's built-in clock told her to wake up. She felt my forehead to see if I had a fever. She then tucked me in, dressed herself, walked to the stove and lit a fire. By the time the rest of us got up, the room was warm. I waited until no one would see me. I layered myself with warm clothes and slipped quietly unnoticed out of the house, heading toward school.

As usual, winters registered below zero temperatures in the northern part of Transylvania, Romania, where we lived. The heavily snowbound country road seemed more slippery than it had ever been. A cold wind blew powdery surface snow against my face. I balanced myself like a tight-rope walker on a dangerous ice laden rope. One slip and I could have been lying in the road mistaken for a dead animal. Only the loud ringing of horse's bells kept me alert.

I had walked about ten houses away from my home when Rose tapped my shoulder. "And where do you think you're going?" she said.

Before I could answer her, she wrapped me head-to-foot in a blanket and lifted me into her arms. "I'm taking you home! Mother must never know about this senseless adventure of yours!"

"I've got to be in school today Rose. The Inspector General is coming this morning." Maybe my voice was too weak for her to hear me.

"I don't understand a word you're saying! I'm taking you home!" She swiftly turned around and started walking back home.

"Please! Please! Please!" I begged Rose. She stopped walking and loosened the blanket around my face. Now she could hear me. "The Inspector General visits our school once a month for one hour. If we students can answer his questions, our teacher looks good. If no one can answer his questions, our teacher gets downgraded. She might be transferred to some hole in the road. Oh, Rose! Please!"

"What's that got to do with you? Don't you know you are very, very sick?"

I paid no attention to Rose's words. "So far, I've been able to answer all the Inspector General's questions. Now my teacher is a first class teacher. But if I'm not there . . .! Who knows . . .! Rose, try to understand!"

"The Inspector General won't understand you; you're incoherent!"

"I'll take a chance. Just take me there. Please? Pretty please?"

Rose uncovered my face and carried me to school. She unwrapped me like a gift package and put me down at the door of my classroom. "Rose! Thank you. I'll leave as soon as the Inspector General does. I won't stay even one minute longer."

"I'll be waiting for you at the door."

I went into the classroom and sat in my own seat. It felt like forever before the Inspector General arrived. As he entered the classroom, we all stood up. He signaled us to sit down. He began pacing back and forth across the classroom, looking, just looking. Then he spotted a giant map of Europe on one of the walls. When he read the signature, he asked, "Who is Livia?" I raised my hand.

"Very good, Livia." He smiled. I was thrilled. No one was equal to me! Back at the podium, the Inspector General was asking the first question. I raised my hand. "Yes, Livia?" He remembered my name! I opened my mouth, and to my surprise, I heard a sound coming as if straight from the depths of the ocean. Even *I* had no idea what I was saying.

"What is she doing here?" The Inspector General looked at the teacher.

"I don't know, Sir," the teacher said.

I had to leave the classroom. I was crying. Rose wiped away my tears.

"At least you tried," she consoled me.

Rose repackaged me in the blanket and carried me home. She took full responsibility for my behavior. As for my teacher, she married the Inspector General, and I learned that I wasn't indispensable after all.

Accompanying Rose to the Fields

It was a chilly autumn morning. I heard a clatter outdoors. I scurried to the all-purpose room window where I saw an empty wagon drawn by two horses parked in the middle of our backyard. My sixteen-year-old sister Rose appeared next to the wagon as if out of nowhere. She held a bundle of blankets under her right arm. She lowered the bundle into the wagon and sat down next to a peasant driver. I couldn't imagine Rose near a wagon, much less *in* a wagon! Since *I* was terrified of horses, I'd assumed any right-minded human had to be scared of them.

I put on a heavy jacket and rushed outside. I asked Rose where she was going.

"I'm taking food to our field-workers," she said.

Goody, goody, I'd have a chance to go to the fields! I'd have a lot to tell my friends! I'd talk so much; they'd never be able to shut me up! But how do I go about asking Rose to take me along? I debated with myself. Just ask her, a voice told me.

"Would you take me along? I'll be a good girl," I said to Rose.

She gave me one excuse after another. "Our fields are located at the outskirts of the village," she said, "the road to our fields is too rough; there will be no seven-year-old children to play with; I'll be so busy, I won't have time to take care of you." She continued with endless excuses. My eyes filled with tears. Rose could never see me cry. In retrospect, I think she pitied my scrawniness, my helplessness, my insecurity. So once more, she gave in. "Hop in!"

She put me on the seat next to the driver. "I'll be right back!" she said.

I'd never been so close to horses. I dreaded feeling their tails swishing almost in my face. What if the horse in front of me stepped back and swept me off of the wagon with one swing of his huge tail? What if I landed under the wagon and was squashed to death? I was drenched with fear and drowned in terror! I couldn't decide whether to scream or cry. Maybe both at once?

At last, Rose returned. She wedged me in between herself and the peasant driver. I wasn't happy. Luckily, she noticed my tenseness. Before long, I landed in her lap, her strong protective arms embracing me. I was feeling safe and calm.

The wagon began moving! Gradually, the very familiar village street changed into foreign rural scenery. The ride was rough, but I didn't miss a single detail. I kept elbowing Rose. "What's this? What's that?" Somewhere between the last house in the village and an almost-endless stretch of fields, I saw a life-size statue of Jesus' crucifixion. Some passers-by stopped before the statue, crossed themselves and walked on. Others rested in its shadow. I'd seen processions with Jesus' image painted on canvas before, but this sculpture looked so *real*. I shuddered.

The wagon made a left turn, then another left turn. When it stopped, I knew we'd arrived. The driver secured the reins and the whip at the left-hand side of his seat. He then jumped off the wagon and disappeared. When he returned, he carried two burlap bags. He took the bridles off the horses' muzzles and wound them around a pole. He separated the horses and strung the feedbags over their heads fitting each bag to a horse's mouth. After the horses finished their last oats, the peasant took them to the river to drink. While the peasant was away with his horses, Rose took four boards and secured a seat in the middle of the wagon for me. From there I could see the landscape all the way to the horizon.

As Rose busied herself with the workers' lunch, I watched the neighboring fields. In the field to my right, I saw peasant women pulling potato plants from the ground. They separated the potatoes from the earth-embedded roots. They cleaned them from the dirt with their bare hands then dropped them into burlap pouches strung around their waists. When the pouches began bulging almost-to-bursting, some of the women doubled-over. They then began shuffling toward a loading area and piled the potatoes onto huge potato mounds.

In the field to my left, I saw women plucking corn ears from the stalks. After shucking away the yellowed leaves, they stuffed the ears into burlap pouches around their waists and delivered them to wagons.

I heard a steady pulsing sound coming from a distance. "What's that funny thump-thump-thump?" I asked Rose.

"You're hearing the peasants threshing the wheat they've just harvested."

"What's wheat?"

"Wheat is the plant from which wheat-flour comes."

"You mean the flour Mother uses to make bread?"

"Yes."

"Why do we buy flour when Father could grow wheat next to the corn and potatoes?"

"Father is a businessman. Farmers grow wheat."

"Why doesn't Father become a farmer?"

"Slow down with your questions; I got to feed the workers."

I remembered promising Rose to be a good girl, so I stopped asking questions and directed my attention to our field workers. I saw peasants crowding around our wagon, holding their bowls and wooden spoons. The women were moving their bowls and spoons from one hand to the other, while wiping the dirt off of their hands on the burlap pouches. One of the men spit a glob of something onto the ground; the air filled up with an intolerable tobacco-stench, sneaking into my nostrils. I began silently praying. "Please, God! Don't let me get sick! Not now! I promised Rose I wouldn't be any trouble to her! You remember, don't you, God?

Please!" Just as I had nothing more to beg of God, Rose took the lid off of the pot of soup she'd brought from home. A heavenly aroma filled the air, neutralizing the tobacco smell. God was great! God was good! He'd rescued me from disgrace. "Amen!" I murmured.

Rose ladled out the meat-and-vegetable soup to the workers. As a treat, she gave them *varzar,* (a casserole of corn meal, butter, sour cream, and green scallions). Rose helped herself to some food and offered me a taste. To my surprise, I liked both the soup and the varzar. If only my mother could have seen me gulping down all this food, she'd have been so happy!

After we'd finished eating, Rose took the dishes to the nearby river to wash them. "Stay put; I'll be right back," she said.

Suddenly, I realized I was alone with those terrifying horses. What if these horses ran away with the wagon? They could cross the river, dive into the woods, and get themselves tangled up in the trees. If they panicked, they'd snap their harnesses or smash up the wagon. I'd be all alone with the maddened horses. No one, not even Father, would be able to find me. Fortunately, Rose reappeared. I must've given her some strange look for she asked me, "What can I do for you?"

I stalled, trying to find something to say. "I think I need to go," I blurted out.

Rose put away the dishes, picked me up in her arms, walked toward the river and stopped in the first thicket of bushes. She put me down on a patch of grass, and positioned herself in front of me.

"Do what you need to do."

I squatted. Minutes passed, but nothing else. In the end I admitted I didn't need to go; I was just afraid of the horses. Rose carried me back to the wagon. She took four or more boards, walked several yards away from the wagon, dropped them on the ground, pushed them around with her feet, and formed a platform for me.

"You want to sit or stand?"

"Stand!" The clouds covered the sun, so Rose decided my jacket wasn't warm enough. She got a blanket and wrapped me in it. I felt warm, and my eyelids grew heavy. Had it not been for the noise around the wagon, I would have dosed off standing.

"What's going on at the wagon?" I asked. "The peasants are lining the walls of the wagon with long boards." Half the length of these boards was sticking out above the level of the wagon, making it deeper. "The deeper the wagon, the more potatoes it will hold."

"What holds the boards together?"

"The potatoes. They'll press against the boards."

The sun was setting. I wished there weren't so many clouds since I wanted to see the big fireball going down the horizon. Soon, Rose picked me up from the platform and, still wrapped in my blanket, she carried me up to the front of the wagon. Now I could watch the peasants at work. No sooner did I see the wagon-bottom covered with potatoes, than the whole wagon was full of potatoes to the top of the extended boards.

Some peasant women threw three blankets over the potato-mountain. I wished I were riding on top of this sky-high heap on the way back home. Maybe wishes *do* come true, for the next minute I heard Rose saying, "Libelah we'll be sitting on top of the potatoes on the way back."

"How will we get up there?"

"The same way anyone else would get up there." Rose had to be joking. She couldn't climb up there with me in her arms, could she? The peasants reached the top of the potato-mound as easily as cats climbing trees. They stepped on the wagon wheels, held on to the edges of the boards, and zoomed straight to the top. Rose undeniably was teasing me. She placed me in the driver's arms and before I could blink, she was standing in the driver's seat. Then it began, as if a game. The driver passed me to Rose, who swiftly passed me to the nearest woman on the mound, who swiftly passed me to the woman on the very top. I was just turning to make out the woman's face when I landed in Rose's lap, my hands freed from the blanket, her strong arms bear-hugging my tummy.

As the wagon started moving, two women began singing songs I'd never heard before. When I compared their songs to the Jewish songs I'd heard, I decided I liked the peasants' songs better. They *did* something to me. I wished I could go to sleep with those songs and wake up hearing more of those songs. Years later, I learned these songs were folk songs speaking of pain, sadness, yearning, nostalgia, reproach and protest. Even today, the *Doina*, a shepherd's melody played on a flute, moves me deeply.

After we passed Jesus' statue, the wagon stopped. All the peasants except our driver and another male peasant who sat next to the driver jumped off the wagon. Almost immediately, I missed the women and their songs. Just as I was thinking nothing could ever make any sense without these folk songs, something mysterious ran across the road and the horses panicked.

Horrible, terrifying snorting noises mixed with the driver's calming, "Whoa, whoa, whoa," reached my ears. Now the wagon was crisscrossing the road like a mindlessly bouncing ball. The blankets that had protected the peasants from the damp potatoes a minute ago were rolling in the road. Potatoes were flying in every direction.

Rose and I were sliding around on our blanket. I couldn't understand what Rose was yelling at me. The bouncing wagon distorted her voice. I wanted her to be saying, or maybe she was actually saying, "Don't be scared! Nothing bad will happen to us! Trust me!"

"I do trust you," I whispered, surprised at my own contorted voice. I began praying in my mind: "God is good! God is great! Please, God! Please help us! We don't want to die, God! Please! And don't let me cry! If I cry, Rose will get upset. You could make her talk to me, though. Thank you, God!"

Then I heard Rose saying, "We have to get rid of the blanket before it takes us into the street! We have to get to the bottom of the wagon!"

We were on top of a mound of potatoes and she wanted us to get to the *bottom*? Impossible! But for Rose nothing was impossible. One minute we were sitting on top of a blanket, and the next minute the blanket was in the street. She was interchanging her hands around my tummy as she held me down, sometimes her hands hurting me. But I was brave, I kept silent. Now her free right hand or left hand, depending which of them held me tight to her stomach, was removing potatoes underneath her, around her, in the back of her, in front of her, throwing them into the street. Her feet weren't idling either. She kept peddling as if she were riding a bicycle! Suddenly, I was no more in her lap; I was between her legs and pushed deeper and deeper into a mass of damp potatoes.

I shouted, "We're sinking! We're sinking!"

"That's what we want! The deeper we get, the better our chances!" I heard.

The entire run-away episode probably lasted no more than five minutes, but to me it felt like an eternity! We were already in the heart of the village. Hysterical voices shouted. "Get out of the street people! Get inside your houses! Now! *Oy vey is mir!"* (Woe is to me!)

I heard a collision and our wagon was standing on its back wheels. Potatoes were pouring over us like a mighty waterfall, but Rose kept protecting my head with her arms and hands. After a big *boom*, our wagon was standing on four wheels again! We were buried shoulder-deep in potatoes! While Rose was struggling to free us from those potatoes, I saw our family and some strangers peering at us.

"Thank Heaven!" cried out my mother, throwing her arms up as if praying. Father, my brothers and a few strangers reached out to us, helping us to the ground. Then I was in my mother's arms. The next morning I woke up in her bed.

The following morning, I learned our wagon had been in a head-on collision with an oncoming wagon. Our driver and his companion and the driver of the other wagon had only minor bruises. The seven-year-old child I was then had no way of describing her ordeal to her friends, but even after all these many years, I remember the nightmare as if it had happened yesterday.

Mr. Thomas and My First Novel

When I was ten, my teacher Mr. Thomas, gave me a book to read. "You're ready for it." he said. It was a novel, a moving story about a French revolutionary sentenced to die. He spent the last three days before his execution at the window of his prison cell, waiting for a glimpse of his beloved. He didn't sleep or eat; he was afraid if he did, he might miss her visit. Just as he caught sight of her, the guards took him away to the guillotine.

I read the novel aloud to Rose on Saturdays in the orchard, while our parents were resting. We were sobbing like small children. At night, I whispered the novel's long phrases as Rose and I lay in our bed. Rose always fell asleep within five minutes after her head touched her pillow, but I continued reading silently. The next morning she'd say, "I know where you left off last night." I never mentioned the extra pages I'd read. Instead, I'd start with the words she remembered before she fell asleep the night before.

Mr. Thomas, Mother and I

The year was 1931. I had just graduated from 4th grade. I was returning from an errand my mother sent me on when I saw Mr. Thomas, my most favorite teacher. I greeted him. He stopped me. He asked me to take him to my parents. "Uh . . . Sir . . .? What . . . ? My voice died in my throat.

"It's nothing to worry about Livia; I think you'll be pleased with my visit." I thought Mr. Thomas was the smartest teacher in the world. That he would visit my home or talk with my parents was more than I would ever imagine.

When the two of us walked through our front door, it was as though I'd brought royalty. My mother's face turned yellow. Rose wiped a chair clean, and Mother wiped it a second time. Mr. Thomas introduced himself, shaking hands with Mother. By some miracle, Mother regained her composure, inviting Mr. Thomas to sit down.

"You sit down, Mrs. Szabo," said Mr. Thomas. Mother pulled

up a second chair and the both of them sat down. "What do you say to your daughter's A+ report card, Mrs. Szabo."

"My entire family is very proud of her!" Mother's face lit up. She must've remembered the times when she kept telling me that I had more brains than all the people who made fun of me put together.

"Do you understand, Mrs. Szabo that your daughter is high school material?" Mr. Thomas began. Mother looked at him as if waiting for more information. "If I were you, Mrs. Szabo, I would consider sending your daughter to high school."

Mother knew that high schools were found in big cities and that high school education was for rich people in that it involved tuition, room and board, books, uniforms and other things. "But Mr. Thomas, we are not rich people," Mother said, her eyes lowered.

"Don't worry Mrs. Szabo; I could help."

"In what way, Sir?" Mother was all ears. "The principal of Liceu Domnita Ileana, the most prestigious all-girl high school in Sighet, is my personal friend. I could recommend your daughter for a four-year scholarship, but you must do the rest."

After Mr. Thomas left, Mother looked at me. "You shall go to high school!"

She spoke with so much conviction, I was flabbergasted.

"What about room and board, Mother?"

"I'll take care of that; I'll speak to my rich cousins in Sighet!" Indeed, her rich cousins agreed to take turns and give me free dinner. I should mention that dinner in Europe was and still is consumed between one and two o'clock in the afternoon. Uncle Yossel, my father's younger brother was quite generous. He agreed to give me free Sabbath meals, which consisted of both Friday evening dinner and Saturday lunch.

My First Year in High School

My elementary school records had just missed the deadline to enter Liceu Domnita Ileana High School in the fall of 1932. My relatives, who agreed to take turns and give me free dinners, were expecting me in the fall of that year as well. To avoid offsetting the time sequence, my mother decided to register me at the Zardo, an all-girl Catholic high school for the fall of 1932 in Sighet, Romania.

Mother had also made a deal with a distant relative. I was to tutor two of her children in return for room, a glass of milk for breakfast and a bowl of soup in the evening. A week later, I informed mother that the glass of milk in the morning did not quench my hunger. Mother could hardly believe that her scrawny Libelah had gotten an appetite. Not only had I gotten an appetite, I could eat anything that was called food. At home Mother would engage the help of my older brother Chayim to make me eat some food. Chayim would tell me stories; I was his best audience. He'd impersonate animals, stand on his head and make cartwheels. I loved Chayim's delivery of the stories; he'd practically play them out.

Upon learning that the milk alone did not satisfy my appetite, Mother made arrangements with a courier to bring me a big, white loaf of bread once a week. Could it be true? I was entrusted with a loaf of bread to handle it whichever way I saw fit? Who could be equal to me?

I got busy planning. I'll use one slice of bread with my breakfast milk, another slice I'll take to school and eat it on my recess, and another slice I'll be eating with my soup in the evening.

My first recess in school turned into a disaster. I couldn't afford to buy juice of any kind to wash down my dry slice of bread, so I began hiccupping! My schoolmates looked at me as if I were a Martian, hiccupping for no reason. As daughters of rich people, they would indulge in cake, butter rolls, sandwiches and all kinds of juices from the man with the cart.

I must solve the problem once and for all, I thought. And solve it I did. The next day and the days following, I retreated in a corner during school recess and struggled with my hiccups without anyone staring at me.

As months went by, my body began craving more and more

food. It practically turned into a sponge. On my main meals, I'd guzzle up the food before the rest of the people at the table had a chance to check what was on their plate. Luckily, my relatives would give me two and three helpings sometimes. Still, I had not let my mother know about this sudden change. It never occurred to me that I had begun growing and developing. Moreover, in my ignorance, I believed it was a sort of curse because I fell in love at such a young age. Yes, you've heard me right; I fell in love. It was a thirteen-year old unfulfilled love.

It happened on the first Friday at Uncle Yossel's home. School ended at 3:00 p.m. I dropped off my books at my sleeping quarters. I changed into my holiday high-school uniform—a navy-blue pleated skirt and a white blouse with a Peter-Pan collar. I looked forward to eating my first Sabbath meal with Uncle Yossel's family. I had his address: Number 2 Avram Iancu Street, the apartment next-to-the last on the left-hand side in the courtyard.

I walked across a patio. I saw three doors. Someone must've heard my footsteps for one of the doors opened showing Szidi, Uncle Yossel's eighteen-year-old daughter. She was dressed festively. We greeted each other and embraced. We walked into the kitchen where Piri, Szidi's sixteen-year-old sister sat at an imposing looking table, her nose glued to a book. "Piri! Libush is here! Say hello!"

"Hello," Piri mumbled without looking up.

At the same moment, Aunt Esther swept in. "How are you, Libush, my dear child?"

"I'm fine, Aunt Esther. And you?" I asked.

Instead of answering me Aunt Esther looked at the clock. "Oh! It's time to light the Sabbath candles! If only I had my shawl," she glanced at Szidi. My cousin disappeared for a minute. Soon, she returned carrying a silk shawl. She wrapped it around her mother's head, an intricate knot ending at her left ear. Aunt Esther lit the Sabbath candles in a five-branched candelabra. The oversized table was covered with a beautiful tablecloth. Expensive looking plates and silverware gave the table a real festive look. After the blessing of the Sabbath candles, we sat down at the table. We talked about my parents and my school.

Twenty minutes into our conversation, Uncle Yossel and his three sons: Yankel, Feivel and Tzali returned from the synagogue. "Gut Shabbos! Gut Shabbos! Gut Shabbos!" Uncle Yossel greeted us.

"Gut Shabbos!" we all answered.

Aunt Esther looked at Szidi. "Ask Ferenz to join us."

Szidi hurried out of the kitchen and returned with a boy of about eleven years of age. He wore a khaki uniform and a cap initialed, L.D.V. standing for "Liceu Dragos Voda," one of the all-boys high schools in Sighet.

Just as the boy's eyes locked with mine, Aunt Esther rushed to introduce us, "Libush, this is Ferenz, my brother's oldest son. He lives here. He's attending Dragos Voda High School."

Aunt Esther then turned to the boy. "Ferenz, this is Libush, the daughter of your uncle's older brother. She'll be having her Sabbath meals with us. She's attending high school in Sighet." Ferenz touched his cap in a mock salute.

Uncle Yossel, wearing a skullcap, sat at the head of the table. Aunt Esther sat opposite him. I sat on the girls' side, and the boys sat facing the girls. Suddenly, Ferenz asked, "What high school are you attending, Libush?" I wasn't wearing the barrette with my high school initials.

"The Zardo. But I've been accepted at Liceu Domnita Ileana for next fall."

"How old are you Libush?" Aunt Esther asked.

"Twelve," I said.

"Twelve and that small? I thought high schools don't accept children!" Ferenz nastily cut in.

You know something, big shot, I thought? *You're* the child here! *You're* six-years old! You can't pull my braids, so you insult me! I hate you! I hate you!

Ferenz then looked at my uncle. "My Uncle Yossel's niece attends a Catholic high school?" he said, this time smiling.

As I noticed the gold cap on his right eyetooth, something strange happened to me! A rush of sensation made its way through my entire body. It began at the top of my head. It kept creeping downward: slowly, slowly, slowly until it reached the tip of my last toe. Weirdly, I didn't hate Ferenz anymore. Moreover, my *body* wanted him; every part of my body wanted him! My *arms* wanted him! I wanted his arms to hold me so tight until I felt my bones crushed! My lips wanted him to kiss them! What previous experience did I have concerning kissing? None! Still, I wanted him to *bite* my lips! I wanted him to stroke my breasts that I so often touched to make sure they didn't sag like my mother's. To top it all off, I wanted him inside me! To stir me up! To rip me apart! To *attach* himself to me! To become *one* with me! To never *leave* me!

Suddenly, I heard, "Libush, stand up! Your uncle is saying

Ferenz

Kiddush (the blessing over the wine)." I stood up as Uncle Yossel said Kiddush. He then washed his hands, said a blessing over the *challis* (loaves of egg bread eaten on Sabbath), and passed a slice of challi to each of us at the table.

Someone served fish; someone removed the dishes and the fish forks; someone served chicken and noodle soup; someone served chicken and chicken stuffed neck; someone served stuffed cabbage and *tzimmes* (a honey-sweetened carrot mix). Finally, someone served dessert. Everyone but me seemed to be there in both mind and body. My heart was beating for two. I'd acted as though I'd never been taught table manners. I'd tried to eat soup with my fork; I'd held my knife in the wrong hand and I'd chased after the spoon falling to the floor.

Dinner ended. I felt the walls, the ceiling, the floor, even the furniture crowding in on me. I excused myself and walked out of the kitchen. I stopped on the porch. It was chilly and dark. Or *was* it dark? Or *was* it chilly? Where was the sunshine coming from? Why were all God's creatures singing? Why were the people smiling at me? . . . A mild breeze whispered in my ears: Libush, you're in love; you're definitely in love! Well, if love feels like that, I don't object at all, I thought.

Someone was standing next to me, tapping me on my shoulder. It was Ferenz. "It's chilly, Libush," he said. He draped his jacket over my shoulders. I slightly trembled; I felt as if he were still inside his jacket, embracing me. "You're shivering! Let's go inside." He put his arm around me and led me into the kitchen.

Inside the kitchen, I thanked Aunt Esther and Uncle Yossel for the Sabbath dinner. I said good-bye to everyone in the room. I put on my coat and headed toward the door.

"Wait Libush," said Aunt Esther, "Yankel will see you home. And don't forget to be here tomorrow for the Sabbath mid-day meal at 12:30."

The following day, I arrived at Aunt Esther's apartment at exactly 12:30. She and Uncle Yossel were just coming home from the synagogue, arm in arm. She was wearing a beautifully styled silk dress and a lot of jewelry.

"Gut Shabbos!" I said in greeting.

I'm not sure whether Aunt Esther greeted me or not. But as soon as we were inside the kitchen, she asked me to accompany her to her bedroom. She wanted me to help her out of her dress. I did so. She draped the dress around a chair. I looked at her. Wow! I'd never seen so much flesh squeezed into a single garment. "You'll unlace my corset," Aunt Esther interrupted my train of thought. I tried. I tugged the laces one way. When that didn't work, I tried tugging it in the opposite direction. Nothing happened. "Never mind! You country people probably don't wear corsets! I'll call Szidi!" Aunt Esther said. "Sorry, Aunt Esther," I sounded apologetic. Szidi was a whiz at undoing her mother's corset. Zip! Zip! Zap! She put the corset away and unlaced her mother's shoes. She then brought a pair of red-silk slippers. She helped her mother walk into them. I hoped I'd never have to do Szidi's job. I thought I'd rather die than look like Aunt Esther. I was glad girls of my generation watched our figures. For us, being heavy was definitely out!

Szidi helped her mother into a pretty, floral, comfortable dress, then left. Aunt Esther asked me to lock the door. I got the jitters. I knew I'd behaved oddly at the dinner table the night before. I hoped we were having a discussion about table manners. "Relax, dear; let's sit down and talk."

I pulled two chairs up. My hands were shaking. "I told you to relax," she said, a false smile on her lips. My heart was racing. Aunt Esther was more observant than I'd supposed. She'd not only noticed my odd behavior the night before, but she'd known who caused it as well. "Listen, Libush," Aunt Esther said, "My brother, Yeno, makes children's dolls. He also owns a stationery store. Ferenz is his older son; his younger son, Moti is not ready for high school yet."

So . . . ? I thought. This has something to do with me?

"Yeno has chosen a wife for Ferenz," she continued. "She's an orphan. She comes from a very good, and very wealthy family, a *very* wealthy family! In time, she'll inherit a fortune!"

Good for her, I thought. The saga I just heard escaped me totally.

A year later, I was enrolled in Liceu Domnita Ileana. I was still obsessed with Ferenz, regardless of whether he was taken or not. His smile followed me everywhere: I went to bed with his smile; I dreamed with his smile; I woke up with his smile; I ate with his smile; whoever I looked at, it was Ferenz smiling.

In my daydreams, I'd be feeling Ferenz lying beside me, endlessly caressing me. These fantasies brought me hours of incredible exhilarations, an almost delirious joy and a symphony of all my senses. Even my night dreams were extensions of my daydreams' fantasies. During my waking hours, my imagination followed Ferenz to dances, parties, *everywhere*. If he was dancing with another girl, I'd simply become that girl. I wondered if I had some unique, magical ability to invoke mental images and fit them into my real life. Or was it my mother's teachings? She would say *"Libelah, whenever you want to know how a person feels you project your own face on top of that person's face. And, in your imagination, you become that person."* My exceptional imagination helped me a great deal.

I kept a special journal with Ferenz entries. Those entries were entries of love, yearning, passion and sometimes tinged with rebuke. More than a few entries were letters. I wanted to send them to him with the postal service, but never did. Here's an example:

> Dearest Sunshine:
>
> Today I saw you at dancing school: You were surrounded by many girls! Sometimes you danced with a girl more than once! You danced with the tall, blonde girl, three times! How I hoped you danced with me! Finally, you did grant me the last dance before closing time! Oh, my love! You call that dancing? Our cheeks didn't even touch, and your heart was further from mine than ever before!
>
> You didn't know my heart was beating for two. You'll never know, much less understand, my pain! Nor will you know that

every time you thought you were dancing with those other girls, you were really dancing with me! By what new witchcraft you ask? You won't find it in a text. I simply replaced my face with the girl's face you were dancing with and there, it was I who twirled in your arms! It was I who felt your smooth cheek, your warm breath, your racing heartbeat!

Last night, as I closed my eyes, I saw moonlight beaming on your pillow, on your face, on your form! And you looked sad, alone, bereft, lost! My heart ached for you, my love! I wanted you to know I was caressing your hair, your forehead, your nose, and your lips! I wanted you to know I was willing your pain away!

If only you knew how much I loved you! I want to whisper my love for you in the sunshine, in the moonlight, in the spring air, in the vivid blue sky, in the emerald green grass, in the rainbows of flower-colors. I want to shout my love for you from the top of the tallest mountain! You will make your choices . . . I choose you! I want to be with you! You are the sun; you alone give life to me; we could spend an eternity together; even that wouldn't be enough; I want you longer than always and more than forever!

Yours . . .

Forever in love . . .*Livia*

Toward the end of my second year at Liceu Domnita Ileana, I almost woke up. I'd been still daydreaming about Ferenz, writing imaginary love letters to him, and, oddly enjoying both my good fantasies and my agonies and desperations.

I decided to find a way to make my fantasy life a reality. I wanted a relationship with Ferenz he'd at least know about! He'd have to notice me, only I couldn't depend on an accident. I must shape my own future. But what would cause a boy to notice a girl? Like *really* notice her? My mind had always been my drawing card, but Ferenz had met my mind without noticing the person who went with it. That left my body! I had filled out quite a bit, but I wasn't a beauty.

If beauty couldn't do what was necessary, I was back to my

body again. My gym teacher had mentioned that I was among her most gifted students. Let's say Ferenz saw me in one of the more interesting gymnastic routines?

I decided Aunt Esther's kitchen would be the ideal place. He'd catch me performing when he returned from school and stopped into the kitchen for a drink of water, or a bite of Aunt Esther's baked goodies before retiring to his room.

For my plan to work, I'd have to be in Aunt Esther's kitchen while she was still cooking the Sabbath meal. In an Orthodox household, every kind of work, including cooking, had to be finished before Friday's sunset.

I asked Aunt Esther's permission to watch her preparing the Sabbath meals. I told her I really loved her cooking. If only I could learn her secrets, perhaps she'd allow me to show my mother some of her recipes. I lied to her. I also lied to some of my professors. Every second or third Friday, I'd feign some health problem and they'd dismiss me from classes early.

One Friday Aunt Esther said, "Libush! Watch me making the *bratten* (pot roast without vegetables). This is for your mother. You wash the meat; you take the knife, holding its tip at a slant; you make little holes in the meat, the more, the better. You fill each hole with a piece of garlic then make a mixture of oil, paprika, salt and black pepper. You coat the meat with it, then you heat oil in a dutch oven. You brown the meat, just the outside of it; you put a little water into the dutch oven; and cover it and let it simmer. Of course, you check it from time to time so the meat won't burn."

"Piroshka open the window; let the smoke get out!" Aunt Esther said to her maid. "You see, Libush, I forgot to tell you when you put meat into hot oil, it splatters and it smokes. Your mother will know what to do."

I held back a smile. Who're you kidding Auntie, I thought? I have no intention to tell my mother how to cook; she can teach *you* a thing or two!

For more Fridays than I want to remember, I'd hear Aunt Esther telling the sleep-in maid who helped with the cooking, "Piroshka, the flame's too high; the flame's too low; put a few more carrots in the fish; why's the lid on the chicken soup bouncing? Do something about it! No! No! Don't take it off! Just move it a bit so that steam escapes! Let me do it! Is there enough fat in the skillet with the stuffed chicken neck? Let me see if it's brown on both sides! Take the lid off of the soup. I want to taste it; it's tender all right; take it off the stove! Okay, take the *cholent* to the baker and on your way back, bring the challis!" Cholent was always the mid-day Sabbath meal. It consisted of fatty meat, beans or potatoes, and barley prepared on Friday and kept in the oven to cook slowly.

During my first "cooking lesson," I was edgy; my mind was busy with my plan. As I'd foreseen, Aunt Esther would have to relax in a chair before I could put on the show I'd intended for Ferenz.

Finally, on the third Friday, Aunt Esther sat down in a chair to relax. Hallelujah! "Would you like me to entertain you, Aunt Esther? You worked so hard!"

"Some other time, child. I need a nap before Yossel comes home and gets ready for the synagogue."

"This just takes a minute, Aunt Esther." Before she could say anything, I'd taken off my skirt and blouse, put them over a chair, and was standing in my gym suit, doing splits, bridges, headstands, and candle-sticks. I'd intended to do some cartwheels, but the kitchen was smaller than I'd estimated.

"Where did you learn those things? I've seen circus people doing such tricks!"

"We have gym lessons in school."

"Dear, do you know that young girls shouldn't be doing splits?" Aunt Esther looked worried.

I faked ignorance. "Aunt Esther, I don't think I understand. Are you worried about tearing tendons or ligaments?"

"No! Uh . . . You know . . . Uh . . . Let's just say . . . Uh . .

. A girl, a woman isn't built like a man . . . Uh . . . Just take my word for it and don't do splits!"

Aunt Esther left the kitchen for a nap and I continued with my gymnastics. I felt I might collapse into a lump of melted muscle and Ferenz hadn't even shown up.

Weeks passed. I'd lost track of all the Friday afternoons I'd spent in Aunt Esther's kitchen doing gymnastics. Then . . . I had to be hallucinating! I thought I saw Ferenz' silhouette in the kitchen window! The thought that he might be watching me caused an adrenaline surge in me. Now I was strong, powerful, and invincible. I began doing contortions I'd never dreamed of. I was an automatic, over-wound toy, literally flipping from one bizarre position to another.

Suddenly Ferenz entered into the kitchen. I reached for my skirt and held it over my gym suit. "Don't put your clothes on, Livia! Not yet! You look so uh . . . nice in your gym suit!" His eyes were jumping all over my body.

I knew I looked good in my gym suit, but I wanted to hear Ferenz compliment me again. "Thank you for the false compliment."

"Livia, I don't give a compliment unless it's due."

"Thank you. When did you get here?" I feigned ignorance.

"A few minutes ago. I watched you through the window; you're a terrific gymnast."

"Thank you again."

Now I was doubly happy! Ferenz had seen me doing gymnastics, *and* his compliments seemed genuine! How I wanted to climb into my own glowing feelings and never emerge from them! Instead, I heard my voice saying, "You'll excuse me? I need to change."

"Sure. I'll see you at supper. You're fantastic!"

That Friday ended my gymnastics in Aunt Esther's kitchen. I wanted Ferenz to have my performance he just witnessed stored in his memory forever. I wanted him to keep fantasizing, to keep creating images of me.

Sometimes I wanted to slow the clock and the calendar. In

1938, times were changing too fast for any of us to comprehend. My older sister Molly sponsored my father to America. The next year, Rose married Boruch Illovitz and moved to Viseu De Sus. Chayim left for Iaşi to live with Yosef who was married to Mina. Mother, Yitzchak, and Toby moved to Sighet. She rented the front apartment in the same complex Uncle Yossel lived.

Ferenz began noticing me as a *woman!* One morning, he saw me in the window facing the courtyard. He asked me whether he could walk me to school; I agreed. We walked side by side; neither of us was speaking. I glanced at him from the corner of my eye; he glanced at me from the corner of *his* eye. I knew what *my* heart said; I wished I knew what *his* said!

At the street corner where he turned toward his school, he froze his look on me as if trying to memorize my face. Just as I started to feel uncomfortable, he began sighing and whispering my name a few times. The sound of his whispers echoed in my mind through that day, into the evening, and during the night. I wondered what his sighs had meant. Finally, I decided he was in terrible pain, caught in an agony he couldn't talk about.

The next day and the rest of the school year, Ferenz visited our home every morning. As he came into our dinette, he'd close the door softly. The room then filled with sighs, whispers of my name, silent pauses, and more whispers.

One morning, I felt uncomfortable with his penetrating stare. To divert his attention, I turned on our radio, explaining, "This is a short-wave radio; it broadcasts news from Budapest, London, Paris, you name it."

Now, that he'd learned about our radio, he'd arrive fifteen to twenty minutes before leaving for school. Since the short waves came through softly, he'd put one ear very close to the radio and signal for me to join him. At times, our ears touched the radio speaker and our lips almost met. Then, we'd forget the news, and just stare into each other's eyes.

Once, he found a station playing dance music. "Would you

like to dance?" he asked. He held me so tightly I thought he was breaking my ribs. Instead of feeling pain, I felt lightning searing through my body. We melted into each other; his breath was *my* breath; his heartbeat was *my* heartbeat; he was *mine*! We were somewhere in a vacuum. We had to separate; we had to go to school.

We danced every morning. We kept twirling in each other's arms, aimlessly. Sometimes, we'd bump into furniture and his lips would suddenly rest on my mouth. But I'd turn my head away. That didn't stop him from trying to kiss me time after time, after time! If I'd been less self-controlling I'd have obeyed my impulse saying, "Livia! Let yourself go! These longings are normal! We love each other!" But my conscience, my keeper, said, "Livia! No! These lips have kissed another woman! This man will be someone else's husband some day!"

It's true that on hot summer afternoons, I tried to lure him out of his room. I'd put on my three-scarf bathing suit, brushing against his window on my way to the far end of the courtyard where I sunbathed, one of my eyes watching his door.

Usually he'd appear in his doorway, wearing only swim trunks. By calculated intentions, I'd decide to apply my suntan lotion. He'd stand, watching me go through my slow-motion ritual. I wanted him to see, to savor every part of my exposed body! I wanted to punish him. Why should I be the only one to suffer, so long? More often than not, I'd agree to his offer to apply tanning lotion on my back. If his hands strayed to my exposed thighs, I'd gently lead them away.

But, I wasn't always heartless .Sometimes, I'd allow him to catch me in flight, and carry me as if I were a child. Once he lifted me over his head, he had maneuvered me until three quarters of my body was suspended in the air. I screamed, "Put me down! Put me down!"

"Promise me a kiss!"

"I promise! Just put me down!"

As he lowered me to the ground, our bodies touched. I felt a silken, sensuous sensation. Do these sensations have to end? Why couldn't we just float up, up, farther up and dissolve into the clouds? Suddenly, I felt a sharp pain in my ribs! He was tugging me toward him! My mouth was almost touching his. He really expected me to kiss him! Those summers were so beautiful and so crazy, yet I never allowed him even one kiss.

One spring, just before he left for a summer vacation back home to Viseu De Sus, he composed a song without a title. He never admitted for whom he wrote it, but he showed it to me and sang it enough times for me to memorize the melody and the lyrics. At ninety-one, I still remember both. Here is a translation: "My empty heart is filled with pain. My soul's a ruined empty tomb. I am bound for far-away lands. Who knows when I'll return?"

Ferenz had returned all right, and had graduated. The next year, the authorities discovered he was involved in subversive activities. Since the northern part of Transylvania belonged to Hungary, and Hungary had banned communism, he was arrested and shipped to Budapest to stand trial. I wanted desperately to go to Budapest, to witness his trial and to see him again before he'd be sent to prison. I understood he might never return.

My dream materialized. Some of my friends from wealthy families decided to celebrate our high school graduation in Budapest, and invited me to join them as a guest of their rich relatives. All I'd need was money for the train fare. Mother gave me the money I needed. She also gave me money to buy cloth for a winter coat; it would be my graduation gift.

When I arrived in Budapest, I telephoned Ferenz' lawyer. "Yes, yes, Miss Szabo! I understand. However, the only way you could see him at his trial is by bribing the prison guards. You'll need a lot of money." Even as he and I were speaking, I hoped the money my mother had given me to buy cloth for a winter coat would be enough for the guards.

Ferenz' trial took five days. He noticed me there during the first day. He seemed to be surprised and touched. Neither his parents nor his fiancé were present. As expected, he received a prison sentence and was subsequently deported to Auschwitz. He survived, as did his father, and his future wife. His mother and his younger brother died in the camps.

I saw Ferenz once after the war. I spent a night with him in his father's house. We were alone. His father had gone to Sweden to bring Ferenz' future bride home. We both understood that the future was leading us apart; I would go to America to join my father and he would marry the fiancé he did not love at that time.

We spent the evening and part of that night in the garden. I sat on his lap, my hands draped around his neck, my head resting on his shoulder. The full moon and the shimmering stars seemed to bless our love. The heavens held us. Neither of us spoke. I heard his rapid heartbeat, his drawn-out sighs and his solemn whisperings of my name.

About three o'clock in the morning, we went into the house. He looked at me as if saying, "I want you so . . . ! Do you want me . . .?"

I wanted him more than anything in the world, but I heard myself uttering, "The only memories I want of this night are the ones we had in the garden!"

He looked at me as if I were mad. His eyes seemed to ask, "Why, Livia? I know you love me! I love you! Isn't that enough?" How strange! For thirteen years, he had been like a sacred temple, one I'd wanted to enter. Now, when the door was wide open, I preferred to stand outside.

"I'll honor your wish, Livia," he said, his glazed eyes all over me.

He gave me his pajamas; he wore his briefs. We slept in the same bed. Neither of us closed eyes for a single moment. We lay in bed, each at the other end of it, facing each other, staring at each other, our yearnings boiling over. He kept sighing and repeating my name until the whole earth seemed full of his longing. He left the bed a few times. Once, he returned dripping with water from a cold shower. But we each proved to have incredible will power. In the morning, we showered; we dressed; we ate; we shook hands; we wished each other good luck. And I left.

I heard news of Ferenz thirty years later, after I had immigrated to the United States. I learned that Ferenz had held a very high position in the Romanian communist government, and that he had two sons who were engineers. He sent his sons to the United States, expecting to join them later. However, the United States had refused him an entry visa because of his communist background. But Canada had granted him an entry visa, and he had settled in Montreal.

My husband had watched me suffer from recurring dreams about Ferenz. He thought I should see a psychiatrist, but I had refused. No one could ever take Ferenz out of my subconscious, no one! I must do it on my own. I must see him personally and tell him how indescribably happy I am with my husband.

Ferenz' arrival in Canada in the mid-seventies gave me the opportunity to exorcise my fantasy. As I met him, I was in awe. It seems my mind made a leap back to my childhood, I was expecting to see an 18-year old Ferenz that I was so much in love with. Now to me he appeared an unattractive old man. When I came out of my childhood trance, I had the courage to tell him there was nothing left in my heart for him. We never saw each other again.

During my two-year courtship with Sigmund, I came to the conclusion that I'd succeeded in transfering to him all that bottled-up love I had for Ferenz. My husband and I had sixty glorious years together. As about Ferenz, I found out he had Alzheimer's. I wondered whether in his recessive periods, he remembered me. Of course, I'll never know; especially now that he has passed on.

Tutoring in High School

Even with all the difficulties I had with my run-away appetite, I made it to the end of my first year of high school. The next year I entered Liceu Domnita Ileana with a four-year-scholarship. Mr. Sangianu, the principal who awarded me the scholarship, decided to go further. He called me into his office. "You remind me of myself when I entered high school," he said, I was penniless. All I had was my scholastic achievements. Look where I am now; I want to give back." I looked at him as if he spoke in a foreign language. He continued, "You'll be tutoring failing students. I'll provide them for you."

Suddenly, I became a tutor overnight. Parents of children with failing grades, failing grades began from C- downward, were fighting for me. After all, I was recommended by the school's principal.

I close my eyes and can still see me as a thirteen or fourteen-year-old girl with the stature of a child. I'm walking Sighet's streets, late in the evening, in sunshine, in rain, in snow and in sleet, looking for the homes of the failing students I'm supposed to tutor. I can still feel the rapid heartbeat of a scared child when I saw a drunken person staggering in the street. He's coming toward me . . . ! He's too close to me . . . ! I am ducking into a nearby door. After the drunken person passes the door, I sigh . . . what a relief!

Livia in High School

I get out of the door and, as if nothing had happened, continue toward my bread-winning goal.

One day, Yittie Yakobowitz, a classmate of mine, invited me to her home. During my conversation with Mrs. Yakobowitz, we touched on the subject of tutoring. Mrs. Yakobowitz made an arrangement with me. I was to tutor Hedy and Shuli, Yittie's two younger siblings attending elementary school. In exchange, Mrs. Yakobowitz was to give me room and a complete breakfast. Wow! A complete breakfast: orange juice, home-baked bread, home-baked rolls, butter, and a choice of eggs cooked ways I never heard of before. Without delay, I conveyed the good news to my mother and asked her to stop sending me bread.

I shared an imported hide-a-bed with Yittie. I could talk girl-talk with a rich girl! Yittie was beautiful and had a heart to match her beauty.

The rest of my classmates weren't eager to befriend me. I wasn't born in Sighet; I didn't grow up among them. My father was neither a doctor nor a lawyer nor a rich businessman. But there was a bright side to the story. Their parents almost forced them to befriend me. They made them invite me to their homes, in hope that something of my attributes--and I don't mean my looks--might rub off on them. I was known as the strange little whiz kid. Needless to say, the wishes of my friends' parents never materialized; their daughters continued with their spoiled ways.

How lucky could I be? I had a complete breakfast and I tutored children to help me pay for my suppers and whatever else. I had to yet overcome the inability to manage my weekly earnings. Come payday, instead of putting some supper-money aside for the whole week, I'd spend my entire earnings in just four days. I'd visit one kosher delicatessen store after the other. I'd gorge myself on all sorts of smoked meat. I remembered holding my nose when my brothers would eat smoked goose-thighs or smoked veal or smoked tongue for breakfast.

One night, I was so hungry I couldn't sleep. I was tossing

and turning and accidentally woke Yittie up. She assumed I was sick and offered to take me to the school nurse in the morning. I explained to her I was hungry. She wondered whether I had a snack after supper.

"I had no supper let alone a snack." I said. A bell must've gone off in her head for she said. "You know what? I feel hungry, too. I'm going downstairs to the servant's quarters. Won't you join me?"

We ventured through the dining room and her parents' sleeping quarters. Yittie opened the door. I was petrified so I held on to her waist and closed my eyes. We began tiptoeing.

"Why do we act like thieves?" Yittie whispered. "What's wrong with two people who sleep in the same room, getting up at the same time to go to the bathroom at the same time?" I kept silent. Suddenly, Yittie's mother appeared. "Mom, we're on our way to the bathroom," Yittie explained. Mrs. Yakobowitz suggested that we use the bathroom first, since we had to get up early in the morning. "No, Mom, you go first; we're two people; you'll have to wait much too long," Yittie said.

After Mrs. Yakobowitz returned from the bathroom, I went in. Streams of perspiration began running down my body; I thought I'd be drowning in my own water. A few minutes later, I heard a soft knock. "Mother is fast asleep," Yittie said. I sighed in relief.

We walked down about ten steps before reaching the kitchen floor. The night light was on. I opened the refrigerator. I took out a pot with uncooked stuffed cabbage; I put it back. Two rolls of salami stared at me so I took out one. "May I have some?"

"You may have as much as you want."

I asked Yittie for bread and a knife. She gave me a roll. I cut the roll in two and put it on a towel which served as a place mat. I made a sandwich with twelve thick slices of salami. I tried to take a bite, but the sandwich was too big for my mouth. I had an idea. I separated the roll from the salami. I then took a bite of the roll, stuffed my mouth with four slices of salami, put my hand over my mouth and began chewing. I repeated this action until

I'd consumed twelve slices of salami and one half a roll. Yittie was flabbergasted. I felt embarrassed. I asked her if she wanted some.

She smiled, "I only pretended I was hungry. How else would you have gotten into the kitchen with me?" I was moved to tears. She embraced me and said, "Don't cry, we have to go back. I also have to write a note to the cook."

"A note to the cook?" I looked at her in bewilderment.

She must write a note to the cook, she explained. She must tell the cook that *she* was in the kitchen last night, so that the cook wouldn't blame the other servants for the disappearance of the food.

For a while these nightly escapades took place a few times a week. I always wondered what would happen if we were ever caught. Would it be "like mother like daughter?" I'll never know; we were never discovered. As about me, in time I learned how to manage my earnings.

My Physics Grade in High School

In my junior year of high school, I got a B in Physics. A "B" in Physics? I knew the material inside out; I deserved an A. I must do something about it.

I made an appointment with the principal; I presented my case; I even repeated to the principal what the newly hired Physics professor told me; "God deserves an A and the best student a B."

Before giving the principal a chance to think about a solution, I proposed to be re-examined on all of the material to date in front of a committee. He looked at me as if he'd seen a vision and said, "It's the end of the year; you want to be re-examined on all the material you've studied through the entire year?"

I went even further; I said I was ready to accept a failing grade if I answered as much as one question incorrectly. The principal smiled and we set a date. I received an A in Physics.

Why did we, the high school students in Europe, call our teachers professor? As you already know, in Europe high schools were neither compulsory nor free. However, the subjects we were offered in high schools *were* compulsory. Not only were they compulsory, but a great number of them were subjects that in the United States are offered on the university level. As a result, a teacher who wanted to teach in high school had to hold a doctorate in his or her field.

Professor Fichman and I

My French professor, Mrs. Fichman, was on the committee when my Physics professor determined my grade. She was one of three Jewish professors in all the high school system in Sighet. Impressed with my performance, she wanted to know more about me. We scheduled a meeting at her home.

Professor Fichman, along with her husband, a well-known attorney, owned a courtyard with apartments. The Fichmans occupied the apartment facing the street. Their apartment consisted of three bedrooms, two studios, a room for the servants, a dining room, a living room and two bathrooms. Each room was exceptionally big. Just walking into the foyer, it gave a clue as to what to expect the rest of the apartment to look like.

All their furniture was imported. As I entered a vestibule, I faced a big round mirror in a heavy antique brass frame. There were two stands nailed to the wall, one on each side of the mirror, with brass planters holding philodendron snaking down the wall. Underneath the mirror against the wall, there was a credenza with a vase holding fresh flowers. A heavy branched-out brass coat hanger stood in a corner. It looked as if hands from all around were asking me for my coat and hat. There was a brass stand for umbrellas and galoshes. The floor had gold-toned carpeting. The doormat was of the same color.

I entered the living room. The same warm gold-tone coming from the walls, furniture and carpeting received me. Professor Fichman wore a beautiful lounging outfit. She was tall, slender and had a dark complexion housing two big expressive eyes. She had well-proportioned features.

She showed me to the couch. But where should I sit down when the whole surface of the couch was covered with blend-in throw pillows? She saw my confused look. "You may sit on the pillows, but if you would be more comfortable I'll push away some." I sat down. My eyes caught three paintings on the wall. "Yes, Livia, those paintings are originals."

Little by little, she teased my life story from me.

"So much ambition for such a little girl!" she suddenly said. "You deserve a break. I want you to have free room and board right here in my home."

I gave her an inquisitive look as if to say, "What will I have to do in return?"

Mrs. Fichman guessed my silent question. "You won't need to do anything in exchange," she said. I have a cook, a maid and a nanny for the children. You will be sleeping on the living room couch; part of it is a hide-a-bed."

I stared in disbelief, not knowing that tears were filling my eyes. She drew me to her chest. Oddly, I felt very secure.

"Professor Fichman, I eat kosher; I promised my mother to observe the Dietary Laws."

"Oh, we don't.," Professor Fichman smiled.

The door opened and Mr. Fichman walked in. He was tall, slender, had a dark complexion and looked extremely dignified. A smiling Mrs. Fichman met her husband, threw her arms around him and gave him a peck on his lips. She then led him to the couch and introduced him to me. He kissed my hand, a European gentleman's gesture. I'm only a student, not a lady, I thought. My face flushed; I felt it would explode any minute. After Professor Fichman introduced her husband to me, she excused herself, winked at me and they both left the room.

About ten minutes later, she returned. "Our problem is solved, Livia," she said. "An Orthodox family, a watchmaker, is one of our tenants. They keep kosher. I think I can work out something so that you could eat in their home. I'll tell you as soon as I know." She stretched her hand out as if saying, "Good-bye for now." I thanked her profusely and kissed her hand in gratitude.

Two days after I moved in with the Fichman family, miraculously, everyone at school seemed to know me. They appeared to be interested in what I was doing and how I was doing. Some of the students wondered whether I'd ever have to study French at all and still get top grades. The truth was, I studied French harder than I had in the past.

During the time I lived at the Fichmans, I tutored ten students. I was able to pay for my own tuition, buy my own uniforms, wear real silk stockings and even buy presents for my family when I'd go home on Christmas vacation.

I had very little social life in high school. My time was divided between studying and tutoring. However, I began to look forward to my meals with Lilly and Shari, the watchmaker's daughters. At first, the family must have been astounded that the tiny girl I was could eat so much food. Before any of them had finished their original helpings, I was at the end of my third portion! As I became more comfortable with the family, I visited them during my free time.

Both Lilly and Shari were beautiful young women in their mid-twenties. Each of their faces was uniquely striking. Lilly's willowy slenderness, alabaster skin, inky, arching eyebrows, flashing black eyes and delicate coral mouth reminded me of a picture from *One Thousand and One Arabian Nights.*

Shari's coloring was like her sister's, but her features were her own. Her face was rounder than Lilly's, and her dark, wavy hair swept itself upward from a magnificent widow's peak. Her eyes were dark brown and appeared to hold some deep secret.

When these beauties were at home, each of them had some moisturizing cream on her face and a novel in her hand. Yet, when they left the house, always together, each of them looked so lovely you'd suppose they'd come fresh out of a gift box.

They showed me all their creams and powders. They both insisted that I wash my face with hot water and soap, followed by an ice cold rinse to tighten my pores. I have never learned whether or not these sisters survived the war.

The Joint, an Orphanage

Two years into living at the Fichmans, Dr. Danziger, my religion professor, came to me with a proposal, "How would you like to tutor three students at the Joint in return for room and board," he asked me. The Joint was a prestigious orphanage financed by American Jews. Dragos Voda, an all-boy high school was situated across the street from the Joint. I accepted the offer. I couldn't continue to take advantage of Professor Fichman.

However, the main reason I accepted the deal was because the orphanage dormitory windows were facing the recreation room of Dragos Voda. The boy students would flock to this room on their recreation time and talk sign language with the orphans of the Joint. The sign language was silly- blowing kisses, and other funny gestures. Why was I so interested? My love, Ferenz attended Dragos Voda at that time. I hoped to have a glimpse of him every day as he'd visit the recreation room.

I lived in the orphanage during the year 1937. At the end of 1937 and the beginning of 1938 an anti-Semitic party came to power. It had two leaders: Octavian Goga and Gheorghe Cuza.

It was a very cold morning in late December, 1937. Even with gloves and boots, my fingers and toes felt wooden. I was going to school early to help my gentile friend, Maria, with her homework. I wondered what she might need help in today. Every day she was behind in something. Some days she was behind in *everything.*

I walked down the chilly corridor about seven o'clock in the morning. I heard someone calling my name. I turned around, and saw Yittie Yakobowitz, the only other Jewish classmate of mine. If you recall, I tutored Yittie's two siblings: Shullie and Hedy in return for room and a complete breakfast in my second high school year in Sighet, Romania.

"What in the world are you doing here this early?' I asked Yittie. "You should be eating your breakfast at this time."

"I need your help in Physics." She looked distraught.

"Physics? We don't have Physics today."

"We don't? I'm so upset; I forgot what day it was."

"Has something happened?"

"Not yet, but I have a bad feeling."

"A bad feeling about what?"

"With Goga-Cuza's anti-Semitic party in power and my father being rich, I'm worried about progroms."

"Yes, my father told me about *pogroms, not progroms,"* inconspicuously correcting Yittie.

"I'm so upset I can barely make any sense!"

I touched her shoulder in a gesture to calm her down.

"What did your father tell you about pogroms?" Yittie asked.

I explained that pogrom was a Russian word and that it meant riot and devastation. They had happened all through the centuries, even during our century. Sometimes entire villages were wiped out.

"Now you see why I'm upset? I'm scared that these pogroms will happen again, especially with this anti-Semitic party in power!"

I told Yittie that we lived in the year 1937, and that people were more civilized now. Pogroms were part of the past. Did I speak too soon? Thirteen thousand innocent Jews mainly merchants and professionals were killed during the first two weeks of Goga-Cuza's reign. Luckily, France and England sent emissaries to our King Carol II, making him aware of the atrocities that were happening right under his nose. The King gave in to the pressures from the two countries. After forty-four days, he removed the party from power and declared himself Absolute Ruler of Romania.

Yittie wanted to get into the classroom and sit down. I asked her to wait in the next classroom; I was helping a classmate of ours with her homework and she wanted me to keep it a secret.

Yittie hoped I was getting paid well. I told her I was tutoring our classmate free of charge. Her parents had given her an ultimatum: either she improved in her grades or her boyfriend went. I sympathized with her. Yittie asked me why I pushed so hard to get an education.

"I am doing what I am best at," I said.

"You're best at learning?" She looked at me as if she saw me for the first time. She had no idea what *she* was best at, she said after recovering.

I got into the mood and said, "You're best at marrying a rich man."

Yittie laughed.

"Speaking of marriage," I continued. "The only chance a girl had in my village was to become a seamstress and eventually marry a tailor. Would you like to marry a tailor?"

"If I fell in love with one, yes, I would."

"Your parents would disown you!"

"I still think I'd marry a tailor if I were madly in love with him."

"And be without a cook, a maid, and a nanny for your dozen children? And listen to your husband's nightly stories?"

"What stories? "

"Stories about how hard he worked today; how he didn't have strength to eat supper; how Shlomka, the fat grocery store owner refused to pay for the alteration of his pants, claiming they didn't fit, while admitting he gained five pounds that week."

"How do you know what a tailor is talking to his wife about when he comes back from work?"

"In a small village, people's business is everyone's business. When a rumor starts in one side of the village, by the time it gets to the last person in the village, the story barely resembles the original. Please, Yittie, we got carried away in our conversation. Go into the next classroom."

I opened the door to our classroom. I was heading toward my desk which was the first desk as I entered the classroom. Out of nowhere, Maria, the classmate I was tutoring accosted me. "I've been waiting for you for an hour!" She tried to force the satchel with my books from my hands but I held onto it. A scuffle ensued and I fell to the floor, my satchel next to me. She held me down with one of her feet while grabbing my satchel. She took out its contents and threw it across the floor.

"Pick up your garbage, Jew dog!" she shouted. Just as I stood up, a flabbergasted Yittie walked into the classroom. She'd heard the commotion in our classroom and came to see what happened. She walked me to my desk. Maria ordered Yittie to sit at her own desk. A scared Yittie obeyed Maria's orders.

I regained my posture. "What's gotten into you, Maria?" I asked.

"What's gotten into *me*? You Jews are the scum of the earth, you don't deserve to live!"

"Says who?" I looked at her.

"My government! You, Jews, make all the trouble in the world!" she said with her eyes bulging out. When I asked her to name one trouble the Jews are accused of, she drew a blank, but then soon said, "All the Jews in Sighet are filthy rich, and have the most beautiful houses!"

I told her that for every rich Jew in Sighet I could show her twenty poor Jews.

Maria ignored my statement. "Pick up your garbage, filthy Jew, or else!"

"Or else what? You'll beat me up?"

"I don't have to beat you up. I just have to tell my brother, Radu, who's a lieutenant in the police, that you called Goga, the leader of our government, a swine!"

I told Maria I need not to worry because I hadn't called Goga a swine; Yittie could testify to that.

"Just you wait when my brother takes you to the Police, whom will the Chief of Police believe my brother or you a filthy Jew liar!" I realized that Maria was blackmailing me and that I had to pick up my things if I and my family were to survive. I complained to the professors; they did nothing to help me. Maria continued with her malicious behavior for six consecutive weeks after which time the party fell from power. Now she made a 180 degree turn about. She hugged me and kissed me and asked me for forgiveness. She said she must have been crazy and didn't know what she was doing. I told her she wasn't crazy; she knew what she was doing and I wouldn't forgive her. But, I would help her with her homework just as if nothing had happened. The values my mother instilled in me were alive and well.

After the fall of the Goga-Cuza regime, my thoughts turned to the Fichmans, the most lovable family that gave me room and board free of charge for almost three years. I wondered whether they were part of the massacre of merchants and professionals in my town. It turned out that they survived.

At a school social, a gentile colleague of Professor Fichman after having had a few drinks, became talkative, "The Jews are in big trouble, "she said. "But don't you worry; everybody knows that you're different from the rest of your people."

Instead of taking comfort in the colleague's words, the Fichmans became quite alarmed. They immediately liquidated their assets, sent their children to England and left for Palestine. It took fifteen years for them to be reunited.

A WORLD OF MADNESS

The *Anschluss* (The Annexation of Austria)

In March 1938, Hitler annexed Austria to Germany without any opposition. The Jews were the first to suffer. The Germans looted Jewish shops and homes. Jewish writers and lawyers who were unable to cope with a bleak future committed suicide. Thirty thousand Jews had been sent to concentration camps. Those who could, fled Germany and its occupied territories. Albert Einstein fled to the United States to avoid being assassinated by the Nazis. Sigmund Freud, dying of cancer at the age of eighty, fled Austria and went to England. In recognition of his services in psychoanalysis, he was made a Fellow of the Royal Society. In addition, a huge number of Catholics, democrats, socialists, and communists found themselves in concentration camps.

The Munich Agreement

Hitler wanted to incorporate the Sudeten Province of Czechoslovakia into the Greater Reich, since the majority of the people of the province were Germans. To avoid being drawn into a war with Hitler, Neville Chamberlain, the Prime minister of Great Britain, and Edouard Deladier, the Prime minister of France, met with Hitler in Munich on September 29, 1938. The two agreed to the transfer of the Sudetenland to Germany. German troops began their occupation of the Sudetenland on October 1, 1938, and completed it in ten days.

Kristallnacht (The Night of Broken Glass)

After the transfer of the Sudetenland, Hitler decided on another dramatic move against the Jews. He expelled all German Jews of Polish descent to Poland.

Sendel Grynspan, one of the Polish-born Jews who had been expelled, wrote to his seventeen-year-old son, Hershel, who was in Paris. He described the suddenness and humiliation of the expulsion. The Jews were ordered out of their homes, and then taken by train and truck to two crossing points on the German border with Poland. From there, they were driven over the border. They could carry only one suitcase or one bundle with them.

The angered son, Hershel, went to the German Embassy in Paris, and fatally shot Ernst von Rath, the Third Secretary in the Embassy. Herschel was arrested and executed. Hitler approved a massive destruction of Jewish homes and Jewish businesses and synagogues in Germany and Austria.

In the course of a fifteen-hour attack during the night of November 10, 1938, as many as 7,500 Jewish owned shops were destroyed. Many Jewish homes were ransacked. The furniture that wasn't stolen was piled in the street and set on fire. One hundred Jews were murdered that night. Twenty-thousand Jews were arrested during the next few days, and sent to concentration camps. In order to impoverish German Jews, Hitler issued a decree ordering them to make good at their own expense the cost of all damages done to them. A one billion mark fine was imposed on the whole German Jewish community.

In Vienna, twenty-two large synagogues and eighty small houses of prayer were blown up and set on fire. Ninety more synagogues were set on fire throughout Germany.

World War II

On August 31, 1939, Germany announced that Polish troops had broken into a German radio station in Gleiwitz, Poland. They killed the German soldiers in the station, and broadcast an appeal to Poland, calling on the population to attack Germany. In actuality, the assumed Polish troops who had broken into the German station and broadcast the appeal to the Polish population were none other than German soldiers in Polish dress; they killed their own German soldiers! Within twenty-four hours, Hitler ordered the German Army to invade and bomb Poland. The Polish government capitulated seventeen days later.

Theodore Eicke, commander of the SS Death's Head, ordered the killing of Polish civilians. Storm Troopers executed prominent Poles, including teachers, municipal officials, and priests. The SS troops shot Jews randomly. In Wieruszow, German soldiers lined up twenty Jews in the market place and shot them. When a daughter begged a soldier to spare her father, the soldier ordered. "Open your mouth! Wide!" He shot her through her open mouth.

The SS killed thousands of Jews. Survivors of this butchery looked for their children, their parents, their brothers, their sisters, and their grandparents. Jews were thrown from moving trains. Troopers put Jews into ghettos until they could ship them to concentration camps.

Three days after the defeat of Poland, Britain and France declared war on Germany. That evening, a German U-boat blew up the British passenger liner, *Athenia*. The liner was crossing from Liverpool to Montreal. Some of the passengers were American students. Within a few hours, the United States, Switzerland, and Sweden declared neutrality. On September 5, a German U-boat sank four British merchant ships and one French ship.

On September 20, 1938, Hitler signed a decree to legalize the killing of approximately seventy thousand of his own German people. These people were mentally imbalanced, physically challenged or had degenerative diseases.

Germany made a pact with the Soviet Union Germany was to retain the western part of Poland, while the Soviets controlled the eastern part like: Estonia, Latvia, and Lithuania. Finland heroically resisted occupation.

Occupation 1940

Some historians say that 1940 began with the "Phony War." Britain and France fought against Germany on the sea, but not on the land. Russia renewed attacks on Finland without success. In May 1940, Hitler began his *Blitzkriegen* (lightning wars). His troops occupied Belgium, Luxembourg, and France. In June, Hitler occupied Paris. In July, he returned two-fifths of Transylvania to Hungary. Maramures, the part of Transylvania I was living in, became Hungary. Sighet, the capital of Maramures, was now spelled "Sziget," meaning island.

For the Jews in Sziget, life became intolerable. Jews were denied attendance at secular schools. Jewish physicians were denied access to the hospitals where they had treated their patients. Jewish lawyers were forced to take gentile partners. These partners almost immediately became senior partners. Jewish businesses were confiscated and given to gentiles. Original owners were forced to operate their former businesses without any salary.

The postal service became chaotic. My family got fewer and fewer letters from Father in America; envelopes containing money ceased to arrive. Now the upkeep of our household fell on Yitzchak, Toby and me; Rose was taking care of her 2½ year-old son, Shullie and also Mother. Yitzchak found a job as a chauffeur with a gentile engineer; Toby worked in our cousin's brush factory, and I continued tutoring.

Worldwide 1941

The Germans violated the Pact they had made with the Soviet Union and invaded on the morning of June 22, 1941. The conflict lasted nearly four years. The war affected all people living in the Soviet Union: Russians, Ukrainians, Armenians, Georgians, Mongols, and above all Jews.

On December 7, 1941, Japanese bombers and fighter planes attacked United States warships in Pearl Harbor, Hawaii. The next day the U.S. and Britain declared war on Japan. Three days later, Germany and Italy declared war on the United States.

A Short Overview of the Year 1942

In 1942, more than 4,000 Jews died of starvation in the Warsaw Ghetto. Czech partisans assassinated Reinhardt Heinrich, the leader of Hitler's Storm Troopers. In reprisal, the Germans killed 199 men in Lidice, Czechoslovakia, and began deporting women and children to concentration camps.

In August, British soldiers unsuccessfully raided Dieppe, a German-occupied port in France. The Nazis captured 2000 British soldiers and killed 902 Canadian soldiers. The Nazis lost 345 soldiers.

By August 21, Nazi soldiers penetrated Russia as far as the Volga, but the Soviet Army heroically defended Stalingrad.

Pop Vasile, My Gentile Admirer

Hitler returned the northern part of Transylvania to Hungary in July, 1940. People were moving in and out of Sighet, the city where I attended high school, joining their relatives in different parts of Hungary. I was finishing my junior high at Scoala Comerciala. The hateful incident I encountered with Maria two and a half years earlier still haunted me. I transferred to Liceu Domnita Iliana high school. I registered. I was soon informed there would be no senior class because they had only eight students. Coincidentally, Dragos Voda, the all-boy high school, also had only eight seniors registered. To solving the problem, the Hungarian School Board instituted a co-ed class, the first such phenomenon in the history of Sighet's five high schools. We met on Liceu Dragos Voda campus. We were three female students in our class.

I barely got used to the new system when I learned that Pop Vasile, a gentile classmate of mine, liked me. What now? I was still madly in love with Ferenz.

One sleepless night, I came to a conclusion. I must set up a barrier between Vasile and me. He must have no chance to ask me on a date. He must call me by my last name, Miss Szabo, every time he wanted to talk to me.

One blistery cold morning in January 1941, I arrived at school in my usual silk stockings and high-heeled shoes. The boys had nicknamed me "Legs," deciding I had the shapeliest legs in the class. I walked to the stove, kicked off my shoes and began messaging my feet. If the stove hadn't been warm, my tears from the pain in my legs might have frozen on my face.

Zsoltan, the class clown, entered the classroom. Seeing my stocking-clad feet, he shouted, "Guys! Come and look what's happened to Legs!" Four male classmates crowded around me.

"Hey Legs! How come you're not wearing stockings?" Zsoltan asked.

"I *am* wearing stockings!" I raised my voice. "And even if I weren't, it's none of your business!"

"Who wants to make sure that Legs is wearing stockings?" Zsoltan cried out. None of the male classmates made a move.

"How much time before the teacher comes in?" I asked.

"Ten minutes," said Zsoltan.

I reached for my shoes; I couldn't find them. "Zsoltan where are my shoes?" I asked.

"Why do you think I know where your shoes are?" Zsoltan answered.

"Because you're the devil incarnate, and I know you took them!" I replied.

"What about Vasile? He could've done it!" Vasile who entered the classroom together with the rest of the students promised he hadn't done it, and he'd find them for me if he had to turn the classroom upside down. He looked in every desk. When he approached Zsoltan's desk, he put up a resistance. A scuffle ensued that took them to the windows where Vasile noticed my shoes.

Vasile gave me my shoes. I was standing in front of my desk. I stretched out my hand to thank him. Impulsively he pulled me to him and kissed me on my lips.

"You behaved like a peasant!" I raised my voice to him.

"I know Miss Szabo. "I'm awfully sorry; but you already know that I love you," he said apologetically.

"And you already know that I'm in love with someone else! There are so many beautiful girls around; why do you waste your time on me?"

"I'm not interested in any other girls! When I look at you, my heart is seized with passionate love for you, and my mind stops reasoning!"

I laughed. "There's nothing ridiculous about my statement, Miss Szabo." He looked insulted.

"I was laughing because you've quoted from Molliere's, *Tartuffe*. Maybe this quote sounds familiar, too, 'I abandoned my heart to someone else,'" I said straightforwardly.

"But that someone else is not even in town anymore. Besides, he's got another girl!" I made a last effort. I asked him to let go of me if he really loved me, if he wanted to see me happy. "I'll always love you and never stop trying," Vasile said as we ended the conversation.

The next day, Zsoltan was still up to mischief. He approached my desk. He said he had a secret to tell me about Vasile. He whispered something incoherent in my ear. Then he turned to Vasile and said, "I told Livia the truth; you love her so much you'd cut off your nose if she asked you to." Vasile's face purpled; his forehead throbbed; he drew a gun at Zsoltan. Two male students subdued him.

During the spring of 1941, I learned that Vasile and Yitzchak, my younger brother, were seeking sexual favors from the same woman. In Europe during my youth, girls were raised to bring innocence to their marriage. Since there were no such requirements for men, houses of ill repute known as Red District Quarters, were legal. The women in these Red District Quarters were examined by doctors paid by the state for venereal diseases on a weekly basis.

However, some widows and divorcees, in dire financial situations, would accept money for sexual favors. My brother Yitzchak and Vasile met at such a woman's residence.

The next day after school, Vasile approached me, "I will not share my woman with your brother!" he said, anger in his voice. I looked at him puzzled. "Isn't this a matter between you and my brother?"

"You just don't understand! Your brother reminds me of you; I don't want to think about you when I'm with such a woman!"

That evening, I had a talk with Yitzchak. "Stay away from Vasile's woman, please!" Yitzchak laughed. "When I pay, the woman is mine! When Vasile pays, she's his!" I tried to convince my brother of Vasile's unpredictability. "He carries a gun," I said. My words fell on deaf ears.

About two weeks later, Vasile had bad predictions concerning Yitzchak. "I saw your stupid brother last night again. I pulled a gun and pointed it at his forehead. Then I saw you . . . your face peered from behind his! If I'd shot him, I'd have shot you, too! That scared me!"

"My brother is stubborn; he's got a mind of his own," I said. "Tell me what I could do, Vasile, please?" I looked at him imploringly.

"You could come on a date with me!" I was caught between my naïve, stubborn brother and a love-stricken, unpredictable Vasile. I had to save my brother's life. I asked Vasile when he wanted me to go on a date with him.

"Today!" he answered. Today it was! Vasile suggested we meet at the *Molomkert* (the park for lovers). I expected he'd try to take advantage of me. I wore two girdles; I hooked them up to a long-line brassiere. If I'd had a chastity belt with spikes, I'd have worn it.

Vasile behaved pretty civilized, except for his non-stop kissing me. My lips hurt so much, I was crying as he walked me home.

Vasile apologized. "It wasn't easy to control myself," he said. "Try to understand."

I remained silent.

Vasile Serenades Me

Serenading one's sweetheart on May first was a long-practiced custom in Hungary. I had just fallen asleep on the couch in the den when soft Gypsy music drifted in from the street. I knew it was May first. Oh! Please . . . ! It's not . . . ? I tiptoed in the dark foyer. The street lamps cast an eerie glow. I saw Vasile with a group of Gypsies. I sneaked back into the den. Suddenly, I heard Mother's tired voice, "Dear, please turn the radio off. I can't sleep." Rose came to my rescue; she told Mother someone was serenading our neighbor's daughter. The both of them went back to sleep.

Just then, Yitzchak crept into the den. He brought me news; he said Vasile was serenading me. I kept silent. "Maybe this news will make you talk. "Vasile is crazy! One day he wants to kill me and the next he makes friends with me," he said.

"So my date with Vasile worked after all," I said under my breath. Yitzchak asked me to explain my babbling. I told him I went on a date with Vasile to save his life. As if bitten by a bee, he walked out of the den. While rushing down into the basement where he usually slept he uttered, "I refuse to believe you went on a date with Vasile on my behalf!" Was it his guilt that spoke?

I was just getting back in bed when Rose tapped my shoulder. She said I needed to take care of my admirer before his music woke up her son. I asked her what she suggested I do.

"Do what people do when they're serenaded: they flick the

light on and off three times. The boyfriend or admirer gets the message and goes home."

I interrupted her. "What message does the boyfriend or admirer get?" I asked Rose.

"I don't know." Rose replied. "The message these enamored fellows are getting is that their girlfriends or sweethearts accept their gesture and that their relationship stands. If I flicked the light three times on and off, Vasile would get the wrong impression, (giving him an excuse to ask me on a date or to a dance the next day.) Rose kept pleading with me. "How can I listen to music when my husband is in a labor camp somewhere, maybe exhausted, freezing and starved at this time?" she said. She sounded as if mourning him. I refused to flick the light. In the end Rose flicked the light and the music stopped.

I decided to stay home for the next two days. When I went back to school, Vasile, in his mistaken belief that I had flicked the light, proposed we go dancing. I concocted a story. I said I had a bad cold and hadn't recovered from it yet.

Soon after the serenade, we received sad news about Rose's husband. He died of exposure and starvation. For a while I avoided my sister. She realized something was bothering me. One day, she asked me what ailed me. I draped my hands around her neck and turned into a helpless six-year-old child. I began sobbing.

"Now, now, it can't be that bad," Rose said.

"It *is* bad! During the serenade incident, I refused to hear your silent suffering. I can't forgive my selfishness!"

"I forgave you a long, long, time ago. I knew that, consciously, you hadn't done anything to hurt me." She stroked my hair.

I felt vindicated; she lifted a ton of load off of my shoulders. I began giving all my free time to her two-and-a-half year old son, Shullie. For no rhyme or reason, I began talking to him in French. The first words he picked up were: "*comci- comça* (so, so). Of course he never knew what he was saying; he must have liked the sound of the words. It took awhile before he was ready to pick up other

French words. Once he did, there was no end to it; I thought he was the smartest child in the world. He was gassed in Auschwitz as my mother held him in her arms. I wonder how many more geniuses the world lost among the one-and-a-half million Jewish children murdered.

Emigration Papers to the U.S.A

In the beginning of 1942, my father sent emigration papers for us to come to America. We hadn't heard from him in two years since the postal services functioned irregularly, and sometimes not at all.

Being that I spoke Hungarian, I traveled to Budapest, the capital of Hungary, to discuss the issue of visas to the United States with a representative of the Ministry of Interior. In Budapest, I learned that I could not represent my family; my mother would have to come to Budapest herself. I explained to the clerk that my mother was recovering from thyroid surgery and that traveling at this time would jeopardize her health. The answer sounded: "Rules are rules."

Rose

Livia

Ideas began racing in my mind. What if I waited in the hallway in front of the representative's office and attached myself to a group of people or a family as they entered his office? I decided to take a chance.

Four days later, I had that chance. I lined up behind a family of five children, finding myself in the office, sitting on a chair next to the wall. I rehearsed in my mind how to soften the representative's heart when sounds of noisy children opening and closing the door as they left interrupted my thoughts. I was alone in the office with the representative, a middle-aged man. "Your parents just left," he said. "Try to catch up with them." He had a concerned look on his face.

I told the representative the reason I was there, and asked him to forgive me for using dishonorable means to get into the office. He looked at me in disbelief. He debated a while with himself and then took the envelope with papers from my hands. After carefully reading three pages, I heard, "I can issue two visas only: One for your mother and one for Toby. According to the existing laws, children under twenty-one-years of age can join their parents. Toby fits the picture," he said, looking at my reaction. Tears began welling in my eyes. I saw myself saying good-bye to my mother, while holding on to her until the train pulled her away, swallowing her image.

I barely slept that night. The next morning I returned home. We waited for Mother's decision, wishing we were any age but our own. Mother renounced her visa, deciding to stay with all of us.

My personal involvement in the 'Aktzion' in Sziget in 1942

On a hot, muggy, mid-July evening in 1942, I was engrossed in reading a book when I heard three loud knocks at the front door. It was the police. The clock showed 11:00 p.m. I opened the door and invited the two uniformed men into the house. They stopped in the foyer. One officer wore a royal-blue uniform which usually indicated he was of higher rank. His jacket had golden epaulettes, golden buttons, a golden star on each side of his jacket collar and golden trim on his cuffs. He had a feather in his hat and I noticed the look of arrogance on his face. The other officer wore a navy-blue uniform, no ornaments, except for a feather in his cap.

Involuntarily, I took a closer look at the low-ranking officer. I thought I recognized him."Is that you, Lupu?" I asked. The officer eyed me up and down. "Oh, yes, you must be Libby," He said. "You two know each other?" asked the other officer who was extremely agitated. "Sort of . . . .uh. . . . ,"

The high-ranking officer interrupted me and looked at Lupu. "You should have told the Chief of Police beforehand that you knew this family," he said, his voice raised. I tried to address the high-ranking officer, "Officer, uh . . . ," The officer interrupted me, "Lieutenant, Sir, to you!"

"Lieutent Sir, Lupu doesn't *know* my family; I saw him only once."

"I'm not interested in how many times you saw him!" the officer shouted, then turned to Lupu, "I think you ought to leave these premises! Besides, what kind of name is Lupu?"

"Lupu is my Romanian name, just as yours would be Radu."

"You'll never again refer to a superior officer by his Christian name in the presence of a civilian, understood?!" Lupu sighed. "Lieutenant, Sir, you and I have known each other for years; what makes this time different from any other?"

Instead of answering Lupu, the senior officer changed the subject by pointing toward the basement. "Who lives in the basement?"

"We live in the basement, Lieutenant, Sir."

"How many rooms are there?"

"Three, Lieutenant, Sir."

"So, you're subletting?"

"We're not subletting, Lieutenant, Sir."

"You're not subletting, but you're hiding people down there?!"

"I don't know what you mean, Lieutenant, Sir. One room we

use as a summer kitchen; one we use for an extra bedroom; and in one we keep the ice box and such."

"Turn the light on!" The two officers went into the basement. When they reappeared, the lieutenant asked for the head of the household. I told him my mother was sleeping. "I want to see your father, not your mother!"

"My father is not here, Lieutenant, Sir."

"When do you expect him back?"

"We don't expect him back; we hope to join him."

"Where? In his hideout?"

"I don't understand, Lieutenant, Sir."

"Maybe your friend can explain?" He looked at Lupu. "I suppose you warned your friend's father about our visit!"

"Lieutenant, Sir, someone isn't getting it, I said. My father is in America; he sent us emigration papers; I could show them to you." As I turned the bedroom doorknob to go and get the papers, I realized that Rose and Mother had been listening. They tumbled out of the bedroom. I helped Mother to the sofa. Her face was colorless and the veins in her neck throbbed like an over-wound toy. Rose tried to tie her robe over her nightgown. After she got her slippers on, she sat beside Mother on the sofa.

I must have spent more time than anticipated looking for the papers. When I returned and opened the door to the den, I heard the lieutenant saying under his breath, "How much longer is that Jew dog going to take?" I was flabbergasted. Suddenly, I realized something was wrong here. I heard voices in my head saying: Maria . . . Radu . . . Jew dog! Could the shouting officer be Radu Maria's brother? Papers in hand, I asked, "Lieutenant, Sir, you have a sister named Maria?"

"What if I do?"

"I attended Scoala Commerciala with her in 1937-1938."

"She calls herself Maritza now. She's married to the son of the chief of police," Lupu chimed in. I gave our emigration papers to the lieutenant. My heart jumped like a startled deer. My memory re-played scenes from Scoala Comerciala as Maria had thrown my books across the classroom floor, shouting, "Pick them up, Jew dog!" I remembered Yittie mentioning, she overheard a conversation between Maria and her brother Radu that upset her very much. Maria had told her brother she wished she could get even with me someday. Even for what? For helping her get good grades free of charge? What gives? What is the purpose of Radu's visit here?

My head was spinning. I recall saying, "Lieutenant, Sir, you're here to thank me for helping your sister with her schoolwork?"

The lieutenant ignored my question, "Your mother is coming to the police station with us for routine questioning; nothing to worry about," his voice subdued.

"Lieutenant, Sir, Mother is recovering from surgery; she doesn't speak or understand Hungarian. The people at the police station are Hungarians. Remember, the Hungarians reoccupied the northern part of Transilvaia in 1940? They renamed our capital Sighet to Sziget meaning island. Radu then pointed to Rose as if she should go instead. "Lieutenant, Sir, my sister is here temporarily; she's taking care of my ailing Mother; she doesn't speak or understand Hungarian either. However, Lieutenant, Sir, I'd be happy to accompany you to the police station."

"No! Not you! Don't you have an older brother?!"

"I have a younger brother, but he's out with his friends."

"He'd better be home by 2:00 a.m.!"

Rose's son, Shullie, woke up, sobbing. Rose excused herself, went into the bedroom, and returned with a quiet toddler. When Shullie saw the police officers, he began shrieking! The lieutenant was visibly annoyed with my nephew's screaming. He pointed to me, "You! Come with me!"

At the Police Station in Sziget in 1942

I'm not sure who pushed me into that over-crowded room at the police station. I remember wondering why most of the people looked so old, so fragile, so frightened. And why was the air so hot; so full of cigarette and cigar smoke, so full of the smell of perspiration mixed with perfume, so full of terror? Music blared from a radio.

I landed in the arms of a hatless, well-dressed man, probably in his early sixties, smoking a cigar. I regained my balance, stepped back and straightened my clothes. "Sorry, Sir."

"My name is Ezra Horowitz."

"Mine is Libby. In school they called me Livia." Then I heard a familiar voice, "Oy, vey! They're already grabbing children from the street!" I turned and saw Uncle Yossel, my father's younger brother standing two yards from me. By now he was in his sixties. He was wearing his usual black suit with a white shirt and a black Hamburg hat. "Uncle Yossel, they're not grabbing children from the street; I'm here in place of my father. Aren't you here as the head of the family?"

Do you know why the police wanted your father Libby?"

"For routine questioning, I understand."

"Yeah! Sure! Hundreds of people are here for routine questionings! What a farce!" moaned a young man wringing his hands. Uncle Yossel asked the man, "What's your name, young man?"

"Mendel, Reb Yossel."

"So, Mendel, you'll tell the rest of us why we're here?" Mendel kept silent. "Is it that bad, Mendel?" Mr. Horowitz asked.

"Couldn't be worse!" Mendel lowered his eyes. Uncle Yossel spoke again, "For centuries, Jews have been falsely imprisoned but our Jewish communities have always bailed us out."

"What's going on now goes beyond prison, Reb Yossel," said Avraam, a second young man. Uncle Yossel wasn't giving up. "It's always the same; we descend into darkness; we hope; we pray; and we emerge into the light."

"They wouldn't kill innocent people?" Mr. Horowitz asked Avraam.

"Wouldn't they?" He spoke in a whispering tone of voice. "The Germans have issued a decree: four hundred Jews from Sziget, chosen at random, must be eliminated in three days. They call this process: "Aktzion". These three-day Aktzions have been in effect for weeks. They apply to every Jew living in the Sub-Carpathian Region."

"So tonight we'll all be executed on these premises?" Mr. Horowitz whispered. Not necessarily tonight and certainly not here." Avraam said, looking around like a thief. "Maybe we ought to tell the rest of the people here what to expect." My uncle kept pressing, "Why take away their hope? God is the only truth. God's justice is to the end of time."

Mr. Horowitz asked Avraam for a more detailed explanation. Aktzion, Avraam said, isn't just for those of us at the police station; they'll drag our families here. Someone will say we're descended from Polish Jews. That's a lie! They'll say the Polish government claims us; they'll say we shouldn't worry about what we're leaving behind; the Polish government will compensate us to the penny! That's another fat lie!"

Mendel got into the discussion. "By dawn," he said, "we'll be loaded into cattle cars and transported to Kamenets-Podolsk in Poland. If we arrive by daylight, they'll keep us in a synagogue until darkness sets in. Then they'll take us into the woods and tell us to run headlong into a blast of rifle shots. Or, they'll tell us to cross a bridge with the guards shooting us in the back." Avraam gave us a glimpse of hope. "There might be a way out when they'll be marching us toward the synagogue in Kamenets-Podolsk. The guards are Hungarians and most of them are on the take."

Mendel took over. He spoke to a lucky survivor of Kamenets-Podolsk, he said. While on the way to the synagogue, he offered his wife's heavy gold chain to a guard in return for his family's freedom. The survivors have since moved in with his in-laws in a different village. They'd been afraid of being recognized in their own village by the authorities who sent them to their death. Or *thought* they had!

Avraam had his own story: two weeks ago, he talked with a

villager whom the guards shot while crossing a bridge. He fell into the river, wasn't fatally wounded so he swam to the shore. The Jewish community of Kamenets-Podolsk aware of these Aktzions but powerless to do anything about them would send men every morning to check the riverbanks and the woods for survivors. They fished the man out of the sandy bank, nursed him back to health, and shipped him off to another village. Besides nursing survivors back to health and sending them to secret places, these community people are also bailing out children for huge amounts of money thus preventing their death. "Since you two, Avraam and Mendel, know all this, what are you doing here?" Mr. Horowitz jumped in.

Mendel replied, "When Avraam found out about these tragedies, he sent his family to his in-laws in a village that has already had its Aktzion share. He also showed he carried a gold watch and some rings in his pocket." Avraam cut in. Just yesterday, he decided the women in his family must wear their jewelry under their blouses or dresses at all times and have money in their every-day handbags. He, personally, had no gold on his person, but he had money."

Mr. Horowitz offered a gold ring to Uncle Yossel. He refused it. "Orthodox men don't wear rings," he said.

"Don't I know, Reb Yossel," Mr. Horowitz sighed, dropping his wedding band into Uncle Yossel's pocket. Uncle Yossel said nothing, not even 'thank you'. Watching Mr. Horowitz's gesture I said. "You gave away your wedding band!" Mr. Horowitz assured me he had a golden pocket watch and a golden pocket watch chain in one of his vest's pockets. I thanked him in my Uncle Yossel's name. Avraam turned to me. He advised me to hold on to my necklace and the ring I wore. I thought about my family. I wasn't sure about money, but Mother and Rose always wore their wedding bands and their diamond rings. Rose also had a heavy gold necklace she wouldn't part with.

An elderly woman sitting next to me fainted. As she fell to the floor, she cried out, "Air! Good people! Open the windows!"

Ironically, there were no windows. Someone at the front desk turned the radio volume way up. Was it, perhaps, to drown out the woman's cries for help?

My throat felt constricted, but somehow I managed to scream, "Turn that blasted radio down!"

The radio volume went down as a voice commanded, "You! The one who gave the order, come to the front desk! Now!"

I tried to move. Nothing happened. My limbs weren't obeying me. My shoes might as well have been glued to the floor.

The voice in the back continued, "What are you waiting for? A special invitation!?" I still couldn't move. The people around me became restless. "Go, go, already!" they grumbled. "We don't need your problems! We've got our own."

Still, I couldn't budge. Mr. Horowitz gave me his arm; he was sure the detective would understand, he said; it was a natural reaction of a young person. He must have lessened my fear, for I took his arm and began shuffling toward the desk. I saw a nameplate reading, "Detective Barna." On the right-hand side of Mr. Barna's desk there sat a woman, seemingly in her fifties, ready to be interviewed. Mr. Barna, a man in his thirties, scanned me with his eyes from my hair to my shoes. He signaled to Mr. Horowitz to return to his previous place. I was to wait there until he finished the questioning of the woman. Now I had a chance to witness one of the infamous interviews Mendel and Avraam were talking about a short while ago. I paid attention to every detail of the conversation; I recall it as if it were yesterday:

"What did you say your name was?" I heard Mr. Barna asking the woman.

"Mrs. Berliner, Mr. Barna."

"Age?"

"Fifty-two."

"How many children?"

"Seven."

"Married?"

"My husband died two years ago." Mrs. Berliner took out a handkerchief and wiped her eyes, then continued, "may he rest in peace."

"Mrs. Berliner, I asked whether your children were married!"

"I'm sorry; three of my sons are married. They're in labor camps, but their wives and children are living with me. By God, it's hard to feed so many extra mouths."

"Have you brought your citizenship papers with you, Mrs. Berliner?"

Mrs. Berliner looked in her handbag, took out some papers, and gave them to Mr. Barna. Mr. Barna looked at the papers, as Mrs. Berliner kept talking, "I don't know if these papers are the right ones. You see, Sir, my late husband, may he rest in peace, used to handle all our papers. The other day, I looked for the deed to my house and just couldn't find it. It was as if the devil took it. I wanted to borrow some money on it. No one should be without a husband, not even my enemy. People used to say, 'Berliner don't climb roofs at your age'. My husband was a roofer, but he wouldn't listen. He was worried about dowries for our daughters. Now his daughters have no father and I am a widow."

"Mrs. Berliner, your problems are over. My government has taken upon itself the monetary burden of transporting you and your family to Poland, where all your needs will be attended to."

"I don't understand, Sir, what you're saying."

"Mrs. Berliner, we have done painstaking research concerning your case, and found that your husband's great-great-grandparents were born in Poland, and therefore Poland claims you."

"With a name like Berliner, my husband descended from Polish Jews? He'd always speak with such pride about being a descendent of German Jews. Besides, Sir, I have a house with furniture. You should see my grandchildren's belongings."

Mr. Barna became annoyed. "I can't waste all my time with you Mrs. Berliner! The Polish government will compensate you for everything you leave behind! Leave through that door!" Mr.

Barna pointed to the door at the left. Mrs. Berliner uncontrollably started sobbing, shook her head and mumbled something to herself while leaving the room.

Now it was *my* turn. Mr. Barna looked at me as if I were from another planet; it dawned on him I was a youngster among all the adults. He began speaking to me in a soft tone of voice. "So *you're* the one who gives orders around here? Young people your age usually *like* dancing music."

"Not when somebody's fainting next to me and is asking for help," I took on courage.

Mr. Barna changed subjects. "What's your name?" he asked.

"Livia Szabo, Sir."

"How did you wind up here?"

"Lieutenant Radu Popescu and another officer brought me here."

"Are you sure that Lieutenant Radu Popescu was one of the two officers who brought you here?"

"I'm sure, Sir. I attended Scoala Commerciala with his sister, Maria, in 1937-1938."

"Why didn't your father come?" I explained my father was in America and my mother was recovering from surgery and spoke no Hungarian. Mr. Barna was about to say something when a door opened and Pop Vasile, my high school admirer, walked in and approached the desk. The two men shook hands. "Good to see you!" Detective Barna said, offering Vasile a chair. "Tonight's been awful!"

"You'll tell me later. I'll wait," said Vasile. Just then, Vasile saw me. Our eyes locked. He rose to his feet like a man in a trance. "Miss Szabo! What are you doing here?" He sounded surprised. "Two officers came to our home tonight; one of them was Radu Popescu, Maria Popescu's brother. The other one was lower ranking. So, here I am."

Vasile whispered something in Mr. Barna's ear. The detective murmured something back. After several minutes of whispering to each other, the detective nodded as if saying, 'Yes'. I still was mixed up. "Miss Szabo, I'll take you home," Vasile said.

As we were leaving the room, I looked at the doomed crowd I'd been part of until a few minutes before. I felt almost guilty that I might live, yet, what could I do to help *any* of them. I wondered whether Mr. Horowitz's gold ring would buy Uncle Yossel's family's life. Then something dawned on me! Now that I'll be home, I could hide Aunt Esther and her son Abby in our apartment before the police came for them. I was relieved.

Vasile Takes Me Home from the Police Station

I'm not exactly sure what I said to Vasile once we were outside the police station. I know I thanked him more than one time for saving my life. The outside air felt muggy, suspiciously still. In spite of my light organdy dress, I was sweltering, yet I was trembling like an aspen leaf.

"Miss Szabo, you're shivering!" Vasile looked at me, concerned.

Yes, I was shivering, not from cold air but from morbid emotions. Thoughts crowded my mind. Since everything has a price in this world, what would be Vasile's price? Could it be me? I was seeing myself carrying his child, wondering how I could continue living with so many accusing fingers pointing at me. I heard imaginary voices cackling, "You see what higher education has done to her? A bastard by a non-Jew! This bastard may turn against the Jews someday . . . it happened before in history . . . she'll pay for this . . . not enough . . . they never do . . . even Rose, who married into such a respectable family, will suffer. . . . and poor Toby, who'd marry her? Her mother suffered for a lifetime . . . finally she'd had successful surgery on her thyroid . . . and her educated daughter, Libe–she calls herself Livia now--spoils it all!" My mind switched to my father in America. At least my father would take my un-wed motherhood for what it was, a personal sacrifice for our family. He'd see my disgrace as an act of God. But I'd tell him it was all Hitler's doing. I was pregnant because of a madman who was bent on destroying us. Father would probably set me up in an apartment far from the family. I would not want to ever marry. I'd want to raise my child as a Jew; and next, I'd want to write. I wouldn't want to be published. When someone becomes more or less famous, people dig up that someone's life! My oldest sister, Molly has two daughters of her own. What would my misfortune do to them?"

Vasile took off his jacket and draped it around my shoulders as I came to. "Vasile? Did you intuitively come to the police station to save my life?"

"I didn't know I'd be saving anyone's life. I came to say goodbye to my friend, Barna; I've been inducted into the army; I'll be leaving next week."

My mind danced in circles. One week? In a week's time anything could happen! In one day . . . ! In one hour . . . ! I was trembling again.

"Miss Szabo! Are you ill? How can I help? You keep shivering!"

What was I doing, I thought? I've let my emotions control me! Now he might insist on taking me inside my apartment; I'd better control myself. I stopped shaking and returned his coat.

"Vasile, did Detective Barna tell you why the room was overstuffed with Jews?"

"He mentioned something about relocating a few hundred Jews to Poland, but he assured me they would be okay. Detective Barna wanted to know why Maria Popescu's brother would go to your house."

"Because Maria sent him! She wants me dead! She's wanted me dead since 1937!" I blurted out.

"In the past, when I'd mention your name, "Vasile said, "Maria would get furious. She'd ask me how I could love a Jew. What happened between you two?" Vasile continued.

"It's a bizarre story, let's forget it," I said.

We arrived at our gate. I offered my hand, thanked him again, and said good night.

He kissed my hand in a gentleman's gesture, saying, "My girlfriend wants me to get engaged before I leave for the army."

Wow!! He has a girlfriend; he wasn't fixated on me any longer; I didn't have to worry!

He noticed my mood-change. "You're happy because I'm joining the army? Or because I have a girlfriend?"

"Do I know your girlfriend?" I asked, avoiding an answer.

"No. She's from Bucharest."

"I hope she deserves you; you're a great guy, if not the greatest!"

"Now, all of a sudden I'm a hero?"

"Many times over! My children and my children's children will know about it! In fact, the whole world will know about this incident someday!"

"I don't feel like a hero, but I'm moved! I wish I could call you, Livia."

"Instead of 'Miss Szabo'?"

"Yes."

"Then say, 'Yes, Livia'."

"Before I do, could we drink to it tomorrow at Brenner's Restaurant? Would that be okay?"

"It would be my pleasure; except, I don't drink liquor."

"We'll drink beer!"

"I don't drink beer, either. But tomorrow, I'll make an exception. Reserve a table next to the window. I want the whole world to see me toasting the man who saved my life and the life of my family!" I was elated!

The next day, I met Vasile at Brenner's Restaurant at one o'clock. I wore a short-sleeved green summer outfit with a matching handbag and shoes. I felt very alive and very fashionable. Vasile rose to meet me before I reached his table. He greeted me with a line I wasn't expecting to hear, "You look just like you used to."

"I don't know how to take that, because I didn't look like this in school," I said. Vasile pulled a chair out for me; I sat down.

"You didn't look like this in class; you wore a uniform. But on those Saturday evenings, when you walked on the promenade in front of the Corona Hotel with your friends, you looked like a rich socialite. Only I never understood why you wore those wide-brimmed hats. I wondered if you thought you needed to be in disguise."

"Vasile, I *was* in disguise. We had a curfew, remember? Since we weren't supposed to be in the street after nine o'clock, we had to look like strangers. The boys wore white slacks and navy blue jackets instead of the khaki uniforms. I never saw you, Vasile!"

"I sure saw you; I was jealous of any man who even looked at you!"

"Isn't it nice to be able to talk about the past as if we meant nothing to each other?"

He looked at me. "You'll never know how much you still mean to me!"

"In a little while, I'll fade into your memories; let's drink to that."

Vasile poured beer into our glasses, saying,"Just a year ago I'd have given anything to sit here with you. I had hoped you'd go in public places with me."

"Vasile, I don't understand. I wasn't good-looking!"

"When I saw you my heart raced; that's all I know!"

I had to change subjects. "Let's drink to your bride-to-be. I love her."

"You do?"

"She rescued you from your fixation on me. Now you and I can be real friends." Both of us drank. I took one sip. Vasile refilled his glass a few times. Something entered my mind and I said, "Tell your superior in the army that Livia said he's never to send you to the front lines!"

"Livia! That's a touching tribute. Thank you."

"Vasile, I have a confession. Your eyes used to terrify me; I thought you could see through and through me.

"Really?"

"Really. But last night at the police station when our eyes locked, I wasn't frightened at all; I saw compassion and understanding in your eyes."

I never saw Vasile again; he died in the war. In January 2001, I had his name inscribed among the Righteous Christians at the Jewish Community Center in La Jolla, California. He'll be remembered after all.

The Ghetto

On March 19, 1944, German soldiers entered Maramures County. They ordered all Jews to wear the Star of David and observe curfews. Few in Sziget knew about concentration camps, although we'd heard about the "Labor Detachment Camps," which were established just behind the front lines. Jewish men between eighteen and forty-five were recruited to work in these camps without proper food or protective clothing, digging foxholes or clearing minefields. Most of these men, including Rose's husband, Boruch, died in one of these camps.

It was the morning of the last day of Passover in mid April 1944. A pale, haggard looking UncleYossel stormed into our apartment, addressing himself to my mother. "Listen Rochel!" he said. "The Germans have issued orders: All Jews from Sziget are to be taken to an undisclosed place; they are to pack two suitcases per adult and line up in the street they live on."

"When . . .?" asked Mother.

"Today!"

Mother put her hands at her temples. *"Oy, vey iz mir!"* (A woe is to me). Uncle Yossel consoled her with a soothing voice, "Rochel, don't worry; we'll all be together!"

The next thing I remember was Mother saying, "Yossel, we don't have eight suitcases; we are four adults; besides, I don't even know what to pack!"

Uncle Yossel gave Mother a thousand-yard-stare. "Use your

head, Rochel, make bundles; as about what to pack, I can't help you there!"

Mother appeared visibly embarrassed; she opened her mouth to say something, but the words got stuck in her throat. I never saw Uncle Yossel or Aunt Esther or their seven-year-old son, Abby again. I met their surviving children: Yankel, Szidi, Piri, Feivel and Czali after the war.

Around nine o'clock, right after Uncle Yossel left our apartment, we began discussing what to pack. We were four adults indeed. There was my mother, my older sister, Rose, my younger sister, Toby and I. Yitzchak, my younger brother was in an unknown labor camp. I don't recall whose suggestions prevailed. I know that sometime before noon four suitcases and four bundles lay on the floor.

Rose did the packing; I watched her in amazement. She fitted more things in one suitcase than I could've fitted in three. After she locked the suitcases, she reinforced them with ropes. Then, she took another rope and tied together the first two suitcases, then the next two suitcases. All four suitcases went on Rose's shoulders.

I pictured myself loaded with two suitcases: One dangling on my back, and the other somewhere on my chest, when I heard Shullie, Rose's son, asking, "Are we moving, Mommy?" He was looking at the things on the floor.

Caught by surprise, Rose said, "We're not moving, dear; we're going on a trip." She spoke in a happy tone of voice, trying to disguise her true feelings. Shullie wanted to know which bundles were his. To avoid questions and answers Rose said, "All of them!"

I can see a bewildered Shullie as if it were today. He put his little hands on his hips, walked around the heap of luggage and said, *"Comci, comça,* I don't like this design, Mommy; can I change it?"

By now, my sister seemed to have lost her patience for she said, "You can change the design, but you can't move things around!"

A baffled Shullie looked at Rose, "How can I change the design if I can't move things around?"

Rose changed her tone of voice, "I have an idea, dear; try to change the design in your mind, what do you say?"

The child looked mixed up. "I don't understand what you're saying, Mommy."

Suddenly, the air reverberated with a loud-as-thunder knocking at the entrance door followed by shouting, "Rauss! Schnell! Yude!" (Get out! Fast! Jew).

A frightened Shullie buried his little face in his mother's skirt. Rose picked up her crying son in her arms, wiped his tears off his little face and said, "These people are telling us that we're ready to go on the trip; I suppose they were a little too loud, but don't you worry, sweetheart." She kissed him on his little cheeks as she put him down on the floor.

We put on our winter coats. Rose dressed Shullie; she asked him to be a good boy and go with his grandma. She explained she would have to carry most of the stuff from the floor. And carry she did, four suitcases and two bundles, one strung on each of her arms. The remaining two bundles Rose divided between Toby and me.

We lined up in the street. Slushy snow covered the ground. Families began pouring in from everywhere. The men were carrying four to five suitcases on their shoulders and just as many bundles around their arms; some of them had bundles strung around their neck, as well.

The women were busy with their infants while their older children took care of their younger siblings. People were tense and confused. The small children were crying, sobbing, screaming. The sick, propped up by their young, strong family members, were shuffling, moaning and groaning, while rifle butts were flying indiscriminately into people's ribs, and on their heads–*everywhere!*

"Where is Yossel, where is Yossel?" Mother sounded forlorn. Just then, a soldier approached us; we were already forming a column.

"Umdrehen!" (turn around) he shouted. We turned around. We

were now facing Piata Unirii, the heart of the town. *"Vorwärts!"* (forward) the soldier shouted.

We arrived at an intersection. "*Halt*! *Halt*!" We stopped. More Jews, with more suitcases and bundles, with more crying children, with more moaning sick joined our column. From then on, at each intersection, we kept hearing, "Vorwärts! Halt! Vorwärts! Halt!" Some pedestrians from the sidewalk kept spitting at us while others turned their faces away.

About four hours later, we arrived at Kamara Utsa, a poor, Jewish neighborhood on the outskirts of Sziget. The guards pushed us into courtyards, then into apartments in which people already lived. There was no room to unpack. People took turns to eat at tables, and women cooked in shifts. Ten to fifteen families shared a single kitchen. Where did people sleep? On floors, on tables and on benches. Fifteen, to twenty, to forty people slept in one room, depending on the size of the room. Coincidentally, our family landed in Cousin Helen Drummer's apartment. The couple had married about three years ago, had no children, and owned a brush factory in the back of their apartment. They shared their bedroom with us. They yielded the rest of their apartment and factory to people they never knew or met before.

Every morning, between ten and eleven, armed German soldiers would escort us into town to do our shopping. Living under such conditions one would imagine that the people would be miserable. Not so. We hoped the Germans would take us to labor camps where we'd work hard, then return after the war to reunite with our families, and eventually recover whatever we had left behind.

The Cattle Cars

At dawn, on May 14, 1944, after a month of ghetto-life, we heard shouts, "Pack one suitcase to an adult and line up in the street!" German guards led us through dark side streets to the railroad station.

We stopped in front of a cattle-car train. Although I was twenty-four years old, I had never seen a cattle-car train from close up. The doors seemed about a yard and a half from the ground.

I asked Rose how cattle get into these cars, not suspecting that we would be the cattle. "On wide, wooden planks," she said. Rose had barely finished the sentence when my imagination went into overdrive. I saw orderly horses walking up the wide planks into the cars to join their friends, maybe even their families. But wait a minute! Horses don't cry!

As I came out of my trance, I heard soldiers counting and shouting. I saw people being pushed into the cattle cars with rifle butts. I heard sounds of pain. I saw children holding onto their mother's skirts and crying. I saw clothes strewn on the ground. I saw chaos. "What's going on here?" I asked Rose.

"It seems that one hundred people are allotted to a car." I turned my face to the crowd when I heard: *Eins!* (one!) *Zwei!* (two!) *Drei!* (three!) *Vier!* (four!) *Funf!* (Five!)! The counting continued until one hundred. "Rein! Schnell! Rein! Schnell!" (get inside fast)! Amidst the counting, shouting and shoving, I saw a soldier snatching a little boy, seeming about seven-years-old, from his mother's arms. The soldier put the little boy on the ground and said, "You'll go in the next car! Your mother's car is filled with one hundred people, the limit!"

The child clenched his little arms around his mother's waist and said, "Don't leave me, Mommy! Don't leave me, Mommy, please!" His imploring eyes looked up at her. The soldier pulled the child away from his mother, and ordered the woman to get into the car immediately.

The woman started pleading with the soldier, "Please, let me keep the child, my husband died in a labor camp, please!" The soldier got angry, put his rifle to her stomach and pushed her away. She bent over in pain, and fell to the ground, groaning.

The little boy, tears running down his face, looked at the soldier. "Why did you hurt my Mommy?" he asked. "She's a good Mommy! Please call a doctor, please!" Ignoring the child's pleas, the soldier turned around. "You there!" he pointed to a young man, "Take the woman and her suitcase and help her into the car!"

"What about her child?"

"Her child goes into the next car! Rein! Schnell! Rein! Schnell!"

Shocked out of my wits, I asked Rose to explain to me the soldier's behavior. She gave me an unexpected answer, "One hundred people were allotted to a car," she said. "The child's mother was the one hundredth in her car; her child was allegedly an extra number."

"So he separates the mother from her child?"

"You've just seen him doing so."

Just then, an elderly man involuntarily knocked the crying child to the ground with his suitcase. Onlookers made no attempt to help the fallen child. Rose turned to me. "Here!" she said, as she thrust Shullie into my arms. "I have to help the fallen kid!"

My nephew's sudden landing in my arms weighed me down, so I bent forward. A single woman to my right, in her mistaken belief that I was falling, grabbed Shullie from my arms and returned him to Rose. "You stay put," she said. "I'll take care of the little boy." When the woman returned, she was holding a crying, bewildered child in her arms. She checked him out for bruises, and then whispered something into his ear. The little boy stopped crying.

At this moment, the child's mother appeared in the doorway of her car, "Zoli, sweetheart, where are you? Zoli, sweetheart, where are you?" She cried out repeatedly.

The distraught child cried out, "Mommy, Mommy! I'm here! This lady promised me to look for you when the train stops!" His mother had time to throw a kiss to her little boy before the door slammed shut in her face.

It was our turn. A soldier shouted out numbers to one hundred. Rose being the closest to the door, gave me Shullie to hold and pulled herself up. Next, she pulled up my mother, then Shullie, then the suitcases and the bundles. She pulled up Toby and me last.

The rest of the confused and frightened people began pushing into the car. Some hauled their children first, then their luggage; others pulled their luggage first, then their children. Once inside the car, they stumbled, got up, and pushed forward at the shouts of the soldiers. After the last person got inside the car, the door slammed shut. Now, we were in semi-darkness with barely any air since the tiny windows above us were railed up.

Mother decided to set up house next to the door. She saw an empty pail in the corner. She put a suitcase on top of it, sat down, and asked Rose to place Shullie in her lap. There was only room to stand. People propped their suitcases on their heels, stood around them, breathing in each other's faces. Some large families propped up two or three valises next to each other to form resting places for their small children. Others piled up their luggage to chin level to rest their heads during the night. When these artificial towers collapsed, we could hear people screaming, arguing, apologizing, and then everything was quiet again. The children between three and six showed the greatest distress. They clung to their mothers for dear life. Some of them fought one another just to touch a piece of their mothers' skirts. Others sat on the floor, clamping their little arms around their mothers' legs, sobbing, fearing that they might be abandoned. The nursing mothers held crying, colicky infants at their breasts day and night.

I saw people with children pushing toward the corners of the car. "What do you think is happening?' I asked Rose. "They're giving out gifts for children or something?"

"People have needs," she whispered.

"Why are you whispering?"

"Because I know something these people don't. There is a pail in each corner of the car serving as toilet facilities. And the pail under Mother's suitcase is one of them."

"Oh, no! You'll tell mother about it? I whispered back.

"No. She'll find out for herself in time, trust me."

"How do you know about these pails?" I was curious now.

Still whispering Rose said, "When I first pulled myself up

into the car, I saw strange people lining an entire wall. They were groaning, moaning, sneezing and were wearing hospital gowns. I talked to them."

"What did you find out?"

"Plenty. German soldiers brought them there from the hospitals during the night. These four pails were their toilet resources."

I asked Rose how she knew these people were Jews. She said they asked her for water in Yiddish.

Suddenly, Shullie threw up his little hands into the air. "I want my Mommy! Please, Mommy, take me, please!"

Rose took him into her arms and stroked his little head. "You don't want to sit in Granny's lap any longer? It's all right, sweetheart, Mommy will hold you."

The child whispered something into Rose's ear. "Very well, dear; I'll get you your potty." When Shullie stood up from his potty; people around us held their noses. Rose cleaned up Shullie, put him in my arms, and began pressing forward, holding the potty above her head, trying to reach one of the designated pails to empty it. "Excuse me folks, I must get to the corner! Excuse me! Excuse me! Excuse me, please!"

I was standing close to a woman whose infant boy suddenly began pounding on her chest. The woman unbuttoned her blouse and started feeding him. To protect her bare breast from the furtive stares around her, she grabbed her husband's hat and covered her breast as well as her child's dainty little face. I'd expected the baby to cry since, from his point of view, a strange flying object had just landed on his face. To my surprise, the infant continued suckling his mother's comforting milk.

Just as Rose returned from emptying the potty, Mother and Toby decided to use the toilet facilities before it was time to eat. They assumed these facilities were somewhere behind the crowd, or Rose would not have gone with Shullie's potty in that direction. When they returned, they looked distraught. Were they angry at

Rose for not having warned them about the pails? Or was their dignity insulted?

Shullie wanted to eat. We decided to have our lunch. Rose took out some food from a bundle and asked Mother to sit down on her suitcase. "No, no, I'll sit somewhere else!" Mother said. Aha, I thought. She realized that the pail her suitcase rested on was meant to serve as a toilet facility, but she took no action. Rose and I had no clue as to how to handle the situation either.

Rose took two bundles and built a seat against the wall for Mother. Halfway through our lunch, the car filled up with a foul odor and a loud murmur; the pails from the corners had filled up and spilled over; people were standing in human feces.

Small children whose potties had filled up were whimpering in discomfort. Their mothers asked them to "hold it!" When they couldn't hold it, they begged their mothers' permission to go anyway. In the end, after all their confusion, all their shame, they soiled their clothing. Now they were uncomfortable and miserable, so their mothers told them to drop their pants, little girls were told to drop their panties to the floor. The place smelled like a sewer!

Shullie asked for his potty again and I gave it to him. Rose was still eating her lunch. I suggested that Rose put the potty Shullie had just used inside the pail underneath the suitcase. She hugged me in gratitude.

At dawn on the second morning, our train stopped and the door opened about four feet wide. Our family stretched, yawned and breathed in the fresh air. Those from the middle of the car rose on their toes, lifting their heads in hope some of the fresh air might reach them.

Soon, we heard a command coming from a distance, "*Rauss mit den Scheisse* (Out with your feces)!" A minute or so later, three men with pails overflowing with excrement placed themselves in the door opening. They were waiting for the guard's orders. The guard, seemingly overwhelmed by the foul odor seeping through the door opening, fled to the middle of the fields from where he signaled to the men. The men jumped off the train, took the pails into the fields, emptied them, and returned with the empty pails.

The third morning, the doors opened about a foot. I stuck my head into the door opening. I saw an endless stretch of green land from which the morning dew was slowly lifting. Suddenly, from behind a cloud of rising dew, there appeared a peasant. I signaled him to approach the train. At first, he hesitated, and then reconsidered it. He stopped about one yard from the door opening, holding his nose, grimacing in disbelief. I told him we had not had water for the last three days. If he brought me a pail with fresh water, I would give him ten dollars. Within a few minutes, the peasant returned with a full pail of cold water.

Shullie drank first as Mother watched him gulp down the water. After we all had our fill, Mother announced, "The remainder of the water goes for the children and the sick in the car!" In a moment's time, someone snatched the pail out of my sister Rose's hands. I saw the pail floating in the air being passed on from hand to hand until it disappeared from my sight.

The third night was the most soul-wrenching of our three and a half day trip. We woke up to an outburst of infant cries; we couldn't figure out what had happened. In the morning, as the sun's rays seeped through the window cracks, we saw nursing mothers, holding their hysterically crying babies at their bleeding breasts. Little did these hungry infants care that their mothers' milk had dried up because of lack of food. They cared even less that their teeth made their mothers' breasts bleed. In Europe, babies were breast fed up to two or two and a half years of age.

Unlike the other crying infants, our neighbor's little boy whom I watched being fed three days ago was quiet. Too quiet. Rose took a close look at his mother and turned pale like a ghost. The distressed mother was tightly holding down her infant's head against her breast. The infant was struggling for air, while his little body was convulsively twitching in the woman's arms.

Rose grabbed the infant from the woman. "You fool! What

are you doing!?" she said. "You're suffocating your baby!" The woman yielded her infant to Rose, her eyes staring into thin air; she must've been in another world.

Rose moved the infant's lifeless little head from right to left a few times. The infant started gasping for air, then burst out crying. "He'll be all right, he'll be all right," Rose assured us. She asked me to take the jar with marmalade she had reserved for Shullie and open it. She dunked her index finger into the jar and led it to the little boy's lips. The infant tasted something sweet, stopped crying and opened his mouth. Without a moment's delay, Rose's finger slipped into the infant's mouth. I followed in awe as my sister's finger went from the infant's mouth into the jar and from the jar into the infant's mouth, until the infant fell asleep. She then gave the infant back to his father. His mother was still on a different planet.

Around noon, on the fourth day, our train shrieked to a halt as we arrived at Auschwitz. We were holding our breath; seconds turned into a lifetime. Suddenly, the doors opened. A flood of light blinded us; we held our hands to our eyes.

Auschwitz

Then we heard an order, "Leave your suitcases in the car and come out with your hand bags only!" Handbags only? A feeling of dread overwhelmed us. We refused to move; these suitcases held everything we possessed. However, the echo of a few rifle shots fired into the air told us we had to obey orders.

We disembarked. The young adults jumped down first, helping the children, the old and the sick. After vacating the cars, a group of men in striped uniforms collected our suitcases and carried them off. It was the last time we saw them.

We were now on the ramp of Auschwitz. What a sight, what turmoil, what confusion! Shouting SS guards with rifles on their shoulders and vicious dogs at their sides kept pacing up and down the ramp looking for thrills. And thrills they created. Whenever an

SS man would see a family huddled together in fear, he'd loosen his dog's leash. The terrifying, ferocious, barking monster would then jump on the people, bite into their flesh and pull at their clothes as the SS man was enjoying the sight.

Someone screamed out an order. Men began separating from their wives and female children and, taking with them their sons from about fifteen and older, were marched away. Later we found out they were taken to a camp for men in Auschwitz proper. The sick and the crippled remained on the ramp. More orders rang out, this time intended for the women. Mother, Toby and I found ourselves in a group of single women ranging from about fifteen to maybe sixty five. We were surrounded by guards instructing us to make a column, five women abreast. I looked around. I saw a group of women with children from babies to about fourteen years of age. Rose, holding Shullie in her arms, was in that group. Also in that group I saw pregnant women, sick women and crippled women. Little did I know that this group together with the male crippled and sick was doomed to be gassed that same day. But, as luck had it, a German soldier saved Rose's life. How so? While Rose unaware of her fate was looking for her mother to whom she was totally attached, I spotted her. "Rose," I waved. "Mother Toby and I are here!" To get to my group, Rose had to cross a dividing line. A German soldier saw her attempting to do just that. He pushed her back to her group. Rose watched the guard. As she saw him involved in holding the crowd together, she swiftly crossed the line and placed herself on the outside side of our row next to Mother.

Our group was heading toward Dr. Mengele's table to be selected as to who will live and who will die. Oh! Uh! A German guard saw Rose. He realized she was in the wrong group; she had a child. He knew something we didn't. He knew she belonged to the group with children, elderly, sick and crippled who were supposed to be gassed that day. He looked at her. She was young, strong and beautiful, and he made up his mind to save her life.

Why? I could only speculate. Was she reminding him of his sister, or a friend, or someone he very much liked at one time? He lined himself up with Rose. In a soft whispering voice he asked whether or not the woman next to her was her mother. If so she should give the child to her to carry. Upon hearing the guard's words, she became annoyed. She gestured with her hand, as if saying, 'Mind your own business!' But the guard was determined to continue with his rescue efforts. About a yard from Dr. Mengele's table, he forced the child out of her hands and put Shullie in my mother's. Before she became aware of what had happened, she was in front of Dr. Mengele's table. He looked her up and down. She was young and strong and showed her to the right. Toby six years my junior, and I, he motioned to the right as well. My mother, in her sixties, holding Shullie in her arms he motioned to the left to be gassed with the group she belonged to.

The young, the strong, the single, whom Dr. Mengele showed to the right, entered a camp for women called Birkenau. My sister Rose, my sister Toby and I were in that group. The first thing that struck us was a peculiar smell, a sweetish nauseating odor. Three months later, we found out it was the smell of burning flesh.

In the distance, we saw giant, red smoke stacks spewing smoky fireballs straight into the sky. "Aha!" I said to my sister, Rose. "These smoke stacks most probably belong to the factories in which we will be working from now on." When we arrived at Auschwitz, we had seen an inscription on a gate saying, *'Arbeit Macht Frei'* (work sets you free). So we assumed Auschwitz was a labor camp; little did we know that Auschwitz was a death camp.

While marching, I continued spinning stories. "Leave it to the Germans," I said to Rose, "they'll be putting the small children in nurseries, have the healthy, elderly women watch them and we, the young and strong, will work in factories. Rose took my predictions at face value. She livened up. Shullie would be in Mother's care, how lucky could she be!

With high hope in our hearts, we arrived in front of an unending row of tables. Women with scissors in their hands and a smirk on their faces were waiting for us; they cut our hair to the roots. When it was my sister Toby's turn, the woman appeared overwhelmed by the sight of her beautiful, long, wavy titian red hair. She took a handful of her hair and held it out in the sun for a few seconds; it gave the appearance of a burning bush.

Without thinking of the consequences, Toby pulled her hair out of the woman's hands, and rushed to the end of the column. The whole process came to a stop for a moment or so. Piercing glances fell upon the insulted woman. It looked as if her coworkers were daring her to do or say something. And say something, she did, "That smart aleck will not see tomorrow's sunrise!"

My blood ran cold. I stepped forward and kissed the woman's hand. I pleaded for my sister's life; I said she was young and stupid, and would she forgive her. I assured her that my older sister, I pointed at Rose, and I would make certain that she never, ever disobeyed orders again. The woman motioned with her hands shouting, *"Verschwinde verfluchte Yude!"* (Get lost, cursed Jew)

I joined the crowd; I avoided Rose's eyes. Trying to disguise her own state of mind, Rose suddenly said to me, "What do you say now, smarty? Why would the women shave our heads?" She caught me. Something entered my mind and I heard myself saying, "You never know, we might be working with delicate instruments, and our hair would be in the way."

"Hair grows back," Rose sounded consoling. We marched on. Rose and I would normally observe the surroundings wherever we'd find ourselves, but not this time. We kept turning our heads in all directions in the hope of seeing Toby.

Unexpectedly, I lost my balance. Rose tried to catch me, but it was too late. I tumbled down three stairs, taking a group of screaming girls with me. When I got up, I was in front of a door unharmed. "This is a good omen, Sis," Rose said.

The Undressing Room

We entered a tremendous brightly lit room. The walls were painted snow white. In the middle of the huge room there were rows upon rows of columns. Around each column and around the walls there were low wooden benches with numbered hangers on hooks. I took a chance and called out, "Toby, are you here?" A voice answered, "Yes, I'm here!" Rose and I were euphoric; we hugged and kissed.

A deafening voice, coming over the loudspeaker, brought us back to reality. "Remove your clothes!" we heard. "Hang your coats on the hangers and memorize the number on the hangers! Fold your dresses, and place them underneath your coats! Take your jewelry and put it inside your shoes or underneath your dresses!"

The voice continued thundering, "You must carry out these orders to the last detail if you want to get your own clothes upon returning from the showers!" We were naked and embarrassed. We glanced at each other from the corner of our eyes. Then we heard again, "Line up in front of the shower room door! Stretch your hands forward; separate your fingers and open your mouths!" A woman searched us for jewelry. After the search ended, each of us received a bar of soap.

We were pushed into the shower room as the doors closed behind us. The room looked like something out of a science fiction book. All over the shower room, perforated pipes made of sheet metal appeared as if growing out from the cement floor all the way to the ceiling with built-in showerheads.

Toby was alive; we were together again. I felt good and even ready for mischief. "Watch me balance my soap on the edge of one of these perforations before the water comes," I said to Rose. "It won't work," she warned me. "Oops!" It was too late; the soap fell into the hole.

A group of men walked in. Embarrassed and scared out of our wits, we pulled toward the wall. An array of thoughts began crowding into my mind one canceling the other. Are these men here to disgrace us? They are only a handful, and we are in the hundreds. We should resist! We should squash them; that's what we should do. Why think of the worst? Suppose these men are here to explain the enigma of the pipes, I thought. Soon, I caught on; the men were here to shave our pubic hair.

As the last man closed the door behind him, warm water began pouring down from the ceiling. Rose held out her soap. "You wash first."

"No, Rose; I should pay for my mistake." We argued back and forth while time was running its course. In the end, I gave in and began lathering myself. When I returned the soap to Rose, she had only enough time to lather up before the water stopped coming. I had no time to dwell on my guilt; a door opened, and loud voices reached us, *"Rein! Schnell* (Enter fast)!"

The Room Next to the Shower Room

We were in the room adjacent to the shower room. I saw two giant tables. On one table, I saw a heap of old clothes. On the other table, I saw a mountain of used shoes. Behind each table, I saw a woman standing. Around the walls, I saw low, wooden benches with folded towels.

We flocked toward the towels. Before having a chance to completely towel-dry ourselves, the same group of men walked in ordering us to drop our towels to the floor. We immediately obeyed and waited for a sign of what would come next. Soon, DDT disinfectant powder appeared. Bursts of coughing broke out as we protected our eyes with our hands.

After the cloud dissipated, a strict voice ordered us to line up in front of the table with the old clothes. An angry-looking woman threw a stained, faded, raggedy dress at each of us--no slip, no panties. From behind the next table, a woman threw pairs of shoes tied together with a string at each of us. However, not all of these shoes were matching. We'd find a laced shoe tied together with a non-laced shoe, a high-heeled shoe tied together with a low-heeled shoe, and a shoe that looked like size nine tied together with a shoe that looked like size five or six.

How did we look in these clothes? Like hobos going to a Halloween party. Surprisingly, we were in good spirits. Some girls kept turning around, as if modeling their outfits. Others in floor length, food stained, wine stained, open-hemmed evening gowns were gesturing as if dancing with imaginary partners, all the while repeating our hanger numbers aloud. In our ignorance, we collectively reasoned: the German soldiers would be brainless to give us good clothes just to go around the corner to the undressing room to get our own clothes back, so we'd better enjoy our Halloween costumes.

Lager A

We never *ever* went back to the undressing room to get our own clothes. Our clothes and personal jewelry were shipped to Germany, while we, the vulnerable hopefuls were taken to Lager A, known as the quarantine lager and pushed into a barrack. On both sides of the barrack there were three tiered bunk beds made of boards with two blankets in each bunk bed. In the middle of the barrack, there was a low heating unit. There was an aisle all around it.

The first thing we did was exchange clothes. The tall women with dresses barely covering their backsides were looking for short women with dresses sweeping the floor. The heavy women with skimpy dresses were looking for slim women with oversized dresses. But those women with mismatched shoes were stuck with them.

The trading ended. I noticed a group of girls standing in a circle, watching something and applauding. An eighteen-year-old girl was doing acrobatic gymnastics. Why shouldn't I show off *my* talents, it occurred to me? I was good in acrobatics in high school. All I needed for my show was a pair of panties. Most probably,

I could get them from the *Stubbendienst* (a woman in charge with the food distribution and the cleaning of the barrack.).

I went to the Stubbendienst and introduced myself. I said if she wanted another performer for variety purposes, I was available. All I needed was a pair of panties. She looked me up and down and began laughing and laughing! Humiliated to the core, I realized that there would be favoritism in this barrack, and that I would not be among those favored.

Soon, we heard orders to occupy the bunk beds, eight of us in a bunk bed. But these bunk beds seemed to be built to accommodate less than eight people. Before we could figure out which way we would be sleeping tonight: on our backs, sideways, crosswise or head-to-toe, we were ordered to come and get our supper.

We lined up in front of twelve giant pails filled with black, ersatz coffee (which means a substitute coffee). The Stubbendienst gave a tin bowl to each of us with a warning, "Hold on to your bowl! No bowl, no food! And when you're inside the barrack, you stay in your bunk beds at all times, and make no noise!"

The first girl held out her bowl. The Stubbendienst poured a cup of the liquid into her bowl. The girl did not move; she waited for the rest of the meal to follow. After all, she had just been told to come and get her supper. The Stubbendienst must have guessed the girl's thoughts. *"Verfluchte Yude"* (cursed Jew), she thundered; "that is all you will be having for supper as long you stay in this lager!"

It was time to sleep now. We decided on a final sleeping position. We ruled out sleeping head-to-toe although we had just taken a shower. We decided to sleep sideways; digging our derriere into our neighbor's stomach was acceptable. Being small, I was at an advantage. Rose swallowed me in her semi-fetal position. Suddenly, I felt as if I were in a cradle, protected from harm, from evil. I spent the night in a state of semi-consciousness. I heard sleepy, tired, incoherent voices of complaints, defiance, appeasement, discomfort and even pain, coming from every corner of our barrack.

Zehl Apel (Roll call)

At dawn, we woke up to powerful shouts: *"Raus! Raus! Zehl Apel!"* (Out! Out! Roll call!)

"What, what?" some half-asleep girl in our bunk bed asked.

"We have to get ready for Zehl Apel," a second sleepy girl chimed in. "What's Zehl Apel?" asked a third drawn-out voice. "Whatever it is, we'll soon find out," said Rose. Before my sister could finish her sentence, we heard a loud knock on our headboard, "Raus! Raus! Zehl Apel!" Our stiff bodies and interlaced hands slowed us down. But at the sound of a second knock on our headboard, we were filling up the aisles. "Schnell! Schnell!" The Stubbendienst pushed us toward the door. In a harmless gesture to speed up the process, some of the girls pushed one another. A quarrel ensued. Tempers flared; accusation and counter- accusations flew indiscriminately, giving the Stubbendienst an excuse to use degrading language; *"Halt dein Schnabel, verfluchte!"* (Shut your trap, cursed!)

Outside, we stretched, and yawned. We discovered it was still dark. It would be another two hours before the sun would rise and warm up the cold, raw, wet air. Despite the poor visibility, we could see girls pouring out of the neighboring barracks, milling in the heavy clouds of morning fog. The Stubbendienst commanded us to form a column, five girls abreast. We were standing as if at attention, waiting to be counted. The cold air at this ungodly hour penetrated my body, and I visibly began to shiver. Rose showed no signs of discomfort; she still had some natural protective layers to keep her warm. Toby, though slim, seemed also comfortable.

In no time, Rose became aware of my misery. She pulled me in front of her, threw her arms around me, and pressed me to her body to transfer some heat to mine. The Stubbendienst noticed the scene and rushed over. She warned Rose about dire consequences if she did it again. I returned to my previous spot. There must be some way to help myself, I thought. I began doing warm-up exercises when a sharp dig in my ribs coming from the Stubbendienst's fist told me to stop. What now?

Suddenly, I heard, "Pst!" It was Rose. I looked at her. At first, I couldn't understand what she was trying to do. Then, I caught on. She was maneuvering her dress with her hands, giving me some ideas how to stay warm. I tried putting Rose's ideas to work. My hands turned into a machine in motion. Inconspicuously, I rushed them to my mouth to stop the chattering of my teeth, to tightening my dress around my body to prevent the flow of cold air touching my crossed legs, then, I maneuvered them to hugging myself to generate some heat, then, I started all over again.

The counting process finally began. Rounds followed in succession, round after round, after round. How many rounds? Countless! The sun rose, the dew lifted, the air warmed up, and we were still standing for roll call. With time, I learned that the length of this procedure could go on for hours, from three, to four, to five hours, depending on the last woman accounted for. In the beginning, we were in the hundreds of thousands of women in the camp.

Roll call finally ended. Still in rows of five, we marched toward our barrack. We waited for the Stubbendienst to get in first. A few minutes later, we heard, "*Rein* (Come in), one by one, and eat your breakfast in your bunk beds!"

As we entered the barrack, each of us received a thin, almost transparent, slice of bread made of sawdust mixed with flour. We also received a cup of Ersatz Coffee. We were warned to consume our breakfast in our bunk beds. I held the bread in my left palm and secured the coffee in my right hand. I was hungry and decided to break the rules and eat my kingly breakfast on the way to my bunk bed.

No sooner did I slow down when I felt a jolt in my back; the girl behind me ran into me. I stumbled and fell to the floor. In my flight, I threw away the bowl with the hot coffee. My instinct of survival still served me.

The Stubbendienst approached me, her hands on her hips.

"What did you do, *Dumkopf?*" (stupid?) She ordered me to wipe the floor dry. "Of course, would you please give me a mop or a rag?" I said. "Use your dress!" I looked at her in dismay. "I have nothing underneath my dress." The Stubbendienst went into a fit, "I said use your dress, verfluchte!"

All that time, Rose was in our bunk bed, holding a place for me. She saw a commotion, but paid no attention to it, until someone told her that I was the focus of the disturbance.

She rushed to the scene just to hear the Stubbendienst commanding me to wipe the floor with my dress. She introduced herself as my sister, and asked the Stubbendienst for a rag to wipe the floor. The Stubbendienst ordered her to return to her bunk bed. Without a moment's delay, Rose took off her dress, wiped the spilled coffee with it, wrung it out, and then put it back on her naked body. I picked up my bowl and began crying. A grinning Stubbendienst signaled us to go to our bunk beds.

I told Rose how sorry I felt. "Forget it," she said, stroking my bald head. Inside the bunk bed, she gave me half of her slice of bread and made me drink coffee from her bowl. At first, I refused to take the half of the slice of her bread. "You don't want the bread?" she said. "Maybe the floor wants it." I watched in horror how she lifted her middle finger from the bread, and then let it slide downward through her thumb and index finger. I still had time to catch it in the air. This would be her routine during our detention in Auschwitz. I'd hear the same line when she'd offer me some of her soup and I'd refuse. "You don't want the soup; maybe the floor wants it."

After breakfast, we heard familiar shouts, "Raus! Raus!" Now the process went much smoother; we learned a lesson from this morning. The Stubbendienst warned us to remain on the grounds, a strip of land separating our barrack from the neighboring one. We had no idea what to do. Rose stood in the sun to dry her dress; I kept her company. A number of girls decided to sit on the ground.

"Aufstehn, verfluchte!" (Get up, cursed!) We could do many things on the grounds it seemed, but not sit down.

About an hour later, we lined up in a column, five girls in a row. The Stubbendienst separated 100 women, and told the rest to stay on the grounds and wait. My sister and I were among the chosen. We began to move. We made a few detours to the right, then to the left, and then we halted in front of a barrack. The Stubbendienst pushed us inside one by one. We closed our eyes for a while to get used to the darkness; we had just left bright sunshine behind. When I opened my eyes, I saw a low, rectangular wooden box. It stretched from one end of the barrack to the other and held fifty holes on one side and fifty holes on the other. I figured it was a communal latrine. I sat down and waited for nature to give me a sign. But two or three minutes later, before the sign could come, we were chased out of the latrine to make room for the girls left behind. We had no bathroom tissues.

At noon, we lined up for lunch. I saw ten, or maybe a dozen giant uncovered pails with soup. The floating clouds of vapors from the pails brought a pleasant smell to my nostrils. I held out my tin bowl. The Stubbendienst filled it up with a liquid from the very top of the pail, and said, *"Weg!"* (Scram!)

I returned to my bunk bed and started drinking my soup. It tasted like water, no salt, no spices--nothing. Later I found out that the purpose for the salt free soup was to minimize the craving for water. We had no drinking water during our detention in Auschwitz. I asked Rose and Toby how their soup tasted. "Like water," they said. Rose remembered smelling potato soup. Something was wrong; she must find out what it was.

She asked the girls from the neighboring right-hand bunk bed whether they had enjoyed their soup. "What is there to enjoy. Hot, tasteless water?" they said. She got the same answer from the neighboring left-hand bunk bed. The girls from the bunk bed underneath us had a different story; they said the soup tasted like a delicious potato soup. A perplexed Rose asked one of them to explain. "Simple," she said. "The Stubbendienst gave us soup from the bottom of the pail, where all the potatoes and potato peels settle."

"Why would she do that? We got plain water; what's so different about you?" Rose asked. "We are her helpers," she said, pride in her voice. "We clean the barrack twice a day and bring the food from the kitchen. In fact, we've already cleaned the barrack this morning while you all had fun on the grounds."

"What fun?"

"I don't know what exactly you've been doing out there; I know we've worked hard and deserved good food."

"How did the Stubbendienst pick you?" Rose asked. "At random," the girl answered. We found out later that for the mass of potatoes and potato peels that settled on the bottom of the pails, the Stubbendienst would organize for herself jewelry, cosmetics and clothes. These were the clothes, cosmetics and jewelry we brought in our suitcases or in our handbags. Before the items were sent to Germany, hungry inmates sorted them out in warehouses. For a portion of potatoes and potato peels, these sorters gave away the store.

As soon as Rose finished talking to the Stubbendienst's helpers, she went to apply for a helper's job. The Stubbendienst eyed her up and down and said, "You're too big; you look clumsy and lazy!"

"I am more agile than any slim woman you could point out to me," Rose said. The Stubbendienst gave her a sarcastic stare, and went into a spell of laughter until she ran out of breath, her blubbery stomach continually shaking. When she finally stopped laughing, she went into a rapture of panting and dismissed Rose with a sign of her hand.

As Rose described her encounter with the Stubbendienst to me, she looked sadder than I've ever seen her before. It broke my heart. "You know what I think?" I said, "the Stubbendienst is jealous; you're a beautiful woman and she's ugly blubber. I remember when you wiped the puddle of coffee with your dress;

the Stubbendienst couldn't take her eyes off your beautiful naked body." Rose hugged me and thanked me for consoling her. "I'm not consoling you; I speak the truth; you're a beautiful woman inside and out."

Rose caressed my cheeks, "Okay, Libelah; I love you, too." Before long we heard, "Raus! Raus!" The instructions were pretty much the same as this morning. We had to stay on the grounds until the next orders. An hour later, the next orders came. We formed a column five abreast and were taken to the latrines. Now the latrine's seats were covered with human feces from this morning. What did we do? We stood up on the top of the box.

We had returned from the latrines hoping to get into the barrack -- no such luck. The Stubbendienst ordered us to line up for the afternoon Zehl Apel. The sun was still up in the sky and strong. A few hours later the sun was gone, but we were still standing for roll call. The ordeal ended at dusk. We were resting in our bunk beds, maybe five minutes, when we heard, "Coffee! Coffee!" No one wanted coffee, at least not at that time. But who asked us?

At bed time, we decided this night to sleep crosswise. However, Rose was not around. The girls asked me to find her since we must all go to bed at the same time. I walked twice around the aisle calling Rose's name when she grabbed me by my arm.

"You're upset?" she asked, while tightening her grip.

"I'm not upset; *you're* upset; you're hurting me!" Rose let go of my arm. I asked to explain her strange behavior. She had good news for me, she whispered. She met a woman on the grounds, and made a deal with her. The woman called herself an 'old timer.' She was from Poland and had been here since 1941. She stayed in a barrack down the block, and could provide anything for bread.

"Even cigarettes?" I asked.

"I guess, but who wants cigarettes?"

"I do. Have you forgotten that just a week ago I smoked?" I

asked "I haven't forgotten, but I'm disappointed," she said. "You're thinking about cigarettes when you should be thinking about a warm sweater to wear it in the mornings for roll call."

I realized that she had already arranged a sweater for me. I felt ashamed. I hugged her and kissed her and apologized. She took me to a corner of the barrack, lifted her dress, and untied a wool long-sleeved sweater from around her waist.

"What do you say to this beauty?" she asked, displaying it in front of my eyes. Overwhelmed with emotions and tears in my eyes, I threw my arms around her, placed my head on her shoulder and said, "It's out of this world, thank you!"

"Don't mention it," she looked at me, gently loosening my hands from around her. "We have to join the women; they probably want to go to bed. And why do you hide the sweater; we're inside?"

"Inside or outside, the fact is, we're not allowed to wear anything on top of, or underneath our rags.

"Then what use is the sweater for me, if I can't wear it?"

"You'll wear it, don't worry," she stroked my bald head.

"Okay, I'm sure you know what you're doing."

In the bunk bed, Rose slipped the sweater underneath my shoes and my tin bowl. I wished she had put it on top of these things to make a softer pillow. But then I thought she might not trust our bed companions.

The next morning I held out my slice of bread to her. "This is for my sweater."

"You give me your bread when I ask for it! The sweater is on me, and don't say another word!"

Soon, I heard the all too familiar "Raus! Raus!" Rose and I knew we must start working on the disappearance of the sweater's long, undesirable sleeves, and be out of the barrack in time for roll call. We waited until the last girl left our bunk bed including Toby before beginning what turned out to be a tedious operation. I followed Rose's instructions. I took off my dress, put on the sweater and lay flat on my back. She then took an eye measurement of the sleeves, and pulled at a piece of yarn until it took the shape of a loop.

"What in the world are you doing?" I asked. "I'm marking the sleeves," she replied. "I'll be rolling them up to that pre-marked point. Remember, the sleeves of the sweater must be totally hidden under the sleeves of your dress."

Something dawned on me. "What if you cut the sleeves of the sweater to the size of the sleeves of my dress?" I was bursting with pride having come up with an idea of my own.

Rose interrupted my thought. "With what do you want me to cut the sweater's sleeves? With my teeth? Maybe next time I'll procure scissors from the woman."

I felt as if she threw a bucket of cold water over my body. She noticed my embarrassment. "Sorry if I insulted your intelligence; you're very smart, but that's for another time to talk about; please cooperate."

Within a minute, I was in a sitting position, holding my hands up, feeling my sweater on my body and my dress sliding over my head.

The last twelve women were ready to exit the barrack. We had better join them soon if we didn't want to get in trouble. We jumped off the bunk bed, ran to the door and flew right through it. I was standing at roll call, my sweater cuddling my body. I was in seventh heaven. The never-ending counting started. The first round of counting, and the second round, which followed about an hour later, had passed by uneventfully. But on the third round, an SS woman noticed my deformed biceps and its cause. She ordered me to drop whatever I had underneath my dress on the ground. I took off my dress, dragging the sweater with it. I was stark naked. I hardly recall how long I struggled to separate the dress from the sweater. Still, Rose had not given up. Two days later, she got a hold of a man's vest- like sweater. It saved my life.

Cigarettes Rolled in Dirty Newspaper

A week later, Rose had another surprise for me. "What do you say to these guys?" She flashed two cigarettes in front of my eyes. "I love them, and I love you!" I then embraced her and kissed her. I offered her my next slice of bread.

She laughed, "I can afford it; look at me and look at you. But the woman wants a slice of bread for a box of matches, so I'll take your slice tomorrow morning."

"If she could give you some newspaper with the box of matches, I could make six cigarettes out of these two." I remembered seeing how people in Petrova would make their own cigarettes. "That's an idea," Rose said. I got so excited that I began rolling imaginary cigarettes, drawing people's attention. Some women gave me a pitiful look. Others thought I had no feeling in my fingers and was trying to exercise them to regain life. And still others speculated that I had lost my mind, especially when I began blowing imaginary smoke rings in the air and foolishly smiling.

I hardly slept during the night. I paid no attention to my growling stomach. My mind was set solely on tomorrow. Tomorrow I found myself the proud owner of six newspaper- rolled cigarettes and a box of matches. No one was equal to me.

I lit up the first cigarette. Suddenly, a streak of fire with the speed of lightning crossed the length of the entire cigarette, landing on my lips. I dropped the damaged cigarette to the ground, looked at it in horror, and only then rushed my hands to my burned lips. Rose was very upset. "Maybe it is a sign that you should stop smoking, yes?"

I nodded, 'Yes.' And to convince her of my determination, I removed my hands from my mouth and said, "Take the matches back to the woman; maybe she could give you something else for it. As for the cigarettes, I have no use for them!" I dropped them to the ground and squashed them. Rose looked on in bewilderment, while I felt I had discovered a new strength in myself. We talked about what to get instead of the matches from the woman. Rose suggested a flask.

"A flask?" I asked. "Yes, a flask to fill it up with extra coffee in the morning. After someone smuggles it out of the barrack, we can sip small amounts of it while idling on the grounds."

I came to the conclusion that acquired knowledge does not take you through life's ups and downs; it's common sense that does it. Rose had barely three grades behind her, but had common sense, compassion, kindness and understanding enough for an entire regiment of people.

I volunteered to be the Smuggler.

It was a daring enterprise, but Rose thought I could do it. First, we had to fill up the flask with hot coffee. How? Toby and I were to go for a second and third helping of Ersatz Coffee in the morning. We were to approach the caldron, hold out our bowls while turning our faces to the extreme right or left making believe we were talking to some girls. We fared pretty well. But all hell broke loose when the Stubbendienst lifted her eyes and saw us. *"Genug, weg, Schweinen Hund!"* (You had enough dirty dog, scram!)

Hurrah! We had a flask filled to capacity with hot, boiling coffee. Rose prepared me for the contraband which consisted of a two-step process. She took a strong string she obtained as an extra gratuity with the flask deal and tied one end of it around the flask's mouth and the other around my waist in such a fashion that the flask would dangle between my legs above my knees. The string around my waist was to be untied only in case I was caught.

I'd have to walk with my legs spread apart to avoid the flask's hot contents coming in touch with my thighs. But how could I be unnoticed by the Stubbendienst when I walked out of the barrack? If you have a sister like Rose anything is possible.

She organized a group of tall girls to make a protective shield around me. They would appear being absorbed talking with one another, while slowly inching themselves toward the door with me trapped in their midst. Rose promised to reward them with coffee upon reaching the ground. She'd also reserve some coffee for the weak, who were panting like heat-exhausted dogs.

Sometime in the middle of June, following a few weeks of observation, the Stubbendienst decided to disturb the suspicious cluster. She pushed the girls aside. There I stood, the eye of the storm, frozen in place, my legs spread apart. *"Was ist loss, verfluchte?"* (What's the matter, cursed?) the Stubbendienst shouted, while shaking my shoulders with all her might.

"Ouch! *Ouch! Ouuuch!"* I screamed as the flask swung back and forth, burning the inside of my thighs. Rose rushed to the scene while the women of the assemblage ran out of the barrack.

"Weg! Weg!" The Stubbendienst chased Rose away.

Rose retreated within a yard or so. She spoke to me in Yiddish in a soft tone of voice. "Don't worry, Libelah," she said. "I got you into this mess; I'll get you out of it; you just follow my instructions."

"Halt dein Schnabel, verfluchte!" the Stubbendienst shouted at Rose. My sister paid no attention to the Stubbendienst's uproar; she continued talking to me. "Lift your dress; expose the flask; let her see it." I followed Rose's instructions.

The Stubbendienst was at a loss for words seeing the flask with a string tied around its mouth suspended between my legs. She wanted me to lift my dress further up to find out where the string led. I lifted my dress; I was naked to my waist. She looked at the contraption from all sides, and then howled, *"Los lassen die Flasche!"* (Let go of the flask!)

I looked at her, confused. Without wasting time, she grabbed the string above the flask and began pulling at it with all her strength. I felt an unbearable pain coming from different parts of my body: from the inside of my thighs, as the flask hit the skin, and from my waist, as the string choked it. I cried out in pain, *"Bitte, bitte, mochte ich das aufbinden?"* (Please, please may *I* untie it myself?)

"Why do you ask for her permission? She'll never give it to

you; untie it yourself," Rose spoke softly. I untied the string from around my waist, watching the flask fall to the floor--what a *relief!*

The next day Rose got me some salve for the burns on my thighs from the old timer whose name was Galena, she'd learned.

Dr. Mengele and His Selections

Rose also had lots of news to tell me. Galena spoke to her about Dr. Mengele, who makes selections. I gave Rose a probing look. "Don't worry, Libelah," she stroked my head. "Whatever selections mean, we'll go through it together; we'll never separate!"

I kept on looking at her. "All right," Rose gave in. "Galena warned me about the upcoming hot weather and advised me to stay out of the sun at all times."

"Go on!"

"During his selections, Dr. Mengele shows the girls with blisters, especially oozing blisters, and those who are emaciated, to the left. All those shown to the left are then loaded into a truck that takes them to the gas chambers."

I was dumbfounded. She hugged me and began repeating the same mantra over and over, "We'll never separate; we'll always be together!"

Rose felt she had a duty to spread the news about Dr. Mengele's selections, and the upcoming weather. She also felt she must help in any way she could. And help she did. She suggested that while waiting for the Stubbendienst' helpers to clean the barrack and let us in, we, the girls on the grounds, make huddles, like football huddles. The girls on the inside would be protected from the sun for a while, and then they'd switch with the girls on the outside. Also, to protect our arms from the sun—we had short-sleeved tatters—Rose suggested that we remove our arms from our sleeves and put them inside our dresses.

One day, a girl had no time to put her arms back into the sleeves of her dress before entering the barrack. We usually helped each other. To this day, I can't figure out where things went wrong.

As the girl was entering the barrack, the Stubbendienst noticed her. She asked her what had happened. The girl got tongue-tied, she couldn't utter a word. The Stubbendienst became angry and pushed her with all her might. The girl fell face down to the floor; she had no hands to break her fall. Blood began gushing from her nose. She probably broke it. The Stubbendienst took her to the infirmary, and we never saw the girl again.

A real tragedy, related to looking for shade, happened in a neighboring barrack. It was an unbearably hot day in July. According to the lager rules, we, girls, were forbidden to leave the grounds on our own under any circumstances. A girl, possibly affected by the sun, strayed into forbidden territory. She found an empty barrel, crawled into it and fell asleep.

At four o'clock, as usual, we lined up for the afternoon roll call. The sun beat down on our bodies mercilessly. Three rows down a woman fainted. Her neighbors had to hold her up so she could be counted. The girl's head slumped forward as the two helpers buckled in under her lifeless weight.

The Stubbendienst tapped Rose on her shoulder, "Come!" she said. She led her to the spot, and ordered her to hold up the fainted girl. A second later, someone appeared in Rose's place next to me.

I watched Rose in action. She took the unconscious girl's right hand and draped it around her neck, holding her hand down close to her chest. She then took her left hand and placed it around the girl's waist in a strong grip. Miraculously, the unconscious girl appeared standing almost straight next to Rose, her head slightly slumped.

An hour later, Rose returned to my row and switched back with the girl who replaced her. "You ought to be commended for the good job you did," I said, but . . . ,"

Rose interrupted me, "But what?"

"I was never more confused than when I saw the fainted girl standing on her own for a while then falling unconscious again.

What happened?" I asked. "The girl did not fall unconscious again," Rose replied, slightly smiling.

"What are you talking about? I saw it with my own eyes," I said. "Well, when the girl regained consciousness, I asked her whether she would be able to stand on her own feet."

"'Not for a while,'" she whispered. "So I told her to pretend she had fainted again, and I volunteered to hold her up for as long as it took."

The sun went down, and we were still standing on roll call. The stars came out, and we were *still* standing on roll call. Around ten o'clock -- or at least it seemed like ten o'clock we had no notion of time, all hell broke loose. Sirens went off. SS men with dogs at their sides combed the entire camp; they were looking for the missing woman, the one who fell asleep in a barrel.

An hour later the SS men found the missing girl. Roll call ended, but so had the girl's life. The SS men must've pumped at least ten bullets into her body. It sounded as if a stream of fire-crackers went off.

Delousing and Blood Drawing

The following day, the main event was delousing, a process of disinfection, removing lice and other parasites. Similar to the showers we took upon our arrival to Auschwitz, we'd go into the undressing room, remove our rags we'd wore for six weeks, take a shower with chemicals, return to another room where women behind tables would throw clean raggedy dresses and mismatched shoes for us to wear for the next six weeks. The day after delousing, it was blood drawing. Our blood served as transfusions for the German wounded soldiers. At the end of the involuntary blood giving, each of us received two slices of salami.

In retrospect, I cannot help thinking how Hitler's mind worked. On one hand he had inspired a whole nation, especially the Hitler Youth to believe that the Jews were subhuman, vermin, and infectious viruses. Yet on the other hand, he found it useful to mix *our* blood with the blood of his superior race.

This brings to mind Mark Twain, who in 1899 wrote the following:

> *"If the statistics are right, the Jews constitute but one percent of the human race. It suggests a nebulous, dim puff of star dust lost in the blaze of the Milky Way. Properly the Jew ought hardly to be heard of, but he is heard of, has always been heard of. He is as prominent on the planet as any other people, and his commercial importance is extravagantly out of proportion to the smallness of his bulk.*
>
> *His contributions to the world's list of great names in literature, science, art, music, finance, medicine and abstruse learning are also very out of proportion to the smallness of his numbers. He has made a marvelous fight in this world, in all the ages; and has done it with his hands tied behind him. He could be vain of himself, and be excused for it. The Egyptian, the Babylonian, and the Persians rose, filled the planet with sound and splendor, then faded to dream-stuff and passed away; the Greek and the Roman followed and made a vast noise, and they were gone; other peoples have sprung up and held their torch high for a time, but it burned out, and they sit in twilight now, and have vanished.*
>
> *The Jew saw them all, survived them all, and is now what he always was, exhibiting no decadence, no infirmities of age, no weakening of his parts, no slowing of his energies, no dulling of his alert and aggressive mind. All thing are mortal but the Jew; all other forces pass, but he remains. What is the secret of his immortality?"*

Of course, Hitler himself had heard of some of these great Jewish minds of the 18th, 19th and 20th centuries to whom Mark Twain was alluding in this passage. He had heard about Dr. August von Wasserman's reaction test, and that his own people, as well as the world's population used it to detect whether or not they had syphilis.

He had heard about Dr. Paul Ehrlich, a German Jew, who had discovered the cure for syphilis, and that the German people, as well as the world at large used his cure.

Hitler had heard about Albert Neisser's method to detect gonorrhea, and that the German people, along with the rest of the world used his method.

He had heard about Ludwig Traube who discovered digitalis, used to treat heart ailments, and that the German people and the rest of the world have used his method.

He had heard about Oscar Minkowski who discovered the role of insulin in diabetes, and that the Germans as well as people all over the world used his treatment.

Hitler had heard about the Shick reaction cure of diphtheria by Dr. Bela Shick and that his own people as well as the rest of the world benefited from it.

He had heard about the Nobel Prize Winner Robert Baram whose method of treating ear and brain damage saved the lives of millions of people, including many of his own.

He had heard about Kasimir Funk who discovered the nutritional value of vitamins, thus helping to eradicate three deadly diseases: beriberi, scurvy and pellagra. Beriberi results from a deficiency in vitamin B1. Pellagra results from a deficiency in the vitamin niacin, and scurvy results from a deficiency in vitamin C.

He had heard about Zalman Waksman, who discovered streptomycin, and that his people and the rest of the world have used it.

These are but a few Jews making up the list of great names--names responsible for the well-being of humanity.

And then we have Sigmund Freud, the father of psychoanalysis. And we also have Albert Einstein and Lisa Meitner who ushered in the atomic era. These Jews were Hitler's contemporaries. They lived in his native country, Austria.

Today, the Hitler Youth are old men. They know that the late Dr. Jonas Salk and Dr. Albert Sabin were two Jews who have discovered the cure for polio. This discovery has saved the lives of millions of children all over the world, including *German* children, maybe their very own. Do they still believe that the Jews are subhuman, vermin and infectious viruses–the lessons they were taught in school?

But let's return to Lager A in Auschwitz and the blood giving. Although Toby physically suffered from blood giving, they couldn't find her veins, still she looked forward to blood-giving. I always wondered whether the thought of the reward, the two slices of salami, tricked her mind into tolerating the pain.

One day, an SS woman came to our grounds; we had just returned from the latrines. She ordered us to form a column, five women abreast. She counted two hundred women, and cut off just in front of the row where Toby, Rose, I and two other women were standing.

As the SS woman headed toward the front to start a recount, Toby seemed to have concocted a plan in her mind. She left our row and attached herself to the last line of the chosen group, thus increasing the line from a required of five girls abreast to a disallowed row of six girls abreast. I watched in horror how Toby pushed and shoved and elbowed a girl whose place she wanted to take. The confused ousted girl kept aimlessly spinning. She looked as if struck by lightning, her eyes asking, 'What happened? Just now I was in a row with my friends, and here I am in no man's land.' She seemed about to fall to the ground when Rose caught her hand and settled her in the empty place left by Toby in our row. Before long, the SS woman returned and led away the column.

Rose and I assumed the selected girls were taken to give blood. We waited one hour, two hours, three hours and Toby had not returned. The same afternoon, Rose saw Galena. She asked her whether she had an explanation as to why it took the girls so long to return from giving blood.

Galena gave Rose a serious look and said, "The selected column of girls is not giving blood; they'll be transported to Germany to work in ammunition factories." Rose then asked, "Do you know where we can find Toby? We'd like to say goodbye to her."

"She's on the grounds in the vicinity of the shower rooms," said Galena, "but I wouldn't advise you to go there; it's very dangerous."

Against Galena's warning, Rose decided to find Toby. Not to say good-bye, rather to appeal to the consciousness of any two girls in her row who might understand the pain of family separation and agree to let Rose and I take their places. We wanted to be together with Toby, Germany or no Germany.

We walked through forbidden territories. At any minute, we could've been discovered, mistaken for escapees and shot to death. But luck was on our side and we found the girls. We barely recognized them. They looked clean and wore regular dresses. No way would any girl in her right mind consider changing places with us, I thought. Still, I volunteered to approach the column; Rose made herself scarce. I located Toby. She looked like a vision. Her wine-colored dress, set against her light, fresh, radiant skin, made a picture I carry in my heart to this day. She also looked so happy and contented.

I was waving and throwing kisses at Toby, tears running down my face when an SS woman appeared out of nowhere pointing a truncheon at me. Next, I felt the truncheon coming down on my face, on my head, on my back, on my derrière, and on my legs until I lost consciousness. As I came to, I found myself in my barrack. Rose was rocking me in her arms, sobbing as if mourning me. I had no broken bones but I had black and blue marks all over my body. For weeks on end, I could neither sit down nor lie down without making noises of pain. But life went on.

During a scorching afternoon in July, we were terribly thirsty;

we had no drinking water. We saw the Stubbendienst bring a pail of water for her helpers to clean the barrack. Rose suggested we surround her and beg her to give each of us one sip of water, then go back and bring another pail of water for her helpers. The Stubbendienst laughed.

In our desperation, we tried to force the pail out of her hands. She was strong; she pulled to her side; we pulled to our side; most of the water fell to the ground. Whatever was left in the pail, she herself spilled on the ground, "Here" she said, laughing. We laughed, too. Not in irony, rather in happiness as we saw a puddle of water on the ground. We fell on our stomachs, trying to reach for the water. Rose looked on in horror. She anticipated what was coming. She reached out for me but it was too late. I was trapped in the middle of a tug-of-war of hundreds of screaming women piled one on top of the other, pushing, scratching, pulling at hands, at tatters, at legs, and at arms. Had any of the girls reached water? Hardly. They had reached wet mud; the water was absorbed by the dry ground in just a few seconds after the Stubbendienst spilled it.

During the next two weeks, the SS women formed more transports. They sent some transports to the front for the pleasure of the German soldiers, while others served as guinea pigs for Dr. Mengele's inhuman medical experiments. Galena told Rose what some of these experiments entailed. To test the endurance of a woman, they'd amputate her leg, or sterilize her, or remove a breast or both without administering anesthesia, much less painkillers. Or they'd submerge the girls in ice cold water until they'd pass out, then revive them, then submerge them again until they could no longer revive them. Or, they'd actually kill them and use their flesh for growing bacterial cultures. Rose would not share with me this information until long, long after the war ended.

The rest of us, whom the SS women had not chosen as part of the transports, were tattooed a number on our inner left arms. These numbers had replaced our names; we had become non-persons.

The morning following the tattooing, some of us were taken to Lager B, the lager of the working women, and some of us were taken to Lager C also known as the lager of the rejects, where inmates would be starved and abused while waiting for room in the gas chambers. Rose and I found ourselves among those who were taken to Lager C.

Lager C

My sister Rose and I entered Lager C. We saw two rows: one outgoing row, consisting of the former occupants of lager C, and one incoming column, consisting of us, the newly arrived from Lager A.

Our incoming group stopped in front of vacated barracks. Counting and shouting, SS women separated us into groups of 1500 inmates. Each group then occupied a numbered, vacated barrack. The column Rose and I were part of arrived in front of Barrack #29 and stopped. Someone from the outgoing column called out our names. I looked around. Was I dreaming? I saw cousin Lilly waving at us. We waved back. Before the next thought, I saw Lilly run up the stairs of Barrack #29 where she faced a shapely, exquisitely- featured, dark haired, light complected woman in her early forties. Lilly gave the woman one of her winning smiles. She kissed her hands while pointing at us. She talked to her a bit more; ran down the stairs and threw a kiss at us and disappeared.

Barrack #29 began filling up with inmates. When Rose and I got to the top of the steps, the woman Lilly had talked to a few minutes ago pointed at us and said, "You wait here!" She then showed us to a space behind the main entrance to the barrack.

Rose and I were wondering what Lilly had been up to. I had a good feeling, though. Lilly was a cousin my age, born in my native village Petrova. We went to elementary school together. We shared secrets together; we had the same dreams; we went through indescribable hardships just to get a high school education; we loved each other. The last time Rose and I saw Lilly was in the shower room as we arrived at Auschwitz.

We were waiting patiently in the space behind the main entrance of Barrack #29. Suddenly, the woman Lilly approached a few minutes ago appeared in front of us; she was out of breath. "It's not easy to handle 1500 unruly inmates all by myself," she said, a faint smile on her lips. She asked us to follow her.

We entered a small room with a window facing the street. Underneath the window there was a table covered with a fancy tablecloth and two chairs next to it. A two-tiered bunk bed with baby-blue, silk-trimmed blankets stood against the wall opposite the window. Close to the bunk beds and against the adjacent wall there was a small table with a water pitcher and a bar of soap in a soap dish. A rich-looking flowery towel rested on a towel hanger on the wall next to the table with the pitcher.

The woman introduced herself, "I'm the Block *Elteste* (barrack senior). You can call me Fraulein Helen." We followed her example and introduced ourselves. Fraulein Helen informed us there were two highly responsible positions to be filled in her newly occupied barrack: one was to take charge of the *Brotkammer* (pantry) and the other was to work as a Stubbendienst. We knew what the job of a Stubbendienst entailed; we had one in Lager A and an awful one, too. We were in the dark as to the job in the Brotkammer. Fraulein Helen talked about our cousin Lilly. She liked our cousin very much. Lilly was in charge of the Brotkammer in Barrack #9. She considered our cousin Lilly to be a very bright, competent and trustworthy young girl. That's why she accepted her recommendation for the filling of these two important jobs.

Fraulein Helen knew exactly which job to give to whom. She looked at Rose and said, "You'll be the Stubbendienst in my barrack." She described the job to Rose: she was to bring coffee from the kitchen twice a day, once in the morning and once in the evening, and hand it out to the inmates; she was to bring soup from the kitchen around midday and give it out to the inmates;

she was to return both the empty coffee pails and soup pails to the kitchen. The inmates were to consume their food at all times in their bunk beds. Rose was to clean the barrack twice a day while the inmates were to stay on the grounds. She was to control every activity of the inmates. She was to wake them up at a certain time; line them up for the morning and the afternoon roll call at a certain time; take them twice to the latrine at a certain time; make them go to bed at a certain time; and upon entering the barrack, make them immediately settle in their bunk beds and remain quiet. They could only whisper.

Did I hear correctly? My sister Rose would be a Stubbendienst?! I just hoped the inmates would not take advantage of my sister's compassion, understanding and goodness. I hoped! I hoped! I hoped! I hoped!

Fraulein Helen interrupted my thoughts, "I'll show you to the Brotkammer."

"I'm ready to start my job, whatever it entails, Fraulein Helen."

"Not so fast. You'll be working during the night," she said, while opening the door to the Brotkammer. From her room, across an aisle that led to both the front door and the inside of the barrack, was the Brotkammer. The entire wall facing the door was lined with shelves. A giant picnic table was the only other furniture in the Brotkammer.

Fraulein Helen explained the job to me. I was to cut 150 loaves of bread into 1500 slices, and give one slice to each girl upon her return to the barrack from roll call in the morning. If I were one slice short, she warned me, it would be *my* portion. If I were two slices short, it would be my portion and my sister's. If I were three slices short, it would be my job. I also learned that part of my job would entail cleaning Fraulein Helen's room on a daily basis, and secretly doing the cooking for her on an electrical hot plate.

I would have no problems concerning the cutting of the bread, I thought. While Fraulein Helen was mentioning numbers, my mind already made the final calculations. I'll have 150 loaves of bread;

I needed 1500 slices. I'll cut each loaf into 10 slices and voila—I'll have 1500 slices—a cinch!

Then, I heard the bad news. I was to take one loaf of bread and reserve it for a trustworthy person, a person who knew how to organize food from the chefs in the kitchen. What kind of food? Food like: salami, raw potatoes, barley, butter and what not. The same woman was to stand guard on the front steps of the main entrance of our barrack. If an SS woman or an SS man would as much as come in view of the *Torwache* (guard), I was to be alerted. I was to disconnect the hot plate and hide it together with the food either underneath the bunk bed, behind the bunk bed, or under the bedding. I was then to spray the room with perfume to neutralize the smell of cooked food.

In my dilemma of finding a trustworthy woman, I went into the barrack. I couldn't understand the darkness. Rose read my mind and said, "Except for a window in Fraulein Helen's room and one in the Brotkammer where you'll be working, there are no windows in the barrack of Lager C. I've known this for a long time; Galena mentioned it to me in Lager A., Rose continued."

"You mean the woman from whom you got a hold of my sweaters and the other things in Lager A?" I asked. "Yes; she's in this barrack." Rose said.

"Could you introduce me to her?"

"Sure, but before I do, I want to show you something." She pointed to a bunk bed at the bottom of the first three-tiered row. "This is our private bunk bed," Rose said. "Only you and I will sleep in it. We will not share it with six other inmates like we did in Lager A." I suppose these privileges come with our positions. I wished we could thank Lilly for everything she had done for us.

Rose was beaming. We walked through the barrack. Girls from the bunk beds looked at me as if I had horns. "Don't worry about the girls' stares," said Rose. "I told them I had a sister here and you'd be working in the Brotkammer."

Suddenly I saw, as if an apparition, a woman in her late fifties with long gray hair standing in front of me. Rose smiled and said, "This is Galena; she'll help me with my chores."

A bell rang in my head and I whispered in Rose's ear. "I have a better job for her. I need a trustworthy woman who knows her way with the chefs in the kitchen." I repeated almost verbatim the conversation I had with Fraulein Helen a short while ago. Rose looked at me, smiled and said, "I have a feeling Galena won't disappoint you; she's a great person and trustworthy indeed." I hugged Rose and thanked her. I got the woman I needed.

I still had a problem with the slicing of the bread since I was missing one loaf. My initial calculations were no longer valid, and my job became complicated. I lost count of how many times I would pre-mark each loaf of bread individually to get to the right size and the right number in the final cutting. I would start my job around one o'clock in the morning, allowing myself an hour or two for playing around with these loaves before the final process. I developed calluses on the inside of each of my fingers. By four o'clock in the morning, I was standing outside for roll call with the rest of the inmates.

At the end of roll call, Rose would have the girls stay put, while rushing to the kitchen with her helpers to bring the morning coffee. I, on the other hand, would go into the Brotkammer and wait. Each girl upon receiving a cup of coffee from Rose would enter the barrack and walk in front of the door of the Brotkammer as I handed out her daily slice of bread.

About eight o'clock in the morning, I'd begin the cleaning of my barrack senior's room, a job I loved best. She had things that reminded me of an outside world to which I once belonged.

Sometimes, I'd brush my face against the silk-trimmed blanket, and then frightened, I'd check it out for dirty spots from my face. With time, I decided to wash my face in the dirty water Fraulein Helen would leave in the basin. I'd turn my dress inside out and dry my face with it. Why inside out? After wearing my dress for six weeks before going to the delousing, I believed the inside of my dress was cleaner that the outside.

Once, I went even further; I used Fraulein Helen's towel to wipe my face. I prayed she would not walk in on me, but she did. I jumped away from the basin, her towel still in my hands. I must've looked like a guilty ghost. Holding back a smile, she calmed me down. The next day, there were two towels with different designs hanging on the wall. One of them was mine.

Fraulein Helen behaved beyond my expectations; she would leave food for me on her plate every day, food I cooked for her. Suddenly, I regained my menstrual cycle. We ceased having our monthly periods as soon as we arrived in Lager A. I assume we were given a special medication in our soup that caused the cessation of our menstrual cycle. My sister Rose was the best proof. She recovered her monthly period only as she began eating regular food after the liberation.

Fraulein Helen had a boyfriend named Stefan, a very handsome fellow in his late forties. He was the *Capo* (supervisor), of the male inmates that cleaned the latrines.

Once a week, Stefan would come into our lager as his people would clean the latrines. He'd put his confidant Yanik on the lookout and rush over to see Fraulein Helen. He'd always bring some food with him. At one time, it would be half a chicken, at another time, it would be a piece of fillet of fish of some sort and still at another time, it would be an intact roll of salami.

On the days Stefan visited Fraulein Helen, I personally stood guard. Upon detecting the slightest movement in the street, I would knock at Fraulein Helen's door. I would tell her approximately at what distance I saw a movement or a shadow of some kind. She would then figure out when Stefan was to leave; he would always leave through the back door.

Once, we had a very narrow escape. Just as in the past, I was busy casting my eyes in all directions when an SS man walked out from the fourth barrack down the street, heading in our direction.

I alerted Fraulein Helen just in time. Before I could turn around, Stefan was out of the room, running toward the back door. Luckily, the SS man had not stopped at our barrack for inspection.

Another time an SS man was four barracks away from our barrack when I alerted Fraulein Helen. After Stefan left, Fraulein Helen called me into her room. As soon I opened my mouth to say something, she began slapping my face. "What have you been doing stupid? Day-dreaming while on guard?! You know what could've happened if the SS walked in on me?!"

"May I explain?" I looked at her, my face burning and my eyes tearing. "You want to explain? Out!" she commanded. I turned around; I was about to open the door. "Stay, come here, please," she addressed me in a soft tone of voice, her hands touching my shoulder. "I want to apologize," she said. "You're an intelligent girl; you understand what made me so angry?" I nodded yes. She took a towel, soaked it in cold water, wrung it out, and held it against my cheeks, which must've been red and swollen. She repeated the process twice, and only then asked me for an explanation. "I could see no logical explanation for what happened," I said, "other than the SS man was already inside the neighboring barrack when I began guarding." In the end, we agreed that I would stand guard the whole day when Stefan would come into our camp.

I remember one time when Stefan rushed out of Fraulein Helen's room half-dressed. I was standing guard, my eyes strained, when a young man out of breath rushed up the stairs ready to storm the door. "You can't pass this door unless you tell me who you are, and what you want," I said. "I can't waste an extra minute," he said. "I've got to reach Stefan; I know he is with Helen."

I let him into the barrack, and said he could talk to Stefan through Fraulein Helen's door. He informed Stefan that an SS man was on the way to the latrines. Before the young man had finished his sentence, Stefan dashed out of Fraulein Helen's room with only his pants on. He threw his shirt to the young man, almost covering his face. I watched them both flee, and marveled at the skill the young man used in helping Stefan put on his shirt on the run. "What's your name?" I heard my voice trailing off in the barrack. No answer reached me.

The next week, I met the same young man on the front steps. Now, he seemed more relaxed. He introduced himself. He spoke in German. "My name is Yanik, what's yours?"

"Livia,"

"I'm Stefan's confidant."

"Your boss has not arrived yet."

"I don't think he will be seeing Helen today. I have a package for her; won't you please take it from me?" Yanik said. "I rather you give it to Fraulein Helen yourself," I said. We entered into the barrack. I knocked at Fraulein Helen's door. "What's the matter?" Fraulein Helen asked. "Stefan's confidant is here, he wants to talk to you, I said." Fraulein Helen opened the door and Yanik went inside.

I saw Yanik many times after that. He came either to give warning signals to his boss, or to bring food in his absence. Luckily, we never had a mishap. Whenever I saw Yanik, I'd think of Ferenz, my first love. At those times, I wouldn't sleep at all. I'd go straight into the Brotkammer around one o'clock and start my job. When I wasn't thinking about Ferenz, I'd think about Rose, about what a caring, understanding and compassionate Stubbendienst she made.

Unlike the Stubbendienst from Lager A, who would not mix the soup of the potato peels or potatoes, Rose would mix the soup after each helping. Unlike the Stubbendienst in Lager A, who would have the barrack cleaned by helpers, each for an extra bowl of soup, Rose decided to clean the barrack by herself, giving the extra portions of soup for the weak and emaciated. Unlike the Stubbendienst from Lager A, who would expose us to the dangerous sunrays for hours on end, Rose negotiated with Fraulein Helen to let the inmates stay in their bunk beds up to the time she had to take them to the latrine. Mixing the soup, cleaning the barrack on her own, and letting the girls stay indoors was not all she had done for the inmates. She'd also check their dresses for tears and fix them. She'd sit on the heating unit at night under a dim light and sew and sew. She'd sometimes fix their shoes, as well. How did she get a hold of her sewing kit? Galena who, by now, was under my employment brought it to her.

Once, on my free time, I asked Rose if she had a job for me. She gave me that motherly smile. "What a coincidence," she said. "I was just going to ask you to bring me half a pail of coal from the bin; I need it for the heating unit." I asked," Why not a full pail?"

"I need half a pail only." I knew she was lying. She must've thought a whole pail of coal would be too heavy for me to carry. She also told me that there was a shovel in the coal bin, and that I should use it. I had no problem in finding the coal bin. When I opened it, I saw a familiar face, except she was a corpse sprawled on top of a heap of coal. The shovel Rose mentioned before was under one of her legs. Her stomach was as big as a mountain.

I knew this face from Lager A. She was breathtakingly beautiful. She was newly married when she arrived in Auschwitz. Four weeks later, she found out she was pregnant, an unacceptable state in Birkenau-Auschwitz. We inmates tried to help her. We'd change our loose clothes with hers. Rose would sometimes offer her own daily slice of bread for a loose dress. We had a feeling only a miracle could save her life. From the size of her stomach, I figured she carried the baby to full term. I dreaded to think how she met with her death. Did she die in child birth, or was she brutally killed and thrown on the heap of the coal in this bin? I was not afraid to look at her. In fact, I admired the serenity in her face. She seemed to be sleeping. I stayed there a few minutes as if guarding her in her sleep. When I had enough of staring, I handpicked a full pail with coal. I didn't use the shovel from under the corpse's foot. I recall thinking. What if I remove the shovel from under the corps' foot and suddenly, the whole mountain of coal, in retaliation of disturbing the corps' peace, slides down and swallows me? I rushed out. I wasn't sure I closed the bins' door, but I didn't return to check it out.

The Upcoming Selection

It was the second Friday in Lager C. I'd just finished cleaning Fraulein Helen's room when she walked in all agitated. "You will not cook today for me; I'll help myself to a plain sandwich," she said and dismissed me with her hand. As I walked toward the door I heard, "send in your sister; I want to talk to her!" her voice agitated still. What could my sister have done, I thought? This morning everything seemed all right. I began praying in my mind.

Back in our bunk bed, I asked Rose what had happened; why Fraulein Helen was angry with the both of us. She hesitated, then said, "Fraulein Helen was not angry with us; there will be a selection today!"

"A selection . . . ?" As soon as I could formulate words I started with questions. "Will we be dressed like when Dr. Mengele selected us on the Auschwitz ramp upon our arrival?"

"We will be naked."

"Naked naked?"

"Stark naked!"

I hid my face on Rose's chest. She stroked my head, "We'll be all right; don't worry!"

"I don't want to ever separate from you," I cried as I hugged her tightly.

"We'll never, ever separate," Rose said. "Whatever the cost, I'm determined to keep you alive. We must live for each other's sake, but . . ."

"But what?"I interrupted her. "We need courage to overcome obstacles."

"I'll try to be brave," I assured Rose, my words trailing off. "From your mouth to God's ears." She wiped off my tears. I felt helpless. If only I could hide under her skin, or melt together with her, I thought. Rose left to get soup from the kitchen. I don't recall how long I lay in the bunk bed in a fetal position. I wanted to be small, crawl into the woodwork, disappear and become invisible.

Suddenly, I heard the voice of my barrack senior, "Livia, come into my room!"

I entered Fraulein Helen's room. I saw half a sandwich of salami on the table. "Eat the sandwich and don't worry about cleaning the dish; I'll do it," she said. I felt a knot in my throat.

I'm not ready to eat right now, Fraulein Helen," I said. She must have realized that Rose had told me about the selection. "Don't worry, Livia; you'll be okay and so will your sister."

"From your mouth to God's ears," I repeated Rose's words. Fraulein Helen looked at me puzzled.

"That was a translation of a Yiddish expression," I said. Fraulein Helen took on a strange look; she seemed to be debating with herself. A minute or so later, she said, "I'm Jewish, but I don't speak Yiddish."

I looked at her in disbelief. "Your cousin Lilly knew that I was Jewish," she continued. "She also knew that Stefan was Catholic and that he was my husband." It seemed Fraulein Helen was eager to talk. From the dribs and drabs, I deduced that Stefan, being gentile, had not been deported to Auschwitz. But upon finding out the whereabouts of his Jewish wife, he worked out a plan. He told the German authorities that he was a Nazi sympathizer and would they send him to Auschwitz to work there in whatever capacity.

Upon hearing of Stefan's smart scheme, I said, "That's what I call true love!" Ferenz came to mind and my eyes filled up with tears. Fraulein Helen looked at me as if for the first time. "How old are you?"

"Twenty-four."

"Have you ever been in love before?"

"Yes, but it was a painful, unfulfilled love."

"Don't worry, you're still young," she said and put her hand on my shoulder. Her touch felt so soothing; I wished we could stay frozen like this until the selection was over. No, my wish did not come true; she removed her hand from my shoulder with the speed of lightning.

"Now eat!" she said. "We don't have much time before the selection!" She also rattled off, "Call me Helen instead of Fraulein Helen, and don't breathe a word to anybody either about the selection or about me!"

I ate the sandwich forcing every bite down my throat. I wiped my mouth with my hands, placed a kiss on Helen's hand and asked, "May I tell Rose about Stefan?"

"Yes, you may."

During the next couple of hours Rose and I lived through a nightmare. My barrack senior asked me to lock the barrack front door and give her the keys. She also wanted to see my sister again. She spoke in a high-pitched tone of voice. Before long, I saw my sister leaving Helen's room. She hurriedly headed toward the back door and locked it. On her way back, she increased her pace and almost tripped. She told the girls to undress until naked. The girls laughed. "You must be joking," one of them said.

"Girls!" Rose said. "Please, pay no attention to that last remark! This is no joke; these are the barrack senior's orders. You don't think I could make up something like this, do you?" The girls refused to listen to my sister.

I thought I had to do something about it. Maybe if I undressed first, paraded in front of them, they might follow my example. I removed my dress and walked naked through both aisles. I tried talking some sense into these girls. "Listen you all!" I said. "I know my sister is lenient with you; the more reason you should listen to her! You don't want the barrack senior to replace her with a Stubbendienst like we had in Lager A? Remember, girls? My sister lets you stay in your bunk beds when she cleans the barrack; she spares you from loitering outside in the scorching sun and getting blistered up! She also mixes the soup so that you have some solid mass to eat! She gives the weakest of you double and sometimes triple portions; sober up and get undressed!"

Fraulein Helen got into the picture. Red in her face from anger, she walked around the aisles shouting, "Drop your blankets to the floor, undress until naked, and remain in your bunk beds! To me she said, "You Livia keep your blanket; you've followed my initial orders!" The aisles filled up with blankets, and the girls took off their clothes. Not only had they realized that my sister was following orders, but they had also smelled a rat. They began crying, wailing, and talking to their friends across the aisles. They also begged the barrack senior to let them have their blankets back. They were shivering like aspen leaves.

Fraulein Helen ignored the pleas of the inmates and asked Rose to put the blankets in a corner thus clearing the isles. She went to the front door and disappeared behind it. The inmates now called out to my sister; they asked her for forgiveness. My sister assured them of her pardon. Satisfied, the frightened, naked girls wrapped themselves around each other. The back door opened, and Fraulein Helen appeared. She ordered Rose to line up 50 naked girls and take them out to the grounds. She must repeat this course of action until all fifteen hundred girls are on the grounds; she could form a U column if necessary.

In the middle of the grounds, I saw Dr. Mengele, clad in his fancy uniform, sitting on a chair. About five yards to his back, I saw a black military truck with its rear door wide open. From both sides of the rear opening of the truck, there stretched a semi-circle with guards, their bayonets inward. The semi-circle ended at the first row of the five women abreast of the U column formation. Since I was on the outside of the first row of the five girls abreast, one of the guards almost touched me. Had I not remembered Helen's statement, "Don't worry; you'll be all right" and Rose's encouragement, I would have definitely messed up. The formation in view, especially the black truck, looked like a bad omen to me. The barrack senior's instructions reinforced my belief. "Each of you, one at the time, is to advance! Then stop about two yards in front of Dr. Mengele and slowly turn! You are to watch out for

Dr. Mengele's hand signals! When he signals to the right, you are to go back into the barrack and into your bunk beds! When he signals to the left, you are to go into the truck and wait!"

I now realized that Dr. Mengele, with one stroke of his hand to the right or to the left, would determine who of us would live and who of us would die. But why would the guards hold their bayonets on the inward?

Rose had just returned from inspecting the U column of the naked girls. All at once, the barrack senior shouted, "Advance!" pointing to me. My heart sank, my feet felt as if nailed to the ground, and most probably I would have remained stuck in place had it not been for Helen's and Rose's words resonating in my mind. I stepped forward, walked erect, looked confident, and stopped about two yards in front of Dr. Mengele. I began slowly turning. Dr. Mengele looked at me from my waist down. Not one time did his eyes stray above my waist. Without any warning, something turned into my stomach and I felt like vomiting. No wonder. My eyes caught Dr. Mengele's hand rising; the hand that would either send me to my death or back to the living. I just had time to formulate my childhood standard praying words in my mind, "God is good, God is great!" before Dr. Mengele made a full sweep with his hand to the right, sparing my life. The good news would not alleviate my nausea. As I passed by Rose on the way to the barrack, she realized something was wrong with me. When I covered my mouth with both my hands, she understood what exactly had happened. "You must hold it until you get to the rear door of our barrack!" she whispered. "The guards must not see you."

But how could I hold it, when the vomit was pushing forward. I thought running would help; I was mistaken. Somewhere midway to the barrack my hands filled up with a smelly mass, forcing itself through my fingers and on my naked body before I decided it was safe to stop and let the vomit fall to the ground. In front of the rear door of the barrack there was a patch of green grass. It occurred to me to roll in it, thus wiping the vomit from my body.

While rolling in the grass, and turning my face on all sides, another reprieved naked girl returning from the selection ordeal caught up with me. She believed I had had a seizure and offered to help. I explained to her my predicament; she shrugged her shoulders and said, "You could've wiped your body and face with your hands, then wiped your hands in the grass." I was not ready to admit my stupidity, so I said, "You're right. But you know what? I had fun rolling in the grass."

Inside the barrack, the girl hugged me and said, "I hope the rest of us make it back as well." She dressed, then asked me for a blanket. I took her to the pile and said, "You're in charge now of all of these blankets. Place two blankets in each bunk bed. I need to rest before starting my job in the Brotkammer. In reality, I just wanted to get dressed, go into my bunk bed, immerse completely under the blanket and lay and lay and lay there.

Although I had covered my ears with my hands underneath the blanket, I could still hear cries of joy, of sorrow and Rose's voice, as she was calming some hysterical girls. I don't know how long I was cocooned under the blanket. I recall Rose trying to free my head from underneath it to allow me to breath in some air. "How many went into the truck?" I asked Rose, looking in her eyes. "Twenty," she answered. Unfortunately, twenty innocent girls will go up in smoke today, I thought.

The next morning around eight o'clock, I went to clean Helen's room. Unlike any other morning, she was in her room as if waiting for me. I stopped at the door; she greeted me warmly. "Didn't I tell you yesterday you would be all right?" she said, a smile on her lips. "The way you are built from your waist down told me you'd be all right."

I asked Helen to explain, I couldn't make out anything of what she had said.. "I saw you were built a little heavy from your waist down," Helen said.

"You mean I have a big derrière?" I told Helen how I was always self-conscious of having too much in the wrong places; how at fourteen I already wore a tight girdle; how every morning before going to school, I'd endlessly roll on the floor in hope of shrinking my backside; and now I heard that the build I so hated was helping me survive?

Helen was even more explicit. "When Dr. Mengele looks at the inmates from their waist down, he wants to see flesh on their buttocks," she said. "The more flesh, the longer they can withstand the daily hardships. Besides, there's no room in the gas chambers."

I was horrified, "So he sends off the emaciated girls first?"

Helen paid no attention; she just kept on. "You Hungarians are flooding the camp; there's no end to the trains arriving here every day!" She spoke as if we Hungarians volunteered to come here. She then caught herself and stroked my cheeks. "You don't have to worry; this madness will come to an end and before long, we'll all go home."

The damage was already done; I looked down. I couldn't face her. Suddenly, she said, "Look at me; I didn't mean to hurt you; I'm sorry." I continued to look down. She put her hand under my chin and lifted my face. "Do you know what I did for you?" I looked at her for an explanation. "I fattened you up," she said. "You wouldn't know it, but I left more food on my plate for you than I myself ate, not that I starved as a result. I wanted you to put on a few pounds. I didn't worry about your sister; she's a little on the plump side."

Spontaneously, she led her fingers to her nose. "You brought in some awful smell. I must ask your sister what's going on in the barrack," she said.

"Nothing is going on in the barrack; the odor is coming from my body and my dress."

She looked confused"What do you mean, the odor is coming from my dress?"

I related to her what had happened yesterday on my way back

from the selection. She gave me the following instructions: I was to take off the dress; I was to wash my body in the water she had just used; I was to use her washcloth and the towel she gave me the other day and I was to wait for her until she returned with a clean dress. Before she left, she took a bottle of perfume and released a drop in the water that I was to wash myself in.

A minute or two later, Rose entered the room holding a blanket. She could hardly believe her eyes, seeing me standing in the middle of the room stark naked. I rushed to explain, "Helen wants me to wash myself in her water," I said. Rose kept looking at me as if saying, "Go on."

"Only after I dry myself, I'm to use the blanket you brought for me and wait until she returns with a clean dress."

"As confused as I am . . . please, don't let it slip and call Fraulein Helen plain Helen."

"But Fraulein Helen *told* me to call her Helen. The other day, she took me in her confidence and told me all about Stefan and herself. In my excitement, I forgot to mention it to you," I felt ashamed. "It's okay," Rose said, then picked up my smelly dress and left.

I had just carried out Helen's instructions, when the door opened and she walked in with a new dress. She displayed it for me. It looked like a semi-dressy three-quarter-sleeved dress of the color of wine with a rose appliqué flower on the chest. I fell in love with it. It reminded me of the dress Toby wore when she left for Germany. Helen also brought me a pair of panties. I would be the only girl to wear panties among all the female inmates in the camp. I loosened my hands from the blanket. In my excitement, I forgot about my nakedness. Helen eyed me up and down. Was she jealous? After all, I was only twenty-four years old.

I put on the dress; it molded to my body. The mirror next to me showed my form. I ran my hands over my curves. For a minute I felt guilty for being in such good shape. Thanks to Helen, my body had revitalized. Words of gratitude began pouring out of my mouth as if someone else spoke them. "I thought you'd like the dress; I hand-picked it myself," Helen said, trying to put an end to my praises.

"I wish I could keep this dress and not have to wear it for the next delousing; I'll lose it if I do."

"I don't see why you couldn't keep it; you wear your smelly dress to your next delousing and leave it there."

I told Helen that Rose was giving my smelly dress to a girl whose outfit was in shreds.

"Your sister Rose is a good person," Helen said. I agreed with her. "If there were sainthood in our religion, I would recommend she'd be bestowed with it."

The next words I heard from Helen were, "You could wear your new dress when Stefan visits me." My mind began its tricks. I saw myself in this new dress being admired by none other than Yanik, Stefan's confidant.

Helen saw me lost in thoughts. She decided to bring me back to reality. "We'll be having selections every Friday from now on," she said. I became visibly upset; she made no attempt to console me. I left Helen's room. Rose paid no attention to my mood; she kept admiring my dress. I decided not to tell her about the upcoming weekly selections; she would find out about it on her own.

The next Friday arrived. I found myself the fourth girl in the fourth row of the column of naked girls to stand for selection. I wasn't happy about it. Now I would have to watch the ordeal of the nineteen girls stepping forward before me. I closed my eyes every time a girl strode forward. Soon, my neighbor elbowed me, "You better open your eyes," she said. "In a minute, it'll be our turn."

"What happened to the fifteen women before us?" I asked her in a whispering tone of voice. "They were shown to the right." I was happy for them. Then, the first girl from our row stepped forward. I prayed for her in my mind. I learned she had had diarrhea for a few days and had lost weight. Dr. Mengele looked at her and pointed to the left. I saw human waste running down her naked thighs. She seemed incapable of controlling her diarrhea. Moreover, she began behaving as if she had gone berserk. Instead of going into the truck, she tried to make a dash for freedom, screaming, "I don't want to die; I don't want to die!" Naturally, she ran into the guard's bayonets. Oblivious of her sustained wound, she tried again for freedom. She ran into bayonets here, into bayonets there, she almost made a full circle. Blood covered her entire body, not even an inch of skin was visible, but she kept uttering, "I want to live; I want to live!"

Suddenly, she decided to approach Dr. Mengele. Would she make it? No! You could see that life was slowly leaving her. She began stumbling, as if her head pulled her down, and about midway to Dr. Mengele's chair, she fell to the ground uttering some incoherent words. The guards approached her; how did she dare come so close to Dr. Mengele's chair. They pierced her corpse with their bayonets time and time again. We, inmates, closed our eyes and kept back a scream. To this day, I can hear her desperate cries for life echoing in my mind.

I wondered whether there ever would be an end to this madness. During the last week of September 1944, I got my answer. "There will be no more selections," Helen said to me. When I looked at her for an additional explanation, she dismissed me. She ordered me not to spread the news about the cessation of the selections to anyone except Rose.

The Sonderkommando

During the months of October, November, and December, things began to happen with the speed of lightning. Lager B closed. The SS men brought the inmates from there into Lager C. Some of the girls were shipped to Germany, others were evacuated from the camp, and still others were gassed. Helen spoke to me about the heroic resistance the last *Sonderkommando* (Jewish male inmates who worked in the crematoriums) staged before most of them were killed. They fought with stones, guns and grenades. They also set Crematorium IV on fire, thus rendering it inoperable. When it was all over, most of the Sonderkommando members were dead. However, the SS also sustained losses.

Who were the Sonderkommando? What was their job? Where did they work? How could they have gotten firearms? All this was unknown to me. We inmates of Lager C had no contact with inmates from other lagers or even inmates from other barracks. We had to stay in our own barracks or on our own grounds at all times.

On the morning of October 8, 1944, everything crystallized in my mind. I walked into my barrack senior's room to do the cleaning. The scene in front of my eyes overwhelmed me. Helen, in her night gown, her face hidden in her hands, was sitting in a chair hunched over the table, her hair almost covering it.

I tiptoed to the table, bent over, and looked from all sides, trying to make out what had happened. I saw two red, swollen eyes peering through the mop of hair belonging to Helen. She threw her arms around me, buried her face on my chest, and held me tightly, as if preventing me from escaping her. She looked pitiful and helpless. As dumbfounded as I was, I still had the presence of mind to say, "Whatever your problems are, please do something about your appearance; don't force trouble upon yourself. You don't want an SS man or an SS woman to walk in and find you looking like this."

She gave me a warm appreciative look, and asked me to come back a little later. When I returned, she looked her own self again except for her red eyes. She had also made her own bed, put away a few things strewn here and there and cleaned up the table. She wouldn't even let me throw out the water from the basin. She wanted to see me at nine o'clock that evening to talk. "How will I know the exact time?" I asked. "I'll give you my wrist watch."

"Are you sure you want to do that?"

"I'm sure I want to do that; what's the matter, Livia?"

"I don't trust myself," I said. "It's such a precious thing; I might break it. Or, who knows, someone might take it from me."

"Why would anybody take it from you?" Helen asked. "It's not food. As about breaking it, do you intend to wrestle with it?"

"I don't know," I said. "It's a funny feeling to be stripped of everything, then six months later, to be entrusted with a worldly item, a wristwatch; I'm scared."

"Don't be scared," said Helen. "I'll fasten it on your wrist myself."

Helen and I had a liverwurst sandwich for lunch. I instructed Galena to alert me at the appearance of anyone, especially when Stefan showed up. I thought I saw the latrine commando this morning. However, Stefan had not shown up. It occurred to me that Helen's unusual distressed mood might have something to do with Stefan's absence.

I dreaded to see her at nine o'clock that night. This morning I thought her mood had something to do with us inmates. Now, I wasn't sure. At nine o'clock, as I entered her room, she met me with tears in her eyes. "I don't know whether Stefan is alive or not," she said, showing me to a chair next to hers. "He's no longer in charge of the latrine commando. I saw a strange face this morning."

"Did you see Yanik?"

"No."

"That's it," I said. "They were probably transferred to another lager."

"All lagers are closed except Birkenau and Auschwitz, the man's lager proper."

"I still think there was a switch in Capos, and Stefan and Yanik are now in Auschwitz proper," I said. She wished she could accept my explanation. She suspected Stefan was involved in procuring firearms for yesterday's Sonderkommando rioting, and was apprehended and killed.

"I had no idea that Stefan was in charge of firearms besides being a Capo," I said.

"He was not in charge of firearms. He had connections among

the Polish and Russian war prisoners in a nearby forced labor camp. Some of those prisoners must've worked in ammunition factories, smuggling out firearms, and Stefan was one of the in-between men."

"What do you know about the fate of the Sonderkommando in yesterday's uprising?" I asked, in hope that our conversation would lead us to good news about Stefan.

"Four hundred Sonderkommando members were killed, and a few broke out of the camp."

"See?" I said, interrupting her. "Stefan might be among the escapees. For what I think, he is right now somewhere in disguise, making his way to safety, waiting for you."

"Hopeful thinking. The truth is grim. A few miles from the breakout point, the escapees barricaded themselves in a deserted barn. A group of SS men caught up with them and set the barn on fire."

"There could still be survivors."

Helen embraced me. "I thank you for this conversation," she said. "I can see that hope makes you girls survivors." I had the impression she was in no hurry to shorten my stay in her room. I took advantage and asked her to enlighten me on the history of the Sonderkommando, especially, why we the inmates here in the camps had no knowledge of their existence until yesterday. "The SS men were not anxious for you to find out about the Sonderkommando. They would've had to deal with uprisings on a regular basis. I, too, was in the dark about the history of the Sonderkommando until yesterday."

I learned more about the Sonderkommando than I was prepared to hear. They were groups of Jewish male inmates chosen from their barracks and assigned to work in the gas chambers and the crematoriums. They numbered about 840. To forestall any emotional problems resulting from their jobs, the SS men replaced them every three to four months. To keep the rest of the camp population in the dark about the abominable jobs they were doing in these infernos, the SS men gassed the outgoing commandos or shot them in the back of their heads.

Before elaborating on the jobs of the Sonderkommando, Helen described, first, the gas chambers. When she arrived in Auschwitz in 1941, the gas chambers consisted of concrete bunkers with openings in the roof. SS men then threw poison pellets into these bunkers full of naked people: children, mothers, fathers, grandparents, and cripples. The poison gas was but a strong insecticide. It took two to four days for the people to die. To drown out the victims' desperate screams, the SS men would gather trucks around the bunkers and run their motors until the last voice fell silent.

Helen continued, "In anticipation of the arrival of the hundreds of thousands of Hungarian Jews, like you in the spring of 1944, new and more efficient gas chambers were built. They resembled the delousing rooms with perforated pipes and built-in showers into the ceilings." she said. "The difference was that the built-in showers were dummies; no water was coming from them. The 3,000 naked people crammed into each of these gas chambers were expecting water to come through the perforations of the pipes. Instead, Zyklon B, a poisonous gas replaced the water. Five minutes later, the people were dead. The Sonderkommando squad, in their large rubber boots, flooded the pile of bodies with powerful jets of water. The separation of the bodies was a hard job. They knotted thongs around their wrists and dragged their slippery bodies into the elevators, which took them into the incineration room. A second Sonderkommando unit cut the hair off the bodies and yanked the gold teeth and gold bridges out of their mouths. A third Sonderkommando unit threw them into the burning ovens."

At this point, I let out a scream, "My God, my own mother and Shullie went through all this?!"

I remembered Mother holding Shullie in her arms as Dr. Mengele showed her to the left. The child stretched his little hands in the direction of Rose, his mother, and cried at the top of his lungs, "Mommy, take me with you, please! I'll be a good boy from now on; I'll eat hamburgers, just take me with you, please!" Shullie was not fond of hamburgers. He must have thought his mother left him with his grandmother in punishment because he wouldn't eat hamburgers.

Helen placed her hand on my mouth to silence my screaming. "You don't want Rose to dash in here thinking that I beat you?" she said. "Do you want to leave the room?"

I turned my head from side to side. 'No.'

Helen removed her hand from my mouth. "Now take a deep breath." I followed her advice. "Do you feel better?" she asked. I said, "No!"

"Do you still want to stay here?"

"Yes, yes," my voice trailed off as I covered my eyes with my hands and was softly sobbing.

Helen stroked my head, "I'm sorry about your mother," she said. "I think my own parents met with the same fate only in different camps. But who in the world was Shullie?"

"Rose's two and a half year old son whom a German guard forced out of her arms. He put him in my mother's arms just before Dr. Mengele pointed to my mother to go to the left."

"Do you realize that the guard saved Rose's life?"

"We realize that."

"I wonder what my little six-year-old, Stasia, is doing in the convent now," Helen suddenly said.

Surprised at the news that she had a little girl, and even more surprised to hear about her decision, I asked, "Why didn't you place your daughter with your husband's relatives?"

"His parents were not happy with his choice of marrying a Jewish woman. But then, neither were my parents happy with my choice of marrying Stefan."

I couldn't explain the reason, but I remember asking her, "What if Stasia won't recognize you after the war, and prefers to stay in the convent?"

"I'd fight anybody for her with my last breath."

The diversion from our previous conversation had calmed me down a bit. I especially admired Helen's motherly courage to fight for her daughter if necessary, even with a giant institution like a convent.

I felt it was time to part, leave Helen with *her* thoughts and *me* with mine. I gave her back her wristwatch, embraced her, and left her room.

Did I share with Rose the information I learned from Helen? Some of it, but only after the war ended. I never described to her what happened to the people after they were gassed.

Time dragged on through October, 1944. I was working on my job in the Brotkammer, cutting loaves of bread and counting slices, when I heard a succession of explosions. I dashed through the door to go to our bunk bed to curl up around Rose and wait for the end to come.

Rose was not in our bunk bed. She was walking around the aisles, quieting down our hysterical women. "Shhhhh, shhhhh, go back to sleep," she kept saying. "No bomb fell, trust me; don't wake up our barrack senior. I'll tell you tomorrow morning what the noise was all about."

When Rose returned to her bunk bed, I asked, "How do you know it was not a bomb?"

"Fraulein Helen told me last night. They are detonating the gas chambers and the crematoriums. We inmates are to clean up the premises tomorrow."

"Why didn't you tell me that last night?" My heart almost stopped beating; I thought I would drop dead."

"You were sleeping so peacefully, how could I wake you up? I knew you'd have to work in the Brotkammer during the whole night. Or have you finished your job?"

"No, I haven't finished the job," I said, and returned to the Brotkammer.

The next day, the inmates of Lager C were out there stumbling, falling, cleaning, and loading trucks with debris. The erasing of the traces of the SS' hideous crimes lasted a few days. Rose and I saw some pipes sticking out from the ground. We figured that these pipes carried the Zyklon B, the poison gas to the gas chambers. We realized the war was winding down. Would we survive? We ardently hoped we would. We clung to hope with every breath. Our camp consisted of endless rows of barracks and narrow winding streets. Concrete poles curbed at the top and ending in floodlights were placed a few yards apart from each other. Eight or ten rows of electrically charged barbed wires connected them. Every thirty yards or so, there was a watchtower with an SS guard leaning on a machine gun. We looked at these towers and wires every day. Did we in our most miserable moments think of going to end our lives by touching these wires? No. I recall in Lager A, when idling on the grounds, we'd refuse to think about the immediate present. We'd take refuge in the past. We'd cook in our minds, sew in our minds, model our creations in our minds, and talk about our love adventures--anything, except the present.

Winter weather had arrived early in the fall of 1944. In Auschwitz, the first snow had fallen and had covered the ground with a white blanket. As the days passed, the blanket of snow grew thicker and thicker. A great number of our women froze to death during roll call. Those of us alive had to hold them up, sometimes four to five hours. They had to be counted.

The Death March

On January 18, 1945, strange things happened. The inmates from our Lager C, the ones who had not been evacuated or gassed, were brought to our Barrack #29. I hadn't seen so many inmates in our barrack since we first arrived there. I could think of nothing except my job. I'd be working through most of the night, and tomorrow morning. I would be seeing new faces.

Rose had her own chores to think about. It was an unusually cold day and she wanted to warm up the barrack thoroughly. She wanted to make the new arrivals feel comfortable. She went to the coal bin in the early afternoon, only to find it was locked. She complained to Helen. To her dismay, Helen told her she would have to do without coal today. Rose had not intended to let me in on her problem, and would have actually kept quiet about it, had it not been for another fall out. Helen told Rose there would be no coffee tonight. We retreated to our bunk bed and talked. We came to the conclusion that something drastic was to happen, but what exactly, we could not figure out.

Around eight o'clock in the evening, Helen called me into her room. She asked me to sit down. "There will be no bread for you to cut tonight," she said, turning her face away.

The news fell heavily on my chest. Thoughts began scrambling in my mind. We couldn't be gassed. The gas chambers were all gone. There was no sign of them. After we inmates cleaned the debris, the place looked as if nothing had ever been there, except for the barracks, the watch towers, and the barbed wires that were still intact. The SS had destroyed the last crematorium a few days earlier; Helen had mentioned it to me in passing. There were only a few non-functional ovens left. She had also mentioned to me the fate of four Jewish women involved in the October Sonderkommando uprising. They were hanged just after Christmas. She was still wondering what had happened to Stefan.

As if through a dream, I heard the words, "Follow me, Livia!" I came to. I saw Helen heading toward her two-tiered bunk bed. She talked fast and breathed even faster, as if she had just come off the run-tracks, and had not had time to rest yet. Was she in a hurry to tell me something, and then dismiss me, so that she could remain with her own thoughts?

I walked behind her. I saw a heap of clothes on her lower bunk bed. She swiftly transferred the items to her upper bunk bed, while showing them to me one by one. I saw two full-length winter coats, two pairs of boots, two pairs of socks, two wool scarves and two slices of salami wrapped in paper.

"Now listen, and don't ask questions," Helen said, seeming

in a hurry still. "The minute you walk out from here both of you put these things on top of whatever you have on now and sleep in them, boots and all. Eat the salami tomorrow morning."

We're going to evacuate the lager, I thought. It took me a few seconds to recover.

"What are you waiting for!?" Helen said. "Take the things and leave the room!" I embraced her and thanked her, tears welling up in my eyes. "Good luck," she said, her voice broken. I left her room, and never saw her again, or heard of her again. Have I forgotten her? No! Not ever!

Rose seemed overwhelmed by the news and the life-saving things Helen gave us. She rushed into Helen's room and thanked her. Helen would not look at her. She just said, "Good luck, you'll need it!"

I asked Rose to help me put on the clothes. She suggested they would interfere with my work in the Brotkammer. "I had forgotten to tell you there would be no bread to cut tonight."

She seemed crushed. We embraced and kissed. For the first time, I saw Rose muffling a cry. Then, as if something entered her mind, she said, "Help me get sewing things like scissors, thread, etc. I also need the blanket we cover the boards with." Unlike the rest of the inmates who slept on plain boards, we, Rose and I, had a blanket to cover the boards we slept on.

"What do you need scissors and whatever else for?" I asked Rose.

"You'll find out later."

When she returned from the spot she usually did her sewing, she showed me what she had made from the blanket. There were two knee-length, slim-legged shorts and two strings to hold them up around our waists. I was speechless. I grabbed my size shorts from Rose's hands and, for no rhyme or reason, pressed them to my heart and only afterwards examined them. They were just the right width to tuck my wine-colored dress inside them. My last delousing dress was large enough to wear it over this ingenious creation. I seemed as excited as when Rose made me my first rag doll and showed me how I could make one myself.

We put on our clothes and silently fell into each other's arms. My mind began racing again. Are clothes the final answer to survival? What role would the weather play? What role would the food play? How would the SS guards treat us? What part would our physical strength and our will to live play? I wished we could turn into pillars of salt and come alive when it would all be over.

I don't recall how long we remained in this embrace before I heard real words, familiar words, words I had heard before, "Remember, we have to live for each other's sake; we have to be brave to overcome obstacles."

"You have something left over of that blanket?" I asked Rose.

"A few strips. I know to whom to give them; I'll wrap them around their necks tomorrow morning."

"What happened to our blanket we cover ourselves with?" I asked. She showed me a bunch of strips. "I'll hand them out to those who need them tomorrow morning."

I looked at her and said, "Are you for real or are you an angel?"

She gave me a peck on my cheek and holding back a smile, she said, "So you've noticed my wings; let's go to sleep."

At dawn, Rose and I ate the salami before anybody else woke up. I heard one of the women telling her friend, "Hey, I smell salami; we'll have salami this morning." Another voice chimed in, "That's why we didn't get supper last night."

I felt guilty. I could not explain anything to these girls, not even why Rose and I looked like human beings dressed in winter coats, boots and all.

It was time to leave the barrack and stand for roll call on the grounds. Rose opened the front door. The strong gust of a wind carrying snow powder told her there was a full-blown snowstorm out there. She stopped the girls at the door. She returned into the barrack for a broom and cleaned the front steps.

We finally made it outside; our arms protecting our eyes. Rose lined us up for roll call. In a few minutes, we were covered with snow from head to toe. I saw a number of women with rags on their feet instead of shoes. They must have been among those who came into our barrack yesterday. Rose saw them, too. She let out a scream, "Darn it!"

I covered her mouth with my hands, "What in the world are you doing? You want to be shot?"

She removed my hands from her mouth and whispered, "If only I had known about these girls. I could have given them our shoes."

"What did you do with our shoes?" I asked.

"I gave them to two of my children; their soles were full of holes."

Yes, she called the inmates 'her children'–and yes, I wasn't her only child and no, I wasn't even jealous.

Roll call was short. We were barely 1500 women. The inmates were looking in the direction where Helen would normally stand. They were expecting her to dismiss them. Helen was not there. Instead, they heard the SS shouting, "The camp is closing; you'll be evacuated!"

The reaction was despair, anxiety and fear for the unknown. The girls begged for blankets and food. The answer was, "*Vorwärts Marsch! Vorwärts Marsch*! (Forward! March!)."

We marched through three or four open gates. The last gate looked closed. While the guards were busying themselves with opening the gate, a group of girls, with the desperation of the doomed, bare handedly stormed a nearby warehouse with food and clothing. Most of them met with their death with only a few exceptions. My sister, Rose, was one of the survivors. This break-in happened so fast, I hadn't even realized that Rose was missing from my side. But she returned, dragging a blanket which she swiftly tied together and threw over her shoulder.

We were now on the other side of the last gate of Auschwitz. The ground was so heavily covered with snow; we couldn't make out the road. The bitter cold pierced through our poorly clad bodies. Snowdrifts beat our faces, while the SS guards were whipping us to an ever-faster pace; to the pace of running. As the howling winds were about to lift our emaciated bodies into the air, we formed human chains by locking arms. Many of our girls gave up. Still, we kept dragging them along, dragging them along until we realized they were dead; only then would we let go.

Rose and I were fortunate to withstand the rigors of the first day. It seemed our reserve energy, coupled with our warm clothing, worked in our favor in the face of the ultimate challenge. The next day my right foot swelled up and I could no longer run. I told Rose to continue without me. "Yeah?" she said. Before I could realize what that 'yeah' meant, I was on her shoulder. She took a knife out of the blanket, cut my boot open, removed it, wrapped a sweater around my foot, put me down, and I could run again. But 200 or 300 feet down the road, my sweater became so snow and ice laden that running was impossible, as it was for the girls from the camp who started out with rags on their feet. With every passing minute more and more snow accumulated on their rags until they couldn't run any longer. The guards mercilessly shot them and casually pushed them to the side. It seemed that all evacuees, male and female, before us took the same route, for both sides of the road looked covered with a black trail of male and female corpses stretching for miles on end.

History remembers our march and the march of our predecessors and the march of all evacuees from all the camps as the, "The Death March."

Going back to my snow-laden sweater, I told Rose she must continue without me. I saw no way out. Carrying me on her shoulders would mean death for both of us.

"Remember my promise?" She interrupted my train of thought. "Whatever the cost, I'm determined to keep you alive."

"Not this time, please, there's nothing you can do."

"Watch me!" she said. She concentrated on the guards. As

some of them turned around to avoid the strong winds blinding them, she walked out of the column. On the run, she took a pair of shoes from a male corpse. She removed one shoe, then the other, then I landed on her shoulder, and then I was back on the ground, running with men's shoes on.

The second day, we were stopped for a fifteen-minute rest at the roadside with the snowed in corpses. I felt terribly tired and terribly cold and wanted to lie down in the snow for a few minutes. Rose vehemently opposed my idea.

"You can sit in the snow, but you cannot lie down! You mustn't fall asleep no matter what!" Rose spoke to me in an unfamiliar stern voice.

"Why? Have a heart," I begged her.

"I'm telling you this because I have a heart. I want you to live; if you lie down and fall asleep, you'll never wake up again!"

She advised the rest of the girls to not lie down and fall asleep. Those who refused to take her advice paid with their lives.

The third day, around noontime, judging from the position of the sun in the sky, we had been ordered off the main road. A knee-deep virgin blanket of snow stretched in front of our eyes all the way to the horizon. We began trotting in the snow. Some of our girls bent down and with the help of their hands, tried to extricate their feet from the deep snow. The guards, in their mistaken belief that these girls were giving up, shot them.

My sister Rose learned from their misfortune. She asked me to embrace her from the back. Now my body was totally leaning against hers. We walked like joined at the hip, making my advancing in the deep snow much easier.

At one point, we saw a dot on the horizon. As we kept advancing, the dot grew bigger and bigger. At dusk, it turned into a shack. The guards pushed us inside with their rifle butts. It was so dark inside the shack; we could lean on the darkness. I trailed behind Rose, my hands around her waist. We stumbled and fell and got up again and, to the shouts of the guards, kept pushing deeper and deeper.

All that time, Rose was feeling with her feet for a place to settle down. She finally found one. However, it was between two sleeping bodies, or we *thought* they were sleeping. She asked me to occupy the empty space as she settled next to the body at my right. Rose assumed the bodies were not asleep and began talking to them. She asked them to kindly move over so that we sisters could be together. She promised them food. The bodies failed to respond.

We then decided to eat. "What are we having for supper?" I asked.

"Canned meat on bread." She opened the sack with food and clothes she had stolen from the warehouse and prepared two slices. I gulped down the two slices before Rose could ask me how they tasted. We decided to save the rest of the food for next time whenever that might be.

At dawn, we woke up to hysterical sounds. We opened our eyes just to see screaming girls pointing at heaps of corpses all over the shack. It occurred to me to look at the bodies near me. I let out an inhuman scream.

"What's the matter?" Rose asked me. "Take a hold of yourself." I pointed to the bodies, "They're dead! I slept among corpses!"

"Come, come, that's not the first time you saw a corpse." She reminded me about the dead pregnant woman lying in the bin on the heap of coal.

"How do you know? I didn't tell you about her."

"I went for coal the next day and saw her," Rose said. "Where was the coal shovel?" I wanted to convince myself she had seen her. "Underneath one of her legs."

"I told Helen about the corpse," I said to Rose. "I hoped it would be removed before you went for coal the next day."

"Well, it was not removed." Rose turned white as a ghost. "What's the matter now?" I asked her. "These corpses are girls from my barrack. I knew them very well!" she replied. In no time, shouts of orders coming from the outside of the shack interrupted our conversation. "Raus! Schnell! Raus! Schnell! Voices told the guards that there was no free passage to the door; the floor appeared solidly covered with corpses. The guards gave a surprising answer. "Pile the corpses one on top of the other!" At the sound of the orders, Rose disappeared in a corner dragging me with her. These corpses were her girls, her children; she could not touch their dead bodies; she felt as if it were just today that she fed them, took them to the latrine, lined them up for roll call and mended their clothes.

And so, amidst protests and screaming and wailing, "Oh, my God, oh, my God!" the surviving girls took on the job; they piled the corpses one on top of the other, watching how mounds of corpses sprang up next to the preexisting mountains of corpses. It seemed that all evacuees before us were ordered to rest here and, just like our girls, they fell to their eternal sleep. The guards came into the shack and began digging their rifle butts into our ribs. "Rauss! Schnell! Rauss! Schnell!" Fortunately, it was not snowing, and the guards had not ordered us to run.

We marched on country roads with neat little houses on both sides. The sun rose and the sun set and we were still marching. I saw light appearing in the windows of those homes with people, most probably keeping warm and appeasing their hunger. And we were still marching.

At last, in the dead of the night, we stopped in front of a barn and pushed inside. Girls fell on top of sleeping cows. They began screaming. The animals had no idea what had happened. The cows stood up and moved in all directions; they wanted to get rid of these human intruders, these human screamers. Some of these intruders used their intuitive sense and held on to the animals' horns. Others, like city girls knowing nothing about cows, were rolling off the cows' backs and trampled to death.

If anybody could save lives, it was Rose. She knew her way with cows. She talked to them, she stroked them, she touched a little here, a little there, and, miraculously, the animals stood still. Meanwhile, I was shuffling behind her. I bear hugged her waist despite the blanket with life-saving food being in my way.

She asked the surviving girls to follow her to the trough. She spotted an opening to the hayloft. She looked for a ladder. Some lucky girls were sleeping on it. Did my sister despair? I don't think so. Solving problems and helping other people was her specialty.

Rose Saves the Lives of thirty, maybe forty Girls.

Rose told the girls who trailed her to stay close to the trough and wait for instructions. Meanwhile, she loosened my hands from around her waist and asked me to step inside the trough and stand underneath the opening to the hayloft. She removed the blanket with food from her shoulder, picked me up into the air and in an instant, I landed on a heap of hay on the other side of the opening. A few moments later, her blanket with food and three other women appeared next to me. I wondered how much longer she could hold up. I began praying to God. I asked Him to give her some of the powers of the Biblical Samson. She needed every bit of strength; lots of girls were waiting to be rescued by her.

No sooner did I finish praying, than I saw Rose in the hayloft, standing next to me. She startled me. What now, I wondered. She took off her coat, jacket and boots, and went down flat on her stomach. Her upper torso almost filled up the opening of the hayloft, while her hands were dangling downward. She asked two of the girls she had just hauled up into the hayloft to lay across her buttocks. What for? To weigh her down to offset the weight of the girls she would be pulling up. She asked the third girl to stand close to her feet and wait for further directions. She now talked to me. I was to listen for the signal word 'Ready'! Upon hearing this word, I was to join the standing girl at her feet, and the both of us were to pull at her legs as hard as we could to slowly bring up her protruded chest with the girl suspended from her wrists. I was all ears, waiting for the commanding word. I overheard a conversation between my sister and the first girl to be hauled into the hayloft.

"Tightly wrap your hands around my wrists!"

"I did!"

"Next, you make yourself light."

"How?"

"You start walking on the wall."

"You're crazy!"

"I'm not! If you pay attention to my instructions, your job will be a breeze."

"You're still crazy!"

Rose paid no attention to the girl's insult; she continued talking. "As the girls in the hayloft start pulling at my legs, you put your right foot on the wall, then your left foot, then tightly holding on to my wrists, you begin walking up the wall."

"Oh my God, my foot slipped!" I heard the suspended girl say.

I began praying in my mind again. Then like through a dream, I heard Rose, "Listen, I can hold you just so long! Ask a girl to get into the trough and push you up by your feet or by your 'toosh'." I also heard the commanding word, 'ready'! Immediately I started my job and together with the standing girl, I kept pulling and pulling and pulling at my sister's legs. Had the suspended girl walked on the wall? She had not. Whatever these girls had done and had not done, we hauled at least thirty of them into the hayloft.

An exhausted Rose put on her boots and her coat. She then asked me for the blanket with the food. To my dismay, the blanket was gone. Some of the rescued girls had stolen it. I began crying; I took the blame for the blanket's disappearance.

"Look at it this way," Rose stroked my head. "Suppose they had taken away my boots and my coat, what then?" She tried to dry my tears. We curled up against one another, covered ourselves with hay, and fell asleep.

At dawn, we woke up to deafening shouts, "Aufstehn! Raus! Schnell!" I saw guards, their bayonets on the ready, standing in the hayloft. The hay in the loft started slowly to swell. Heads, then arms, then legs, then bodies covered with hay appeared through the entire hayloft, stretching, moaning, and groaning.

"Weg mit den Schmutz!" (Take that dirt off of your bodies!) the guards shouted. Hay began flying into the air, in the girls' faces, in the girls' mouths, in their eyes, it even reached the guards. "Verfluchte!" they shouted. *"Pas mahl auf!"* (Watch it!)

We lined up in a column, five abreast. Two guards, one on each side of our column watched over us. The rest began combing the hayloft with their bayonets, looking for girls who had dug themselves in. Unfortunately, the guards found the hideouts. One girl stood up, screamed in pain, then stumbled and fell lifeless onto the hay, blood streaming from all sides of her body.

Sometime the next day, we were loaded into open coal cars with six to eight inches of snow on the floor. Snow was still coming down. Pushed and elbowed, I found myself leaning against the wall of our freight train.

"The metal wall is too cold for you," Rose said. We switched places. Now I was facing her. She asked me to bear hug her and press my body against hers. I felt protected and secure.

Suddenly, she cried out, "I see the girl with our blanket; stay put; I'll be right back!"

What now, I thought. Rose wouldn't take the blanket away from the poor girl. Rose and I were wearing winter coats; the girl must be dressed in rags. A minute or so later Rose and the girl appeared next to me. I watched the girl's demeanor. She showed no sign of being upset. In fact, her face was glowing as she spoke to me about the following plan: The blanket was to serve as a canopy that would shield a group of about twenty girls from the snow fall. The protected group would then interchange every so often, thus assuring each girl in the car a chance under the canopy. I asked Rose who would hold up the blanket. "Interchangeable human hands," she said. Of all the great arrangements, I realized that the girl who stole our blanket had the best deal. She was to remain stationary in the middle of the canopy at all times. Not even Rose or I would join her.

During the night, the snowfall stopped. Three days later, barely 150 living-dead landed at the outskirts of Ravensbruck, another infamous concentration camp. The periphery of the camp looked like a garbage dump. The barrack we were pushed into by rifle butts looked no better. Puddles of melting snow covered the floor. In the bunk beds there were two or at most three boards instead of twelve.

What was happening? It appeared a tug-of-war broke out. Girls were screaming, pushing each other, elbowing each other, while removing boards from the bunk beds. We followed their suit. Rose grabbed a board from here; and I grabbed a board from there. All together, we accumulated four boards. We separated them and slept crosswise, our feet dangling downward. What about blankets? We had none. Still, nothing could disturb our deep sleep, not even the cold, whistling winds coming in through the holes in the walls.

The next morning we explored the barrack. "Come quick!" Rose and I heard an excited voice calling out. We trailed the voice. It was coming from the other end of the barrack. We rushed to the scene. We saw eight or nine intact bunk beds with blankets, boards and all. Gentile women, dressed in winter clothes, their faces and bodies showing no traces of malnutrition, occupied these bunk beds.

God must have planted these women here to help us survive, I thought. No such luck. They chased us away as if we had leprosy. Some of them even waved truncheons at us. We figured these women held positions in Auschwitz-Birkenau. Positions such as: barrack seniors, Capos and Stubbendiensts. They had been evacuated before us. They had collected most of the boards and all of the blankets without any concern for the rest of the arriving evacuees.

Midday, we were ordered to line up for lunch by the same women. They gave each of us a tin bowl filled with soup made of grits and potatoes. For the majority of us this meal was the first in four days. They fell on their knees and tried to kiss the women's boots in gratitude. The women brutally kicked them in their faces.

The next day, we learned these women were assigned to bring food to our barrack on a daily basis. But they did so once every other day or once in three days. Rose decided to smuggle herself into the prohibited camp proper, and try her luck with the inmates there. She talked to them about the food situation in our barrack and asked them kindly to help her with some food. They laughed and turned away from her. So she resorted to playing a deaf and dumb person. She'd place herself in front of an inmate who'd eat--for example her bread or soup--and just stare at her. When they'd chase her away, she'd come back. To get rid of her, some of these girls would throw a crumb of bread on the ground, and then watch her pick it up, by now all mixed with mud or snow.

Those girls who gave her some soup had devised their own sadistic games. They'd hold their bowl high up in the air, and tell Rose to hold hers underneath theirs. Just as my sister was focusing on the few drops of soup coming from the bowl above, the girls moved their bowls an inch or two to the left or to the right. The soup landed on the floor and the girls watched in delight my sister's frustration and disappointment. Sometimes these sadists would ask Rose to replace her bowl with her mouth just to use the same tactics they used before. Raptures of laughter would then break out as my sister would watch in dismay the streams of soup runnig down her clothes. Rose endured these nerve wracking games and would sometimes return with half a bowl of soup and a handful of bread crumbs. She never took a bite before sharing it with me. Whatever the cost, she was determined to keep me alive. Many times I believed that deep in her heart, I was her two and a half year old son, Shullie.

One day Rose was late returning from the camp. I was terribly worried. According to the stringent rules, she could have paid with her life had she been caught in the camp proper. I would normally stay in the barrack guarding the four boards with my life. But on this day, I was concerned about my sister's whereabouts; I was determined to find her. What about the boards? I definitely couldn't save all of them. I took two boards and placed them under my coat from my armpits downward. I held them close to my body and began walking like a wooden soldier. Suddenly, an SS woman appeared in front of me as if from nowhere. How dare I be so close to her! She took her truncheon and let it fall heavily all over my body. As she reached the boards, she decided to pound my head with them. I fainted. When I opened my eyes, I saw Rose crying and kissing my swollen hands.

Suddenly, we saw the group of gentile women coming out of the kitchen with caldrons of soup. Maybe today they would be bringing the soup to our barrack, but no such luck. We followed them. They stopped somewhere in a remote corner. They took off the lids of the caldrons and started eating the soup. Rose approached one woman, then the next, then the next. She asked them kindly for a bowl of soup. They laughed at her.

In her desperation, my sister forced her hand with her bowl into one of the caldrons with soup. In punishment, the woman took the lid from the ground, put it back on top of the caldron, and sat down on it with Rose's hand caught inside. Sounds of a wounded animal coming from my sister in pain filled my ears. Now the woman told Rose to drop the bowl if she wanted her hand freed. Rose refused the woman's proposal. She knew if she had no bowl, she'd get no soup today or tomorrow or ever. Her palms could not replace the bowl.

Meanwhile, two women held me in place about three yards from the scene. They tried to prevent me from helping my sister in freeing her hand. I cried and told one of them that I could convince my sister to drop the bowl. When the woman heard me say, "drop the bowl," she freed me. I walked over to Rose. I bent down to talk to her. My eyes caught the dangling feet of the woman sitting on top of the caldron. Something entered my mind. I grabbed the woman's two feet, and with all my strength, I lifted them into the air. The woman fell backward, the lid slid off of the caldron, and Rose removed her hand with an empty bowl. Why an empty bowl? Because the caldron my sister forced her hand into was only half full. Rose then took hold of my wrist with her other hand and we ran for our lives. The women were pursuing us.

When we got back to our barrack, Rose apologized for not being successful in getting me soup. It was always for me, for me, for me—she came last. Rose fought for me, starved for me and stole for me. She was my God, my mother, my father; whatever the cost. She was determined to keep me alive. In 1984, living in Jerusalem, she was diagnosed with lung cancer. She died the same year. I knew she had cancer; she did not. I had no financial means to go and visit her—spend the last few weeks with her. I encouraged her to write. In six weeks, she wrote 40 pages of poetry in Yiddish. I hold on to them with dear life.

The Death Shack

After three weeks of misery in the isolated barrack in Ravensbruck, we were taken to a small concentration camp called Neustadt-Gleve. What a difference between this camp and Auschwitz. The barracks here had windows but no bunk beds. We slept on a thin layer of straw. In Auschwitz the barracks had no windows but had bunk beds to sleep in. In Auschwitz, we'd take a shower once in six weeks. We'd leave our filthy tatters there and return with clean tatters. In Neustadt-Gleve, we lacked these features. As a result, 400 inmates, including my sister Rose and I came down with typhoid fever.

Overnight we were transported by truck and landed in a shack somewhere on the outskirts of the camp and were left there to die. We were given no food, no medication, just two cups of black Ersatz Coffee; one in the morning and one at night.

The shack had 3-tiered bunk beds alongside two opposite walls. In the middle of the shack, there was a giant platform made of boards filled with dying and dead inmates. Every other day, a group of men would come in, remove the dead and replace them with the dying from the bunk beds. Next to the only free wall, there were chamber pots so close to one another; they gave the appearance they were strung together. The chamber pots always overflowed with our bloody bowel movements that spilled on the floor.

I was lying, burning up with fever, on the third bunk bed on one side of the barrack. Rose, in the same state, was lying in the bottom bunk bed on the other side of the shack. To complicate things, she had phlebitis. Whenever I'd use a chamber pot, which was much too often, I'd have to make a choice: either balance myself on top of the overrun pot, or relieve myself over the spilled, bloody river laden with DDT disinfecting powder. I usually chose the latter, since we had no bathroom tissues.

One night, or maybe it was during the day, I had a nightmare. I dreamed that a group of corpses wove their long, skin-and-bone arms into a coffin and enticed me to get inside the contraption. I let out a scream. I called out for my mother. I asked her to get rid of the corpses; I didn't want to die. She appeared to me in the image of the queen I imagined her to be when I was a five-year-old watching her light the Sabbath candles on Friday evenings. This time, she had a scepter in her hands. She lifted it, and one by one, the corpses disappeared into the thin air.

Following the nightmare, I opened my eyes and, miraculously, felt my fever was gone. Everything appeared crystal clear.

I rushed to Rose's bunk bed. I hadn't seen her since the first night we were brought here. She noticed the big change in me and said, "I feel better, too."

I have no explanation for this happening.

I returned to my bunk bed, fixed my eyes on the platform and began counting the bodies. Suddenly, I saw what looked like a silhouette rising from among the corpses. I rubbed my eyes a few times. No, I wasn't dreaming. The silhouette was now standing on the floor taking on dimensions. I saw a thin face; I could almost see through it. I saw two long arms and two long legs held together by skin and bone. The silhouette struck a pose as if waiting for some music to start. Then, she began ballet dancing around the platform. She looked like a bird in flight. I counted one round, then another round. Then, I heard a crashing noise. I climbed down from my bunk bed, and there, her dead body lay sprawled on the floor.

It was just another morning of moaning and groaning and last-breath choked up noises when I saw a nurse with a pad and pencil in her hand. A doctor trailed her. The nurse called out, "Selection! Sit up in your bunk beds!"

A selection? Here of all the places? How is that possible! I must be dreaming. I could not afford to speculate, for the process had already started across the aisle. I had a clear view of the upper and middle bunk beds. I saw the doctor pointing at sick inmates and the nurse writing down their numbers. I tried to figure out whether the girls who were written up were the victims or the survivors. I concluded they were the victims. How so? They couldn't hold their torsos balanced for thirty seconds. I counted the time the doctor was staring at them, before he pointed at the nurse to write their numbers down.

I wasted no time. I feverishly began spreading the news to all girls within my reach. Some of them were thankful, others were indifferent and still others were grinning at me.

I tried to talk to the apathetic ones. I reminded them of a beautiful world out there waiting for them. All they had to do, I said, was sit up straight and remain motionless for about thirty seconds. Next, I got involved physically. I helped the closest to me to sit up straight. I adjusted their bodies. I pushed up their chins and fixed their hands next to their sides.

Uh-oh! I saw the doctor two bunk beds down, watching me in action. In a flash, I took my position. Suddenly, the doctor pointed at me. How I wished it were a dream. Unfortunately, it was not. I distinctly heard the nurse say to me, "Show me your number!"

I rushed over to Rose. She was in a sitting position. That afternoon, I lived my whole life in two emotionally drenched hours.

I asked Rose how the selection affected her. The doctor had spared her life, she said. She wanted to know what went on in my bunk bed. Instead of an answer, I knelt down on the floor to be level with her, threw myself on her neck, and sobbed and sobbed and sobbed.

She ran her hands up and down my back. She thought my tears were tears of happiness. I told her the bad news. I said the nurse wrote down my number on her pad. Rose loosened my hands from around her neck, looked in my eyes, and said, "I don't think it's the right time to make jokes." She dried my tears.

"It's true," I said. "The doctor pointed at me and the nurse asked for my number." I begged her to let me hang on to her. I wanted to feel the warmth of her body before I went up in smoke.

She became visibly upset. "You must never talk like this," she said. "No one will ever separate us, no one!" She brought my face close to hers and tenderly kissed every part of it.

"Then why are your eyes misty?" I asked. "Because you believe me?"

"I believe the doctor pointed at you for a reason other than what you've just mentioned."

"What would that other reason be; to lead the march of the doomed?" I said.

Rose looked at me. "This is how much hope you have in God?" she said.

"You are my God."

"I'm God's sheleech" (messenger).

My Mother's Lessons

My whole life paraded in front of me with my mother in the lead. About a week before I traveled to Sighet to attend high school, my mother gave me a last lesson on 'empathy', the ability to put myself in other people's situations and feel the way those people feel.

She said, "If you want to know how a person who's made fun of feels, a person who's sick feels, a person who's mistreated feels, a person who's poor feels, all you do is replace that person's face with your own and in your mind you become that person and you feel everything that person feels."

Just when I least expected it, it happened! It was 1970. I lived in New Jersey and worked in New York City. One blustering cold winter morning, I walked into a rest room in the Port Authority Bus Terminal in New York. In a corner, I saw an elderly, frail, poorly dressed woman sitting on a produce box, warming her hands under a blower. Thoughts began crowding into my mind. "Replace the woman's face with your mother's," said one voice. "She must be your mother's age when you last saw her. Do it!" commanded another voice.

I did it. I replaced the face of the frail, elderly woman with my mother's face. In my imagination, that woman became my mother, and I hardly liked what I saw. For the next two years, until she no longer showed up, I'd take an early bus into New York. I needed time to find her in one of the thirteen ladies rooms in the bus terminal. I'd then drop a package of food or clothes in her lap and go off to work.

One day, I noticed she had frost-bitten legs. The next morning, I caught her just as she was entering a rest room. I put my coat, hat and gloves in her lap. I took a new pair of rubber gloves and some ointment from my purse, ointment my pharmacist recommended the night before. I applied the ointment to her wounds; I wrapped her legs with gauze. I retrieved my hat, coat and gloves and left.

I'm not sure how many women walked through that rest room during the time I had worked on her legs. Most of them stopped in their tracks for a few seconds. After their apparent surprise wore off, they went their own ways. I don't know what these women were thinking. I knew what I was thinking: 'You women! You were born with the same sense of compassion I was. Did anybody help develop your God-given sense of compassion or sense of empathy'?

While proud of my deep-rooted sense of compassion, my mind tricked me to the day Mother introduced me to a lesson in charity. "You know who invented charity?" she said, "Your forefathers; the ancient Jews!" If I knew then what I know now as a result of thorough research, I would've told Mother that charity, in its infancy, has existed since time immemorial. Some ancient Indian tribes took care of their poor relatives. The problem was that only a few tribes out of hundreds did so. Our Jewish ancestors took charity to a higher level. They legalized it and made laws concerning the poor. People were required to give ten percent of their income to the poor. People who didn't work but had savings had to give ten percent of their savings to the poor as well. The farmers gave their ten percent for the poor in produce--no one was left out. In fact, the giving became so established that even the poor gave to charity.

There were special charitable organizations that handled the money for the poor. Some of the money went for housing, some for food, some for clothing and some for traveling expenses for the poor. Traveling included looking for a job or visiting a sick relative. Visiting a sick relative was a good deed known as a Mitzvah.

The poor were given money enough to travel to one village or to one town at a time, even if the sick relatives they were visiting lived three villages or three towns away from their own. How so? Their well-being was taken into consideration. After a hard day or two of traveling either on foot, on a donkey, or on a camel, the traveling poor would be exhausted. They would need to clean up, to eat and to rest before continuing with their journey. This was where the villages or towns came into the picture. They were equipped with facilities for the poor to bathe, eat and rest. Then, they were given enough money to travel to the next village or town where they would be treated the way they were in the village or town they had just left. The poor who were traveling to look for work were treated the same way.

The laws for the poor contained many other humane provisions. The orphans and the widows and widowers were exempt from paying interest when they borrowed money.

For instance, if a poor person left his or her coat as collateral, the creditor would have to return the poor person's coat in the evening, assuming the person was using it as a blanket. In the morning the borrower would return the coat to the creditor again.

On the Sabbatical Year, a poor person's outstanding debts were totally cancelled or erased. Also on the Sabbatical Year, the farmers would leave the produce from the corners of their fields for the poor and the wild animals. The Sabbatical Year took place every seven years. Six years the field was cultivated and in the seventh, it remained fallow for a whole year in order to regenerate itself.

In going ahead with my research, I found out that the ancient Jews had created special laws pertaining to the sale of inherited land—all land was inherited. From a closer look though, one comes to the conclusion that these so called sales transactions were actually rental transactions. How so? If a landowner sold his land, he received his land back on the Jubilee Year. The Jubilee Year was celebrated at the end of seven Sabbatical years to which they added one year to round it off to fifty years. Seven Sabbatical years equals 49 to which you add one year and you get to the Jubilee Year. The return of the land to the original owner depended on the Sabbatical Year the land was sold. Suppose a land owner sold his land on the third Sabbatical Year. He would have to subtract three Sabbatical Years from 50, the Jubilee Year. Three Sabbatical years totals 21. Subtract 21 from 50 you get 29. The landowner would get his land back 29 years later. Suppose the same landowner sold his land on the 5th Sabbatical Year, he would subtract five Sabbatical years which totals 35 from 50 which equals 15 years. He would have to wait 15 years to get his land back. Doesn't this look that the land was never sold; it was rather rented out?

Yes, my mother continually talked to me about morals and ethics. And yes, I was her best audience. She'd tell me stories connected to these subjects, and if anything, I liked stories. The stories were always attributed to spiritual leaders like rabbis. To this day, I still recall the name of the Bal Shem Tov, the founder of Hasidism. He was the focus of most of the stories associated with good deeds.

One Friday after sunset the Jews of the town, Bardizsif were gathered in the synagogue waiting for the Bal Shem Tov to perform the Sabbath services. They waited one hour, two hours, three hours, four hours and the Bal Shem Tov had not shown up. At twelve o'clock midnight, he walked into the synagogue, looking tired and exhausted, barely to be recognized. He told the people to go home to their families. "But, Rabbi," they said, "you haven't performed the Sabbath services. We were waiting for you. We haven't said a single prayer on our own. What will happen now?"

"Nothing will happen. I promise, I was involved in a more important job."

"What job could be more important than officiating over the Sabbath services, rabbi?"

"You'll find out in time," he said. In time, the town's Jewish people found out that the Bal Shem Tov did some investigative work, and found out about an elderly widow living in a shack in the woods. He visited her and learned she had no family and no help from her neighbors. He knew the cold weather would set in very soon. So he decided to supply the widow with enough wood for her stove to last the entire winter. The harder he worked the less result he saw; it seemed as though the shack grew larger with every new bundle of wood he brought. Nightfall set in. He was at a loss. Should he serve God, return to the village and officiate over the Sabbath services or should he continue helping the widow? He decided for the latter. The same night an angel came in his dream congratulating him for making the right decision.

The Bal Shem Tov was kind to animals as well. One day, he saw a peasant, his wagon filled to capacity with boards totally mired in the mud. The peasant kept repeatedly whipping his horses. He was determined to get home with the load of boards intact. The Bal Shem Tov got into the picture. He said, "No matter how hard you'll whip your horses, they won't be able to get your wagon out of the mud. Why don't you take part of the load of boards off of the wagon and put it on the ground. Then go home; let the horses rest, and return tomorrow for the boards you left behind.

"That's a good idea," said the peasant.

How could I not like such stories?

Kaporas Ceremony

On the day before Yom Kippur, the Day of Atonement, religious Jews, my parents among them, observed the Kaporas ceremony. During the Kaporas ceremony, a man or a young boy takes a rooster, and a woman or a young girl takes a hen, its legs tied together, waves it over their heads three times while reciting a Hebrew benediction. The slaughtered kapora is then cooked and eaten or given to the poor.

When I was very young, the Kaporas ceremony simply meant I'd have to stand still longer than I wanted to. Rose or my mother waved a chicken over my head as I said a few meaningless-to-me Hebrew words. By the time I was seven, I loathed the ceremony since I had to hold a tied-up chicken in my own hands! At least Rose helped me by putting her hand on top of mine. Together, we'd wave the hen over my head three times. The terrified hen squawked, squeaked, screeched, and squalled, while flapping her wings in my face.

It rained one day, so I stayed in the house. We had just ended the Kaporas ceremony. The chickens awaiting slaughter were penned up in a corner of the all-purpose room, lying on their sides, straining their heads, screaming, flapping their wings, trying to stand, but rolling over in their futile attempt. They were showing every sign of distress I could imagine.

Three roosters lay among the victims. For whatever reason, the largest rooster was pecking its neighbor's coxcomb. It tried to defend itself with its beak and head, causing a big disturbance among the rest of the doomed. They sounded as if a fox had invaded their coop.

The chickens held their beaks open as if they were thirsty. I must give them water before they're taken away, I thought. I put a china soup dish on the table, and then went to pick up my kapora. Aaaah! The hen's panic renewed itself. She flopped about, flapped her wings, and escaped my hands. "No! Please! Calm down!" I muttered. I followed it until it reached the wall. Here my kapora was exhausted and subdued. It made no attempt to escape me even when I lifted it in my hands. Did it know I was its friend?

I looked at my kapora. It was so tiny, merely a baby! I put this tiny baby chicken on the table hoping it would drink water. But my kapora lay on its side with no chance to drink the water. I would have to cut the string around its legs so it could stand, but I needed a sharp knife or some scissors and I hadn't learned to use either.

The door opened with a jerk and my mother entered. My kapora got frightened and rolled down the table, taking the china dish along with it. I began loudly sobbing. Was it because of the broken dish, or was I concerned that my kapora was injured? Mother carried my kapora to the corner to join the rest of the doomed. When she returned to the table, she stroked my hair, whispering, "May the broken dish be your kapora!"

Suddenly, it dawned on me, I had two kaporas. Didn't Mother just say, "May the broken dish be your kapora?"

"Mother, do I need two kaporas?"

"No. Not really."

I asked Mother since I had two kaporas, could she consider the broken dish as my true kapora and give me my hen kapora as a pet? I promised to take good care of it, to feed it indoors, to protect it from the bad cocks.

"What bad cocks?" asked Mother.

"Once I watched Rose feed the chickens in the back yard; it was a disaster," I said. "The cocks went wild. They kept pecking at the hens, then chasing them away as if the food belonged to them only. After the hens ran away, the cocks began fighting between themselves over the food." I suggested to Mother that Rose keep the cocks separate from the hens. "That cannot be done, my dear," she said. "The cocks must be together with the hens at all times." And before I could ask that fatal question as to why the cocks must be together with the hens, Mother gave me the final answer pertaining to my pet kapora. She said that according to our religion, my kapora must die--no ifs, ands, or buts. I tried to look submissive, but I had already made up my mind. I'll never submit my own children to the Kaporas ceremony. I'll give money to charity instead.

Making Cheese

In my childhood, I thought our cow was monstrously big. She gave birth to a calf every year. We children took an interest in each of her calves. We played with each, jumped along with each, and enjoyed being friends to each. But in what felt like no time, our father sold each of our new friends. Our cow was considered special because she yielded more milk than most cows did. That meant her female offspring were in high demand.

We made our own cheese. Mother or Rose set milk aside to sour. When it soured, Rose or Mother boiled it. Almost miraculously, the boiled sour milk curdled. Mother or Rose gathered the curds. They then put the curds into a cone-shaped cloth. I don't recall how long it took for the curds to turn into cheese. But I almost taste the sweet, unsalted cheese.

Churning Butter

When I was about five, during the usual challenge of encouraging me to eat more, my mother tried to talk me into having a slice of bread and butter. It happened during the process of churning fresh butter. Rose sat me on a stack of pillows piled on a chair facing the table. On the table sat a butter churner with freshly churned butter, a bowl of ice water, a serving spoon, and a single slice of bread on a saucer. When Mother put the saucer, bread and all, in my lap, I wanted down. I suspected entrapment.

To keep my attention, Mother brought the churn closer to my face, asking me to look inside and tell her what I saw. "I see milk."

"Libelah, I'll be turning this milk into a big butterball. Do you want to see my magic powers?" Mother scooped three serving-spoons filled with thick, white liquid from the churn, dumping them into the ice water. Instantly, tiny pieces of butter began separating from the whey.

I thought I'd get to see a big butterball! Instead, I saw little pieces. Mother began gathering the tiny butter-specks with the serving spoon, bouncing and rolling them until she had the big butterball. When the butterball became too big to fit into the serving spoon, it tumbled back into the ice water. To my surprise, Mother began chasing the fallen butterball with the spoon from which it just fell. Something occurred to me.

"Mother," I said, "since the butterball was too big to stay in the serving spoon, wouldn't a ladle do?"

Mother hugged me, then fetched a ladle, fished out the butterball with it and placed the butter on a pewter dish. "Let's celebrate your discovery with bread and butter and marmalade!" she said.

"I don't like butter. It's too slippery!"

Mother tried so hard not to laugh that her face turned red and tears rolled down her cheeks. "Butter will help you grow into a big and beautiful girl!" I wasn't an easy child to convince and my stubbornness prevailed. So we decided I'd have bread and marmalade without any butter.

Eventually, the entire village found out about the story with the ladle. With time, the story took on different variations. Some people said I used the ladle myself. Others said I was four-years-old and not five and still others said the story was a fabrication.

About a year later, Mother was discussing my weight with a neighbor. "Butter's the only thing that will ever help that scarecrow child of yours gain weight!" said the neighbor.

"But she won't eat it. She thinks it's slippery," Mother explained.

A few days later, I was looking for my younger brother, Yitzchak. Some ten-year-old boys were chatting good-naturedly. When I asked them where Yitzchak might be, they laughed. "Scram, Slippery! We're too busy for anyone who's slippery!" I felt almost hysterical as I ran back to our house. "Rose! Rose! The boys next door called me "slippery!" I sobbed.

"Don't worry, Libelah, I'll take care of everything." And taking care she did; no one called me "Slippery" anymore.

My Mother's Suitor

It happened again! My mind tricked me to the time I met my mother's rejected suitor. I was still living at the Yakobowits family. If you recall my struggling high school years, you will remember that I tutored Hedy and Shulie at the Yakobowitz family. You might also remember that Yittie on numerous occasions took me down to their servants' quarters in the middle of the night, let me eat to my heart's desire and then wrote a note to the cook that she had eaten the food.

Feigie, the oldest daughter in the Yakobowitz family had married a Talmudist named Efraim. One day, when Efraim's father, Joshua, visited his son, I had just walked into the dining room. Mrs.Yakobowits introduced me to him. He politely asked me for my family name and my place of birth. I said my family name was Szabo and I was born in Petrova. He said he knew more than one family named Szabo in Petrova. I told him I was B'Tzalel Szabo's daughter.

He gave me an unfocused look. I felt he was seeing someone else. "I'd bet your mother, Rochel, is as pretty as she was when

I met her at a wedding a long, long time ago. She was the most beautiful girl there."

I was confused at best. The people in the room exchanged glances as if saying, "What is he talking about?"

Joshua felt he owed us an explanation. "A long time ago," he said, "I met your mother at a wedding. I fell in love with her the minute I saw her. The next day, I sent a matchmaker to your grandfather to ask for your mother's hand. Your grandfather refused me." The Yakobowits family squirmed. Efraim fidgeted in his chair, hoping his father would stop talking.

That night, thoughts formed in my head. If Joshua had been my father, I wouldn't be me! What would've happened had I been someone else? What if I hadn't been anyone?

I could barely wait for school to recess for summer. I was anxious to talk with my mother. I hoped for a real heart to heart talk about a part of her life she never mentioned.

It seemed like forever before I was home for the summer. I told Rose about my mother's rejected suitor. "I can't wait to ask Mother about him! Will it upset her?"

Rose hugged me. "Libelah, you're thirteen; you have it all figured out by now.

I don't have to put words in your mouth any longer!"

"Only this time, please!"

"Okay. Talk to Mother about it when Father is not home. Simple!"

Finally, I was alone with Mother. When I told her about Joshua, her eyes got an odd far-away look. She talked as if she were a schoolgirl in love and sounded like an illusion-filled romantic!

"So? He really touched your heart that afternoon?"

"That afternoon became the rest of my life."

Oh uh . . . Mother is still in love with Joshua, I thought. I took courage and asked, "Mother, can you tell me what happened?"

"Of course. I've replayed the scene in my mind hundreds of times."

"After all these years?"

"Yes, Dear."

"He said you met at a wedding."

"At my best friend's wedding. I was wearing my prettiest dress. And my corset squeezed just enough to bring up color in my face."

"Your face always has good color!"

"The corset made it more pronounced."

"You must've looked like a million dollars! Your ex-suitor told me you were the prettiest girl at the wedding."

Mother's face was all flushed. "I don't know about that. I remember the young girls were standing on one side of the room and the boys on the other side. None of us paid much attention to the music! We kept glancing over toward the boys, but they were just as busy looking at us. One of the boys caught my attention. The attraction must have been mutual. I suppose we were both dazed. I don't remember anything else about that wedding after our eyes met. The next day, a matchmaker came to our home. He told my father that a Talmudist had seen me the day before and wanted to marry me."

"How old were you?"

"Eighteen."

"Why didn't your parents agree?"

"Because Talmudists usually don't earn a living. They and their families live with their in-laws for the rest of their lives."

I asked Mother why the Talmudists don't learn a trade or profession. Her answer was, "They're devoted to learning Torah forever."

My next question pertained to her parents. I asked her whether or not they were poor. Her father had a thriving lumber business. But if all three of his unmarried daughters had married Talmudists, he could have spent his last years in a poorhouse.

"Isn't your sister, Aunt Reizel married to a Talmudist?" I asked.

"She is, but when Uncle Simcha Srul asked for Reizel's hand in marriage, he already had earned a doctorate degree in Theology, and was teaching Jewish History in Bratislava, Czechoslovakia."

Mother's eyes took on that odd faraway look again. Her held-back smile told me she might be reliving a pleasant episode. Her heart seemed to be torn by life's injustices, including her marriage to my father. I decided it was a good thing my father knew nothing about her "true love." Had he guessed he wasn't the man she wanted to spend her life with, it might have hurt him. He loved her dearly and I didn't want him to be hurt. I loved my father.

After our conversation about her suitor, Mother seemed to me like a character in a love story. She suddenly appeared much more complex then I had imagined. She was cheerful and loving toward her children, but serious and dutiful toward our father. I always wondered if she ever grew to love my father.

Aunt Reizel

Sometimes I daydreamed about my Aunt Reizel and her husband Simcha Srul. Aunt Reizel's face was a replica of my mother's. She was petite and as cuddly as a kitten. She carried a ready smile and had laughing eyes.

With his neatly trimmed beard and his gold-rimmed glasses, Uncle Simcha Srul looked like the distinguished, enlightened Talmudic scholar he was.

In the early 1930's Aunt Reizel and Uncle Simcha Srul visited our family on their way back from a vacation. They were a very handsome couple, so sophisticated and so stylish; it was obvious they were from a big city. Furthermore, they seemed very much in love. Aunt Reizel had a certain way of looking at Uncle Simcha Srul as if he were God-On-Earth.

They couldn't have come at a better time. My father and his partners had just renewed a lease on a three-mile fruit orchard on the outskirts of our village.

At one end of the property stood a crumbling, picturesque mansion, which belonged to the absentee landowner. At the other end of the property there was a small, well maintained home for the caretaker.

Aunt Reizel and I were trotting down a narrow trail of dirt mixed with pebbles at the foot of the leased orchard. I was wondering why she chose to wear high heeled shoes on an outing, but decided such behavior must be part of her charm. As if she'd read my mind, Aunt Reizel said: "I hope I won't break my heels."

Break her heels? I thought. What about her ankles? But who was I to even try to make sense of such a sophisticated, enigmatic woman? A few steps further down the road, she stopped walking, removed her scarf, and sat down on it. She looked at me and out of the blue said, "The other day, you asked me if I had a formula for a happy marriage."

"Do you, Aunt Reizel?"

"Yes, my dear. Mutual love, mutual trust, mutual understanding and mental compatibility are very important but those aren't everything". I waited. "A woman must always look her best for her husband."

"Suppose I don't think I even have a 'good' to turn into a 'best'."

"Nonsense! Everyone's got something!"

"But my face isn't pretty."

"Don't be silly! There's beauty somewhere in you! We shall find it!"

"My teeth are overlapped. I'll never be able to smile at anyone the way you smile at Uncle Simcha Srul."

"So child, what do you do for your looks?"

"I practice with the mirror how to smile with my mouth closed. I put a hundred rags in my hair every night. And I roll on the floor to get roundness in my hips."

"I could use some rolling to shape my hips. But at my age, I'm afraid to do it."

I tried not to laugh, but when she giggled at her own joke, I couldn't restrain myself and burst out laughing.

She studied my face for a few seconds. "Move your lips to

the left and smile." I moved my lips to the left and smiled. "Good! Now, move them to the right and smile!" I moved my lips to the right and smiled. "Your smile is better on the right side." I decided I'd smile only on the right side of my mouth. Aunt Reizel asked me to stand, then to walk, then to turn, then to step back and then to step forward.

"Your dress looks like a man's nightshirt. You do have some curves, so show them! How old are you?"

"Thirteen."

"You must show your curves! Men are visual. If they can't see something, it isn't there. That doesn't mean they have no imagination; they do. In short, what pleases men is what they see."

I decided to open up. I told her I was in love with someone who was in love with someone else. Aunt Reizel looked at me but said nothing. I was disappointed; I assumed my admission came to her as a shock.

We stood up and began walking. "Libelah my child, I have a question! What does one do for a ladies room in an orchard?"

"Uh . . . The caretakers have an outhouse."

We were walking toward our destination, when my mother, wearing flat shoes, caught up with us.

"Oh, Rochel! I had such an interesting talk with your daughter."

"Good. I could tell she liked you!"

"We're on our way to the caretaker's outhouse!"

"Do you want my shoes? You'd make better time," said mother. Aunt Reizel refused my mother's offer. I walked behind the two sisters; they were silent. Was my mother glad for her sister's happiness or was she jealous of her? I will never know.

I never saw either Aunt Reizel or Simcha Srul again. They both died along with my mother and millions of other Jews.

Mother, the Spa and I

Mother suffered from an under-active thyroid condition as well as from a stomach disorder. In spite of her many visits to various doctors, she never got so much as a diagnosis. Seventy years later, I got one: "Lactose Intolerance". I should know since I inherited her condition.

In the 1930's, doctors who had no diagnosis for their patients often sent them to the country or to spas with mineral baths. Single women, single men, widows, widowers and divorcees traveled by themselves in anticipation of finding suitable partners at these places. My mother traveled with me. She hoped for a cure for herself as well as some weight gain for me.

Every time we went to a spa, my mother felt better. The hotel meals featured duck, chicken, turkey, fish, red meat and very little dairy. I recall Mother filling my plate with everything served. I would turn the plate to all sides, pick a bite from here, a bite from there, then rub my stomach, meaning I had enough. I never put on any weight.

At the first spa where we spent a summer, I barely escaped death. I was eight-years-old. Mother gave me permission to explore the hotel's grounds during the official siesta (rest time). I had strolled these properties often enough with my mother as hundreds of people were coming and going. The oddest walkers were women with little mushroom-shaped summer umbrellas. These specimens of spa life were always in a hurry saying, "Excuse me, little girl! Excuse me, little girl!" They often bumped into me since they were busy looking at my beautiful mother from the corners of their eye.

This time, my walk felt very different from any other. I didn't see another person, and I felt as if I were the first flower who'd ever grown here. For once, I had plenty of space to arrange my many-colored petals. I was skipping, hopping, almost dancing. My eyes were fixed on the trees' thick, green mantles. My ears delighted in birds making music I'd never imagined existed. I looked at the sky as opaque, milky clouds slipped past. As soon as I discovered a lamb, a bird, a dragon, a bearded man, the wind stretched the figure, distorting, deforming, and thinning it out until it no longer existed.

Snap! It was a sound like twigs breaking! I began falling. At first, I thought I was having a recurring dream of being on the edge of falling into our family's out-house hole! I was going down very rapidly. What I'd seen only seconds before just wasn't there. There was no ground, no grass, no flowers, no clouds, no trees, no sky, no colors; just a thin strip of light above me, as if I were looking at a crack over a closed door.

Now, I was immersed in cold water. First, to my ankles, then to my knees, and then above my waist. My imagination was taking over: The Messiah is here! I'm swimming in the waters of the turbulent Sanbatyon River on the other side of the Earth. And the Leviathan, the great-monster-fish who lives in the Sanbatyon River is transporting me and all the Jews in the world to Jerusalem!

Something's wrong! Where are the others? The story doesn't say we are being transported to Jerusalem one at a time! I'm touching something soft, very soft. It's the bottom of a ditch. I feel scared, upset, lost and helpless. Now, I'm clawing the walls, trying to dig myself out! Falling soil thickens the almost-frozen water I'm standing in.

The next day, I woke in a hospital amid eerie whispers of hypothermia. I'd fallen into an abandoned mineral well where I'd remained five hours before being rescued. Light, any light, was so, so beautiful!

My Brother Chayim

While I was vacationing with my mother at the spa, my brother Chayim was vacationing from me. What am I talking about? Chayim, two years older than I, was assigned by my mother to make sure I ate my daily food—part of it was good, too. You probably remember I was a poor eater. Why Chayim? Because he was the jokester in the family and a terrific story teller. For a story, I'd do anything; even swallow a few bites of food. When Chayim was indoors, I'd follow him like a little doggy. Was I expecting to hear a story or watch him do something funny?

Chayim and Father's Streimel

One day, I tried to draw Chayim's attention. I climbed on a chair, took father's streimel (a furry Sabbath hat) from the armoire in the girl's bedroom and placed it on my head. The contraption was so big it covered my eyes. Then I felt a hand moving the streimel even further down my eyes. I knew whose hand it was. "Chayim, Chayim! Take your hands off, please! Stop clowning! Father will come in and find me wearing his precious streimel; he wouldn't like that!"

"Come on, Sis! It's just a game!"

"A game? I'm not in a mood for games involving Father's streimel! I want that thing off my face!" But Chayim insisted and I gave in. "What do you want me to do?"

"Play along. I'll take you around the room. If you can name five items I will lead you to, I, Chayim-the Merciful, will put the streimel away without even using a chair!"

"Okay! But hurry!"

Forever passed. Then forever started over. "And now my little one, perhaps this object is one you can name correctly?" He moved my hand to an item perpendicular to the walls.

"This must be the cupboard!"

"So it is. And this?"

"This is a window!"

"Very good! And this?"

"This is the table!"

"Ah, so! And this?"

"This is a book!"

"Yes, little one. Name the kind of book it is." I felt its covers; I assumed it was a prayer book.

"Wrong, my little one."

"It's your math book!"

"You guessed it!" Chayim removed the streimel from my eyes. I squinted a few times. I looked at the book. "So it's the book you won't part with!"

"Anything wrong with math?"

"Nothing wrong wanting to be like Father. He's smart at math. But I intend to be a teacher!"

"You're much too young to know what you want to be!"

"Okay! I want to be as smart as a teacher. Is that better?"

"I know somebody who's smarter than a teacher!"

"Who's that?"

"Our rabbi!"

"But he's only smart in Hebrew!"

"When our rabbi was your age, Jews couldn't go to a secular school!"

"What's a secular school?"

"A non-Hebrew school!" Nevertheless, he's smarter than any teacher you'll ever know!"

"Why couldn't Jews go to secular schools?"

"You're too young to understand that!"

"I'm almost ten; you're only two years older!"

"Ten years is too young!"

"I'm not too young to know you skipped cheder (parochial school) today."

"Don't tell Father!"

"Maybe I will!"

"No, you won't!" said Chayim as he put the streimel away, and dashed through the door. He was right. I would never tattle on Chayim. I wouldn't want him to get in trouble.

Chayim, Honeycomb Cubes, Yitzchak and I

On a very hot day in July my brother Chayim, my brother Yitzchak and I were playing in the all-purpose room. We were very, very thirsty. Rose had just brought a bucket of ice-cold water from the well, but Chayim refused to let me have any, claiming I was overheated.

"When a girl is overheated, icy water is usually fatal; we can't afford to bury anyone this year, Baby Sister!"

"Chayim don't be a wise guy. How do you know what we can afford? I suppose you're Father's bookkeeper?"

"Men share secrets, Little Sister."

"You're not a man. You're only eleven! And I'm thirsty!"

"Not a man? Well!" Chayim limped to the cupboard as if he were older than Methuselah. He pretended to peer around for something: Then he acted as if he'd forgotten what he'd come to look for. Finally, he selected a huge pewter mug, and filled it with cold water. "When we get outside, I'll set the mug in the sun. You'll have to watch it until the water warms up. Then you may have a tiny sip," he spoke to me in an unsteady voice.

As we stepped outside, he lifted the mug over his head. "Look who's here!" he said in his normal voice. I saw Father trudging alongside a trapper who was carrying a beehive on his back. Father's face and hands were red and swollen. One eye I couldn't even see. The other was a narrow slit. To look at him, you'd think he robbed the bees of their home and dinner and he was the one carrying the beehive, not the trapper. Surprisingly, the trapper's face was normal. Fortunately, my mother had a good remedy for bee stings!

All three of us children ran into the house. For once, we could hardly wait to wash our hands. As you already know, I was of very small stature. If we had a baby booster seat back then, it would have worked for me even though I was nine-years-old. My seven-year-old brother Yitzchak was taller than I was.

We were restless waiting for our treat of honeycomb cubes. Chayim suggested a game of "patch." Yitzchak and I stood around Chayim at the head of the table. Chayim held his palms parallel to each other. Then, one at a time, each of us were to put our hands on top of his. Once Chayim agreed our hands were in place, we'd have to scramble to remove them before he could slap them. If anyone got slapped three times, he or she lost one honeycomb cube.

I loved watching Chayim perform his ritual motions. Clown that he was, Chayim could make almost anything fascinating.

Sometimes he'd concentrate on my right hand with such intensity and conviction that I'd snatch it away at the slightest tremor, allowing him to tap my left hand which was still resting in his palms. He was so good at tricking me. Yitzchak had lost two of his honeycomb cubes during the game.

Suddenly, Rose walked into the room with a piece of honeycomb on a pewter platter. Yitzchak and I forgot about "patch" and chose places at the table. I stood at the front of the table with Chayim: Yitzchak sat at the far end, almost in isolation.

We each received three, small honeycomb cubes in separate plates. Rose reminded us: "Be good!" Then she left.

His plate in hand, Chayim walked to the other end of the table to collect his prize. When he noticed Yitzchak's red hands, he decided he must have slapped him too hard so, in his guilt, he canceled his winnings. Chayim's generosity was too late. Yitzchak, overcome with bottled up rage, tripped him! The plate flew out of his hands and his honeycomb cubes fell to the floor.

"Idiot!" screamed Chayim. "Just look at what you've done!"

Rose rushed into the room expecting to separate a fight between the two brothers. Instead, she heard a story about "patch" and vengeance. Chayim pointed at his three honeycomb cubes lying on the floor and, in his anger, left the room never to return the rest of the day.

How I missed him! I knew his shows were intended for me, and I devoured each word he said and each motion he made. I used to wonder what Chayim would look like if I were taller than he was. So, one day, I made a deal with Yitzchak. I was to give him a honeycomb cube in exchange for a piggy-back ride. Now I was on Yitzchak's back. I could see Chayim as if I were taller just the way it ought to be! Chayim obliged his newly tall sister with his best show ever. He danced, he sang, he imitated people we knew and he pretended being an elephant.

As I got older, I finally grew to be five feet tall and even gained a little weight. Nevertheless, every time I saw my little brother

Yitzchak, he'd lift me high into the air, asking, "So! How's my little sister?" Often I wondered when I, his older sister, had become his little sister. Did something shift in Yitzchak's mind when he found out how easy it was for him to hoist me almost to our ceiling?

Semietchki: Chayim

Children are playing under my window. I hear a little girl asking for semietchki (pumpkin seeds or sunflower seeds.) I'm wondering whether the little girl will ever know that the word she's using has the power to time teleport me into my childhood.

On a cool, autumn day, Yitzchak and I were peering through the window of our front door. He had to lower himself to see through the top of the window. I, on the other hand, had to stand on my toes to see through the bottom of it.

I saw Father walking alongside a trapper who carried a sack of something!

"I bet it's hazelnuts!" whispered Yitzchak.

"No! He's got semietchki!"

"Pfuy! Semietchki's for girls!"

Father opened the door, letting the trapper come in first into the house. Yitzchak was right. The sack the trapper put on the floor of our all-purpose room was filled with hazelnuts! He was also right when he said pumpkin seeds and sunflower seeds were for girls.

Rose and I had spent some very happy times roasting sunflower seeds, sharing them with friends and nibbling at them on our Sabbath walks. We often shelled them with our teeth until our tongues sprouted tiny semietchki blisters. The sunflower seeds turned my lips black, so I quit eating them.

Chayim's Chore of Shelling My Hazelnuts

We children were never allowed to shell hazelnuts with our teeth. Until the day came in the future when my family finally bought a nutcracker, we shelled every hazelnut with a hammer. However, only Rose and Chayim were allowed to use the hammer.

Shelling a hazelnut took coordination and concentration, especially if we hoped for intact nutmeats as well as intact fingers. A hazelnut sheller had to hold each nut steady between the thumb and the index finger in one hand, while delivering a masterful blow to the nut with the other hand.

Yes, there was another option to shelling hazelnuts. It required lining them up at a distance from each other and hitting them with the hammer. The perfect blows would yield intact nutmeats. The not so perfect blows would cause runaways or globs of hazelnut and hazelnut-shell paste.

Chayim loved to shell my nuts. He found a smart way of rewarding himself for his hard work. Since I accepted nothing but intact nutmeats, Chayim would hold each nut between thumb and forefinger, delivering the perfect blow to his victims.

Kneeling on a chair, I'd prop my elbows on the table, cupping my chin in my hands watching Chayim's expertise with wide-eyed admiration. Sometimes when my face was barely above the nut-to-be-cracked, he'd growl: "Do you want me to work on your face or on your hazelnuts?" I'd give him a disheartened look, then pull back a bit and continue watching.

"How about doing something, Sis?"

"What?"

"Separating the nutmeat from the shells and eating?"

"Sure, Chayim!"

I ran to Rose, asked for a pewter plate and started my new job. When I began rubbing my tummy after consuming a big pile of nutmeats, he asked, "Does that mean you've had enough?"

"Yes." I stretched out like a contented cat before the fireplace.

"Go ask Rose for more."

"More? I had enough."

"Little sister! I want more nuts!"

"Go ask yourself!"

Chayim gave me a long penetrating look. I got the picture! He wants a well-deserved reward; he used his time and risked his fingers so I could have perfect nutmeats!

I took my plate, flew out of the room almost as if I'd grown wings, and asked Rose for more hazelnuts. "Libelah, you already ate the others?"

"Yes, Rose." I lied, of course!

"That's wonderful!" Her grin was almost bigger than her face.

I handed the plate to Chayim and was ready to leave the room.

"Don't you want to watch me shell my hazelnuts?"

"I just watched you shell mine."

"I'll shell mine totally different!" My curiosity took over. "Well . . . Okay."

Chayim lined his hazelnuts in rows like soldiers in formation. Then he began beating them, running after the escapees, hammering the poor souls to death, while endlessly commenting: "You wise guy? You think you'll escape me? What nerve! Now you'll taste my revenge! Hey, you! Don't you dare run off this table! No matter where you try to hide, I'll find you!" Suddenly he'd soften his tone of voice. "You over there . . . come here . . . what a sweetheart; I'll be gentle; I might even spare your life."

Today I understand why he wanted me to watch him shell his hazelnuts. Had Rose come into the room to find him sitting alone, comfortably shelling and eating the hazelnuts, she would have known I'd lied to her when I asked for more hazelnuts.

Chayim, Ignorance and Brutality

I so wish that the incident wouldn't have happened to Chayim in elementary school, the incident that robbed him of his exceptional personality.

One day, Chayim told one of his schoolmates that Jesus was a Jew. The rumor of his 'blasphemy' spread like wild fire and all hell broke loose. Chayim's entire class was ready to lynch him!

Chayim

During recreation time, at least twenty of his classmates threw him to the ground and beat him savagely.

Since I was in the schoolyard, I saw the first blows. Our principal was standing on the upper step of the school's entrance. I ran to him for help. "Stop them! They're hurting my brother! Please!" The principal wouldn't even look at me. He kept gazing at the scene as if enjoying every minute of it.

When the bell rang and the students went back into their classrooms, I ran to Chayim, finding him semi-conscious. The principal was still watching. "Szabo, go get your father!" he called out to me.

Could I leave Chayim? What if he'd be killed? I couldn't carry my brother and I was afraid to drag him, so I rushed to find my father. Two hours later, I got hold of Father. The two of us ran to the now-empty schoolyard. We heard a low moan, then silence. A minute or so later, we heard another moan.

Chayim, eyes unfocused, lay almost hidden in a bush. His breathing gurgled. Father scooped the bloody mess that had been my brother into his arms and carried him to the doctor. He had a fractured skull, broken ribs, and a collapsed lung. He took what seemed an eternity to recover. His recovery was only partial. His body eventually healed physically, but gone was his exceptional personality. More than my other siblings, I dreamed about the Chayim I knew before the incident.

My father confronted the principal who only had a warning, "Teach your son to think before he speaks!" It seemed he was as ignorant about the fact that Jesus was a Jew as were his students.

Ignorance is the root of hatred. It does not think, but babbles. Once, in my elementary school, I asked a classmate of mine, a peasant girl, whether she knew who gave the Ten Commandments. She looked at me suspiciously, almost as if I'd spoken in a foreign language. So I said, "You know, the Ten Commandments: Don't kill. Don't steal. Don't lie. And so on?"

"Sure I know who gave the Ten Commandments!"

"Who?"

"The gendarmes!"

"Why the gendarmes?"

"Don't they punish you when you do those bad things?"

My Brother Yitzchak and the Simchat Torah Incident

In my village Petrova, as I already mentioned, the Jews were Orthodox, fundamentalists. Men went to the synagogue to pray every day, twice a day. Women attended only on Shabbat. Men and women sat separate: men sat in the synagogue proper while women sat in an enclosed balcony from where they could see all men's activities. The Jewish fall Holidays ended in the festivity called Simchat Torah.

I wanted to see the Simchat Torah festivity; I was about eight-years-old. I asked Rose to take me to the enclosed balcony reserved for women. Tonight there were lots of girls in the balcony. Some stuck their heads through the wall's openings to gaze at their admirers. Others were anxious to see their fathers and brothers in prayer. And still others, very young, were trying to make out what the celebration was all about. I was waiting for the festivities to start.

Finally, all of the scrolls had been taken out of the Ark (the sacred structure that holds the Torah). Now they were being carried in triumph through the aisles of the synagogue seven times. Each procession was followed by a lively interlude of singing, chanting and dancing. Young boys carrying Simchat Torah flags with lighted candles stuck in potatoes or apples were trailing behind the euphoric crowd of the scroll carriers. I watched wide-eyed as men took one corner of the talit (prayer shawl) touching it to a Torah scroll, then kissing the now holy place on the talit before sitting down in their seats. I was singing, humming and counting.

During the seventh procession I saw Yitzchak. Was I dreaming? His flag was on fire. Oh, my God! In my imagination his whole body was engulfed in fire. I turned hysterical.

" Somebody! Please! Help my brother! He's on fire! Please! Please!"

Rose buried my face on her chest. "Libelah! Libelah! Yitzchak is all right! He's not on fire! He's not even in the Synagogue! He dropped his burning flag on the floor and ran outside! He's smart!"

I calmed down, but I wanted to see Yitzchak. Rose helped me walk down the stairs. I felt weakness in my knees. We didn't have to look for Yitzchak. He was within eye-sight leaning on the synagogue's entrance door. Maybe he felt weakness in his knees like I did. Without another word, Yitzchak, Rose and I walked home. I leaned on Rose's arm. Yitzchak refused her help.

As I lay in bed that evening, I remembered how it all began. The eve of Simchat Torah was nearing; Father had returned from his business about noon time. Yitzchak, six-years-old, his eyes lowered, approached him. "Father would you make me a flag for the Simchat Torah festivities? For once I can tell my friends that my father made me the Simchat Torah flag and not my sister, Rose."

"Sure!" Father looked at Yitzchak, his face flushed.

Yitzchak and I intently watched as Father selected a beautiful red apple and carved out a candle-sized space in it. After he secured the apple on a pointed stick to which a flag was attached, he fitted a candle into the apple's waiting hollow. Now it looked like a perfect match, as if that apple and that candle had waited maybe five thousand years for the meeting.

Yitzchak was so excited that instead of thanking Father, he ran out of the house to show off his flag to his friends. One of the older boys asked to see the flag. Yitzchak handed it to him. The boy turned around and scooped out almost the entire apple under the candle with his pen knife before handing the ruined flag back to Yitzchak.

"Here!" The boy smirked. "Take this to your father and ask him to repeat the miracle again! Then come back to me!"

Yitzchak looked at his destroyed flag and began crying. His friends were moved by his tears. Hershel, whom the boys nicknamed "the brain," decided that wrapping some paper around the candle might keep it in place. Maybe none of them understood enough about fire, or how the candle could ignite the paper.

In the synagogue, when it was time, Yitzchak joined the procession of chanting men and boys as if his flag were intact. But during the seventh procession, the candle touched the paper it was

Yitzchak and his wife on their wedding day

wrapped in and started burning. Yitzchak's flag became a torch. My little brother was terrified and threw the burning glob on the floor of the synagogue. A man removed his black silk caftan, threw it on the flame and stamped out the fire.

My father assumed the "Great Synagogue Fire" had been an accident. He thanked the man who saved his son, the building and the entire congregation. However, two days later, our hero, the fire fighter, brought us the bill for the mending of his caftan. That's when Yitzchak admitted to father he knew his flag was damaged but had no idea who the boy was that destroyed the apple.

Father went next door to ask my brother's friends who had damaged the apple. Oddly, no one knew the boy responsible for this prank. However, Father had noticed the furtive looks which the boys had exchanged almost as if they were swearing each other to secrecy.

"Hmmm?" said Father to the boys. "I suppose the gendarmes will have to find out who he is. I've heard they don't use torture these days. I hope it's true." He looked at the children almost as if he never expected to see any of them again. Scared out of his wits, the youngest child named the villain.

Mother and Father and the evil-doer's parents met, and they went to the Rabbi to decide on a fair settlement. The rabbi decided that the two families split equally the cost for the mending of the caftan.

Yitzchak and I at a Poor Bride's Wedding

Once, when I was about seven-years-old, my mother gave me permission to attend the wedding of a poor bride. She dressed me in my best. Since I was unnoticeable in stature, she placed me at the very end of the crowd of people trailing after the bride, heading toward the rabbi's back yard where he would officiate over her wedding. I felt excited but scared. I began praying in my mind "God is good, God is great; God, I'm so scared; I'm so tiny; suppose somebody in front of me makes a wrong move and squashes me to death? I don't want to die! I want to go to the wedding! I also want to go home and see my mother; she always tells me I'm smart and I shouldn't worry about people teasing me. When people are teasing me, I cannot help it, but when Yitzchak my younger brother teases me I don't like it! He thinks he's so strong, he can fight a lion. I know he cannot fight a lion. But I don't say it. I don't want him to be angry with me; I like when he carries me on his shoulders; I can look down at things, instead of straining my neck to look up at things; I don't have to stand on my toes and hold on to the edge of the table just to see what's on top of it. God in heaven, would it be too much to ask you to make me tall like other children my age, so that the village fool doesn't haunt me; doesn't always say, Libkela, you have a bibkelah on your nose. Every time he says that I check my nose for a bump but luckily, I don't have one. Thank you, God, for that. And another thing, God, please, don't make me cry; I don't want trouble!"

I had just finished praying when I saw my brother, Yitzchak, standing next to me and complaining, "You and your wedding! Mother made me leave my friends! I was almost winning the game! That'll cost you something!"

"What?"

"I don't know; I have to think!"

"Will a honeycomb cube do?"

"I don't know; I have to think!" While Yitzchak kept thinking; we had arrived at the rabbi's backyard. I pulled at his pants.

"What?"

"I want to see the bride; please put me on your shoulders!"

"That'll cost you something!"

"What? Another honeycomb cube?"

"I don't know; I have to think!" His lengthy thinking gave me a chance to see the whole ceremony.

When I got home Mother asked me, "So what did you see?"

I told Mother I saw a circle of elderly women, the bride and groom being part of it. I saw the circle of people circling seven times, I counted.

"What was the rabbi doing?"

"Praying."

Mother laughed.

"Why are you laughing?" I asked.

"The rabbi did not pray; he officiated, over the wedding." I was expecting an explanation of the word, "officiated," but the explanation never came.

"After the rabbi did whatever you said, someone held a glass of wine from which both the bridegroom and the bride drank," I said. "Some young fellows shouted out the name of the bride, Drink! Drink! Drink! Get drunk!" The same fellows kept laughing when the groom couldn't break the glass with his foot the first time."

"You're smart; you remember everything." said Mother.

Yitzchak and the Engineer's Wife

I also remember Yitzchak by his problem with the engineer's wife. At twenty, Yitzchak was a very handsome young man with an athletic build, sandy blond hair and brown eyes. He worked for a gentile engineer. One morning he told me, he wondered whether the wife of the engineer might be trying to seduce him.

"Any evidence?"

"She looks at me as if she's trying to take my chauffeur's uniform off. The other day, she invited me into her house for coffee while her husband was away on a project. She was wearing a nightgown. Sort of a see-through one."

"Is she young and attractive?"

"She's neither."

The news upset me. Yitzchak noticed the change in my face.

"You think she's up to something?"

"You bet she is!"

"What do you say I do?"

My advice to Yitzchak was to ignore the woman, but to be polite when she spoke to him; to keep busy with his master's car; to ask his master for a bigger uniform. "You didn't want to confront a gentile, jealous husband," I said.

My Oldest Brother Vigdor

What do I remember about my oldest brother Vigdor? I recall he was known in the village as the best built and the strongest Jewish young man. In fact, the people envied him. They believed that with his frame and strength, he would have no problem when inducted into the army.

The people were mistaken. Vigdor's letters from the army were cries for help. The training exercises were too rigorous and his skin was painfully sun-blistered. Some fellow soldiers called him a communist, claiming his red hair proved it. He was very unhappy being a soldier.

Father wanted to help. If Vigdor was in the cavalry, his life would be better, he thought. A Jew in the cavalry? It was possible if he paid for his own fancy uniform, brought a thoroughbred horse and left it for the cavalry at the end of his military services.

And so, a fancy uniform and a horse of a most excellent breed placed Vigdor in the Romanian Cavalry.

When Vigdor came home for furlough in his splendid uniform, he was suddenly the village hero. He greeted everyone with a salute as if each person was his superior in the cavalry. Married

Vigdor

women adored him. Young girls giggled and small children trailed behind him. His noisy spurs on his shining calf-hugging boots bewitched me.

Once, as Vigdor was sitting at the table eating, I bent down and started playing with his enticing boot spurs. I don't remember how it happened; I was five years old, but my left hand landed underneath Vigdor's heels. He was forever upset. He blamed himself for the accident, though the family assured him it was my fault. I was unable to fully use my hand for a very long time. However, to everyone's surprise, I had completely recovered within a year. The cavalry finally discharged Vigdor. He arrived home in civilian clothes, carrying a small satchel. I was terribly disappointed. He looked so ordinary!

My Second Oldest Brother Yosef

Yosef was ten years my senior. My village and all the neighborhood villages held that Yosef was an exceptionally bright young man. There was also a story connected with my brother's smartness. Presumably my mother went shopping for sugar one day, leaving me in Yosef's care. I was 18 months old and Yosef was 11-years-old. While Yosef was trying to entertain his eighteen-month old baby sister, crowing, making faces, imitating a monkey, he heard a loud knock at the door. Should he open it? Hmmm? He opened it, and four of his friends trooped inside. "You'll stay in the house all day watching your bony little sister?" Yankel spoke first. "I love my bony little sister." Yosef also liked his friends. They attended cheder (parochial school) together, played games together and talked about girls together. "See you tomorrow, Yosef," said Ezra, heading toward the door, his friends trailing after him. "Hey fellows, my Mom will be back in a little while, try again," said Yosef. "Yeah? When moms go shopping, they get lost," said Boruch. "Not my Mom! She's smart.! She knows her way back," said Yosef. "I didn't mean lost, lost! I meant they meet other moms in the store and talk and talk and talk, said Boruch."

"What if you take your little sister outside and tie her to the fence right where the big house casts its shadow?" Ezra suggested. "We'll keep an eye on her from my backyard."

"Bad idea, Ezra! My sister is not a dog! But let me think. After a minute or so, Yosef said, "I not only got an idea, I got a plan!" Yosef whispered his plan to Yankel, who whispered it to the rest of the dumbfounded friends. The boys would gather stones, even if they had to unearth them from the street. Yosef carried me into the backyard where the big house cast its shadow. He put me on a heap of rags, took the stones and built a tight wall around me with only my head showing. Yosef intended to keep an eye on me, but had "sort of" forgotten. When he remembered he'd left me all alone with only stones to guard me, he ran from Ezra's next door backyard to the place he left me. Uh, oh! Chayia Engelstein, our next door neighbor, already saw me in my private fortress. Her head cupped in her hands, she ran in and out of our house, then onto the street, looking in all directions, yelling, "Rochel, Rochel, your baby!" Just then, she noticed Mother in the street.

Mother was hysterical when she saw me buried to my neck in stones. "What if the neighbor's pigs were loose? What if those vicious pigs had chewed off her baby's ears? What if a venomous snake had wrapped itself around her baby's neck and choked her to death? What if? What if . . .?"

According to family legend, Father was livid with anger toward Yosef. It may have been for the best that my brother disappeared for three days while our entire village looked for him. Several families dredged the river behind our orchard, expecting to find his body! Yosef was hiding in a fruit tree in our orchard, eating unripe plums, unripe pears, and unripe apples. The third day, as he was scrambling toward our outhouse, Rose saw him. When Father saw his son Yosef alive, he forgot about corporal punishment. He ordered Yosef to memorize five pages from Genesis, assuming such an accomplishment of memory would keep him inside for at least five days. In less than one afternoon, Yosef could recite every verse. That autumn, Father sent Yosef to the most famous yeshiva in Chernovitz, Romania.

The rabbis were amazed. In the two days before the weekly exams, Yosef learned everything the other students needed a full week to learn. During the rest of the week, he was free to go to secular libraries where he studied and studied and studied. His intense secular readings acquainted him with Utopian Communism. The Talmud had taught him to help the oppressed, yet Romania had outlawed the Communist Party. During his first year at the yeshiva, the Romanian authorities arrested Yosef for being a communist. They jailed him and tortured him. They made him swallow sand to get a confession about the communist group he belonged to, but Yosef did not confess. They notified my father who bailed him out and brought Yosef back home.

Now, he had very little in common with his former friends. He moved to Iaşi, Romania, where he met Mina, another ardent Communist. Mina had also been tortured in Basarabia, Romania. One morning, a guard took her from her ice-lined cell into a snow-covered prison-yard. He had two buckets with frozen water. He broke the thin ice over the water, crossed himself, and poured the contents of one bucket over her head. He then threw the water from the second pail into her face, screaming, "Confess! Confess!" She tried to tell him she'd done nothing wrong, but her face was frozen and her lips wouldn't move. She tapped the ice around her lips, managing to chip off enough so that she could speak. "This is what Jesus taught you to do to innocent people?" she uttered. Her words must have resonated with something the guard had once believed in, for he guided her back to the cell, took off his own mouton-lined winter coat and put it over her shoulders and left. She never saw him again, but the guard's coat saved her life.

Mina and Josef eventually married and had two daughters, Bianca and Bella. In 1940, the Romanian Government arrested thousands of communist sympathizers. Mina, Yosef and their children fled to Russia, the "worker's paradise," but found only

Yosef and his family: his wife Bianca, Mina, & Bella

chaos. Refugees from German-occupied territories flooded Russia. These people traveled aimlessly, hoping to be reunited with lost family members. Mina took a six-year-old orphan girl into her own family and together with three other families moved into a cold-water flat.

When Yosef's money was gone, he still had not found work. In his desperation, he began selling cigarettes on the black-market. One day, a desperate, jobless father of six children approached him and asked him how he made a living. Yosef, identifying himself with the suffering family, told the stranger the truth. The stranger was an undercover KGB agent, who sent Yosef to hard labor in Siberia for ten years.

In his work camp, the winter snow was waist-deep. The prisoners used ropes strung between trees to get to their workstation to cut trees. Each morning, the workers bade each other a final good-bye. If a man's half-frozen hands slipped from the snow and ice laden ropes, he was swallowed by the snow. If his hands withstood the cold, he won, but only for that workday. Most of the prisoners died of accidents, exposure, and starvation. Yosef survived.

During the time Yosef was in Siberia, Mina stayed in Russia until August, 1944, when the Soviets occupied Romania. Mina returned to Iaşi with her family. As an active party member, she eventually became a department head at the Ministry of Justice in the government controlled by Nicolae Ceauşescu, the communist leader of Romania from 1965 to 1989. When Yosef returned from Siberia, he also landed a prestigious job: Director of Light Industry in Iaşi. As prominent members of the Communist Party, Yosef and his family led a sheltered life. They had a luxurious apartment with servants and ate at restaurants designated exclusively for party members. They had a yearly four-week paid vacation at a famous resort and regularly received complimentary tickets to all theaters, museums, opera houses and art shows. Their daughters were educated in science, humanities, arts, music and ballet free of charge. Bianca became a biochemist while Bella became a dental technician. Both Bianca and Bella married and their children had nannies.

During Ceauşescu's reign, anti-Semitism raged in Romania and innocent Jews ended up in jails. Mina and Yosef worked as a team saving Jews, believing God had planted them in Romania to do His will. Twelve young Jewish Zionists accused of being enemies of the establishment landed in jail. Mina interceded on their behalf and demanded a retrial. She acted as their defense lawyer and their accusers acquitted them. Mina was able to arrange for the group to emigrate to Israel.

Eventually, Yosef and Mina realized they were part of a political system in which a small group of party leaders enjoyed the privilege of power while Romania lay in shambles. Unemployment was high. Food, gasoline and electricity were rationed. Romanians were trapped for hours in trolley cars and elevators. Refrigerators stopped running while many meals were half-cooked or raw. Amidst all this chaos, Ceauşescu was accumulating gold, diamonds, and art. Mina and Yosef were worried about their children's future. They liquidated their assets, and sent their two daughters with their husbands and children to Israel in 1970. Ten years later, Yosef and Mina joined them.

Molly, My Oldest Sister

In the spring of 1920, I was six months old and my older sister Molly had already left home. From my first memories to the time my family and I were deported to Auschwitz, Molly, to me, meant packages of clothes for each of us. Not just ordinary clothing but special holiday garments that made me feel like a rich American child rather than the village child who couldn't afford such lavish outfits. Whenever I think about my black pure-silk pajamas with delicate, smiling, geishas wrapped in kimonos, tiptoeing across the cloth with little umbrellas in their dainty hands, I'm reminded of Molly.

My family had a good reason to celebrate. Moti, Aunt Rifka's millionaire son, sponsored Molly's move to Mexico City, Mexico.

Molly and her Husband Sam

She was 19 years old. Whatever happened, Molly wound up in America. She married Sam Reisner, and together they had two daughters.

My Sister Toby

Toby, the last of our family's eight children was beautiful. She had fair skin, titian red hair and a well-proportioned nose. She was the only girl who ever dared stand up to the tomboy, Toby Stern, in our village. At six, she wanted to enter the first grade in elementary school, when the official age for starting school was seven. Later, she wanted to be a seamstress. Her "apprenticeship" lasted a week.

When I began secondary school in Sighet at the age of twelve, Toby was seven-years-old. I couldn't have been part of her everyday life. During Christmas vacation, I had to study for the following semester. During the summer vacation, I studied for the fall semester so that I had time for tutoring and earning extra money.

In 1939, Mother and the rest of the family moved to Sighet. Toby was fourteen. I tried to play older sister and be her friend, but she wanted everything of me or nothing of me. Could I have

Toby

included Toby in my social life? Definitely not. Back then, a fourteen-year-old and a nineteen-year-old high school student had little in common. When high school girls got together, they talked about high school boys. When a high school girl and a high school boy got together, they talked about literature, history, math, chemistry and physics, each one trying to impress the other with the vast knowledge they were acquiring in school. The boys and girls who went steady were "a couple" and they had their own language.

Back In The Death Shack

I'm back in the death shack. Rose squeezed my hand, "The men have just entered the shack," she said. I woke up from a minute's travel through my entire life. I kissed Rose. "Don't worry Rose," I said, "I won't go down without a fight; this is not the last time you'll see me."

"From your mouth to God's ears," I heard Rose saying.

I was still in my bunk bed when I saw five male inmates were busying themselves with giving out bundles to the doomed.

"What you'll find in the bundles," said one of them, in a soft tone of voice, "is a hospital garment. We're taking you to a hospital in town; you'll be taken good care of."

I knew it was a lie. If they wanted to take us to hospitals in town, they could have done so at the onset of the disease. I was convinced we'd be gassed that same evening.

I was rehearsing in my mind; I'd refuse to put on my hospital wear. I'd tell them I feel as healthy as they do, maybe not as strong, and how would they like to be in my shoes. I might even make a recovery demonstration. I'll slide down from my third-tiered bunk bed, start walking up and down the aisle, and then ask them to judge. Another thought and my mind would have shattered into pieces when a bundle, four times as big as those of the doomed, landed in my lap.

"Please open it," a fellow said, a faint smile on his lips. I felt enraged and insulted. How dare he laugh at my misfortune! "I refuse to open the bundle!" I said, grinding my teeth in anger. "I know you're taking me to be gassed; you can't fool me!" I blurted out. "And on top of everything, you find it funny!" I clutched my hands around the pole that held together my bunk beds and said, "If you want to take me out of here, you'll have to take me with the pole and all!"

Just then, a naïve girl from the next bunk bed spoke up on my behalf while pulling her hospital gown over her head. "Sir," she said, in a chirp-like voice, "Please forgive my friend for the way she talks to you. She must be so overwhelmed with the good news, that she doesn't know what she is talking about. Please take her with us."

I pitied the girl for not knowing where they were taking her. However, I had to fight for my own life. Or at least maybe plead for my life? I decided for the latter. "You see, Sir," I spoke in a voice choked up with tears, "I have totally recovered from this dreadful disease a week ago. I don't know how long I've been here."

"Six weeks," said the man. "Without medication and food; that should tell you something, Sir," I replied. "This morning, I tried to help the girls sit up straight in their beds. Ironically, the doctor watched me in action. You'd think he'd realize I was recovered and send me back to my barrack. No! He sends me . . . you know where."

"He sends you back to your barrack; check out your package."

"I so want to believe you, Sir, but I don't," I said.

"Maybe this will convince you," he said. He opened my bundle and a dress, a jacket, shoes and socks stared at me.

I realized these were clothes to wear to go back into my barrack. I apologized and thanked him profusely. I also asked him kindly to let me go to my sister, Rose, and tell her the good news. I slid down the pole from the third bunk bed with the agility of a cat. I wondered from where this strength was coming. At Rose's bunk bed, I displayed my clothes. "I'm going back into the barrack," I bubbled. "The Sabbath Fairy Queen intervened! Soon, she'll send you back, too!"

Rose knew very well how the Sabbath Fairy Queen got lodged in my imagination. Our parting was tearless; Rose and I felt it wouldn't be long before our next reunion. I was halfway to the door when I heard Rose say, "Take your food in piecemeal; give your stomach a chance to get used to food again."

"I love you," I said and followed the men through the door. I took Rose's advice. By the end of the next week, my stomach could hold half a bowl of soup and half a slice of bread.

At dusk, about a week later, we heard knocking noises at our barrack. When the noises stopped, we saw our windows were boarded up and our doors were nailed down.

What now? Will the Germans set us on fire, or dynamite us? We expected the worst. We started with hysterics and ended in prayer. One day passed, two days passed, three days passed and nothing. We were terribly weak, and the barrack smelled like a sewer. We must do something! The girls gathered their last bit of energy and broke out of the barrack. To our surprise, the main gate, which happened to face our barrack, was wide open and there was no trace of German soldiers.

Some inmates rushed through the camp to spread the good news and encourage the rest of the girls to break out of their barracks. Others ran into the kitchen, opened the doors and the windows and began throwing out loaves of bread, potatoes and bags of sugar, while making wild noises. One of the girls, a jokester it seemed, opened a bag of sugar and spilled it on top of her neighbor's head.

I stayed inside the barrack for fear the euphoric crowd might run me over. I saw girls crying, kissing, embracing and jumping up and down. Some even danced the hora around the recently created bonfires in which they threw potatoes.

My nostrils filled up with the heavenly waft of baked potatoes and my mouth salivated at the sight of so many goodies piled up to the top of the kitchen fence. Wouldn't it be nice if I stepped out of the barrack, helped myself to bread, and held it out in front of Rose as a welcome gift when she returned from the shack?

It must have been a vision. Rose, holding on to my cousin Lilly, walked into our barrack. I forgot about the whole world around me. We sat down on the floor, and fell into each other's arms. We cried and kissed and wouldn't let go. By the time we looked around, Lilly was gone. Two minutes later, she returned with a loaf of bread and a bowl of water, just to disappear again. Yes, that was Lilly, our cousin, thanks to whom I got to work in the Brotkammer and Rose got work as a Stubbendienst in Barrack 29, with Fraulein Helen in charge; you remember the rest. We had met up with Lilly on the Death March.

With a slightly shaking hand, Rose broke off two small pieces of the loaf of bread Lilly brought us, put them into the water and waited a few seconds. She fished out a small mass and gave it to me.

"This time you eat first," I said.

She smiled, took out the piece of mush, and ate it in about four or five swallows. "That'll do for now," she said.

Around midnight, the crowd decided to end the celebration and get into the barracks. The first thing the girls got rid of was the smelly straw. But could we sleep? Not at all. We feared the Germans might wait for the deep of the night to return and kill us. We sat up against the walls, held hands and prayed. Eventually, we slid down the wall and fell asleep.

LIVING, AGAIN

Liberation

At dawn, we heard the sound of a truck entering the main gate. The dense fog prevented us from distinguishing the soldiers' uniforms. We tried to listen to the language they were speaking.

"Girls, these soldiers are Americans," I cried out.

"How do you know?"

"They speak English."

"Do you speak English?"

"I do; I had two years of English in high school."

We ran outside and waved. The soldiers waved back. They looked at us as if they were seeing ghosts.

"Speak English?" a soldier asked. "I do, Sir," I answered. The soldier wanted to know when the Germans fled. I couldn't answer that; we were locked up. The soldiers gave us cigarettes, canned food and chocolate. They had to move on, they said, but not to worry; the Russian soldiers would pass through here this afternoon and take care of us. They left about half an hour later. In our excitement, we forgot to ask the soldiers about the status of the war. Were they passing through Neustadt-Gleve on their way to victory, or was victory already here?

In the afternoon, the Russian soldiers entered the camp. They were just as surprised at our appearance as the American soldiers had been this morning. They had no food, no cigarettes and no chocolate to give us. Instead, they took the girls to town and gave them permission to go into German homes and take anything their hearts desired.

The girls chose mostly food. During the three-day rampage, they brought back preserved chicken, preserved rabbit meat, smoked meat, liverwurst and salami. Some of the girls also brought back oatmeal, which was exactly what Rose thought we needed for our recovery.

Three hundred girls ate whatever they laid their hands on. Tragically, they swelled up and died. Rose believed the victims should have taken it easy and gradually introduced their stomachs to regular food.

A week later, the Russians took us to a camp; I don't recall the name. We stayed there six months. We would have most probably stayed there much longer had I not fallen upon an idea. I must go into town and talk to the higher-ups, the Soviet officers in charge. I must find out when we'd be returning to our hometowns; winter was creeping up on us.

I knew I could smuggle myself out of the camp and have no difficulties representing the inmates of the camp, but was that enough? Not really. I needed free passage to these high-ranking officers. I was small, skinny and nothing to look at. The guards might mistake me for a child intruder and kick me out!

I spoke to Rose about my plan. I counted on her wisdom. And wisdom I received. "You need an attention-stopping face to accompany you," she said.

"Will you help me find such a face?" I asked Rose.

"Definitely not! I know you have an eye for beauty!"

I barely slept that night. The next day, I found the desired subject. We smuggled ourselves out of the camp and headed toward the Soviet Headquarters. Eyes turned and doors opened straight into the office of the commanding officer. I presented our case. I talked and the officer kept looking at the beautiful girl. I talked and he kept looking at her exquisite face. He promised to meet us at the camp in the staff officer's office tomorrow.

The next morning, I got up early. I went to the staff officer's office in our camp. The officer I spoke to yesterday arrived soon; he asked me to repeat my request. I then knew he had not heard a single word I said yesterday in his office; he was wandering somewhere in fantasy land with my chosen beauty.

We stayed another three weeks in the camp before we were shipped, each of us to our own hometown. I have no knowledge how the story ended between the commanding officer and the beauty.

In Sighet 1945

We arrived in Sighet sometime in November, 1945. To our surprise, we learned that the Soviets had occupied Romania since 1944. Who were these people, we wondered? The Russian faces we grew familiar with in the camp were our saviors. Here, we saw stern, unfriendly faces roaming the streets, soldiers saluting their superiors. The sight scared us. We had no parents, no relatives and no friends. We met some young faces from the past at the Jewish Distribution Institute in Sighet. The Institute was sustained by American Jews. The Institute fed us, clothed us and provided us with sleeping quarters. My sister Rose and I shared a room with two other girls.

One morning, we heard a knock at the door. I rushed to see who the visitor was. A Soviet officer greeted me in German. I answered his greeting. He then politely invited himself inside. Did I have a choice, I asked myself? He spoke a correct German. He asked me questions related to Auschwitz. After an hour or so, we excused ourselves. We had to go to the Institute to have lunch, we said. He stood at attention, and left.

The next day, he showed up again. He focused his attention mainly on me. He said I reminded him of his Jewish wife he left back in the Soviet Union. In my naiveté, I felt flattered. Two days later, he said he was looking forward to taking me to the Soviet Headquarters to dance and dine; he wanted a companion.

I was scared out of my wits. I went to the Distribution Institute and asked for money to leave town. The people I spoke to were very understanding and cooperative. Twenty-four hours later, my sister and I landed in a home in Satu Mare (Szatmar), a neighboring town.

We rubbed our eyes. We saw our cousin Molly, Mother's brother Victor's daughter. She said that the people from the Jewish Distribution Institute in Sighet called her up. "They had two young survivors who needed our help." They were given no names. "It seems you are those two people."

I asked. "Why would they call you as opposed to other Jews in Szatmar?"

"Because they knew we were devoting our lives to helping survivors."

Suddenly, I saw three children. "You're taking care of children, too?" I asked Molly.

"Are you serious, Libush?" she always called me Libush. "These are my children!"

She explained her good fortune. She and her husband Sonyi (Solomon) and their three children were hidden by a peasant family in a nearby village during the war. They were also very lucky, she said, in having recovered their fabric store after the war. By now they were also the proud owners of a nightclub.

We couldn't have felt more comfortable and more wanted in our own parents' home. Molly moved us into the room of her children's governess. Yes, she had a governess for the children, a cook, two other servants and a chauffeur.

During our stay there, we learned that our brother Yitzchak returned from a labor camp and was now in Bucharest, the capital of Romania,

Soon, Solomon's head sales representative traveled to Bucharest and took me with him. I visited Yitzchak. We fell into each other arms and stayed that way for quite a while. I asked him if he'd heard anything about Yosef, Chayim and Toby. He heard about Yosef and Chayim, he said, but not about Toby. "So where is Yosef?" I could barely wait for his answer. "In Iaşi, Romania, with his family." That was good news. I waited for Yitzchak to continue. "I've heard nothing about Toby," he said and stopped. It was a bad omen. "Where is Chayim?" I broke the silence. "He died in one of the labor camps."

Poor Chayim. He never made it. My childhood paraded in front of my eyes. How hard he tried to make me laugh, then watch from the corner of his eye how I'd take a swallow of food between my giggling. Whenever I'd concentrate on his performance and neglect my food, he'd stop in his tracks and say something like, if I didn't continue eating, he'd walk out of there. Of course, I would promise to eat. And when I'd finish my food, he'd run to Rose or Mother and with great pride announce his accomplishment. How I'll miss him!

I cried myself to sleep. In the morning, I asked Yitzchak about his plans. Rose and I were aiming for Germany, I said, and from there to America. Yitzchak intimated he had just met a young girl and wanted to stay there a while longer. I remembered my father's address by heart. I wrote to him. I told him we had news about Yitzchak, Yosef and Chayim, but not about Toby. A few weeks later, we received a letter from father with good news; Toby was already in America and staying with him.

How I Met My Husband, Sigmund

My sister Rose and I stayed with Cousin Molly in Szatmar, Romania, from November 1945 to May 1946. The same month, an underground Zionist organization smuggled us to Budapest, then to a transitory displaced persons' camp in Salzburg, Austria. The camp was run by American soldiers. We lived in military barracks and ate soldiers' rations.

Following a few weeks of idling, I applied for work. My educational background landed me an office job.

It was the first morning on my job. I walked into a small office with my manager, Stanislav, a young man from the Soviet Union. At a desk about two yards from mine sat a young man in his mid-twenties.

"This is Miss Livia Szabo," said Stanislav to the male clerk. "She will translate German documents into the English language." The serious looking clerk, of medium height, brown eyes and good features, stood up, gave a mock salute and sat down again. "Miss Szabo," the manager continued, "This is Sigmund Krancberg. Look at him; he's afraid of his own shadow, but don't underestimate him; he does an excellent job. In fact, he even does my job on top of his. I'm too busy testing the waters; there are many, many interesting girls in this camp."

Stanislav's behavior upset me. I had heard of this young man before. Rumor had it he took advantage of defenseless inmates. I had no answer as to why no one denounced him to the American soldiers.

As Stanislav left the office, I approached Sigmund. "Do you smoke, Mr. Krancberg," I asked. "Yes, I smoke; call me Sigmund."

"Are you related to Sigmund Freud?" I slightly smiled. I tried to soften his stern expression; I succeeded. "Not that I know of," he said holding back a smile. I liked his answer. He had some sense of humor after all, I thought. I took out a pack of Chesterfield cigarettes and offered him one. He hesitated to help himself. "Come on, Sigmund, take a cigarette; I have plenty!" I said. Sigmund took a cigarette and put it on his desk. He then pulled up a chair for me from Stanislav's neighboring desk. I thanked him and sat down. I took a cigarette and browsed for a lighter in my handbag. He asked me for my lighter. He held it out for me to light my cigarette. I realized I was dealing here with a gentleman.

He lit his cigarette, took a few puffs and held his breath. I was expecting to see smoke come out from his nostrils. I was mistaken. He opened his mouth, brought his lips forward like a fish and began blowing in intervals. One by one, tiny smoke rings took off into the air. I lost track counting the rings. Just as I thought I'd seen the last of them, more began escaping from his mouth. He seemed to enjoy my surprised look. "I could never do that; I've tried it many times," I said. "I haven't smoked in a while. The office manager treats me with a cigarette sometimes, but I rarely see him."

"You'll have cigarettes galore, as long as I'm working here."

I waited until he finished his cigarette; mine had burned out in the ash tray while I savored every puff he made. I wanted to find out more about Sigmund's personal life, but no smart questions entered my mind, so I rattled off, "I'm getting my cigarettes from America; my father and two sisters of mine live there. I only wish I had more friends who smoke so I could support their habits. Be assured I'll support yours."

"Do you know that cigarettes are the most sought after item in this camp and outside of this camp? Among other things, cigarettes buy you diamonds, gold and whatnot."

"Do they buy you freedom as well?" I heard myself say.

Sigmund's probing eyes ran all over my face then he convincingly said, "Freedom is a state, or quality of being free; there are countless freedoms."

His reasoning impressed me. "Are you a philosopher?" I asked.

"Philosophy is the closest thing to my heart; I'd like to teach it someday."

My heart made a leap. I'm talking to a future professor of philosophy! Didn't I dream, at one time, of becoming a professor of literature, and, at another time, a professor of foreign languages? Wow! I had met someone with a thirst for knowledge. Maybe he could help me quench mine. We could make a great team. I felt something was connecting me to this young man. I became energized; I turned into a new me!

Something I had purposely brushed over a short while before began gnawing at me. "It's none of my business, Sigmund. But why in the world would you take such humiliation from Stanislav? He portrayed you as a 'nebbish', a nonentity, a nobody! He has a very bad reputation in the camp. People like you and all those who don't stand up to him are contributing to his abusive, immoral and scandalous character! He's also a black marketeer!"

Sigmund skipped over the part of Stanislav's immoral character and said, "Almost every male survivor in this camp is a black marketeer; maybe even some women, for what I know. It's survival of the fittest; we live in a world recovering from a war!"

I had a notion that our soldiers were the bravest and most honest people in the world, so I chimed in, "But Stanislaw is turning our American soldiers into black marketeers as well!"

"American soldiers are human; they're not saints," he said. "Whom do you want these black marketeers to deal with? There are no civilians in this camp; there are only survivors and American soldiers." He must have found me naïve and a senseless debater, for he blurted out, "I would advise you to keep things to yourself! Just a short while ago, you drew my attention to the way Stanislav treats me! It's easy for you to say; you have cigarettes; I, on the other hand, have to do things that I normally wouldn't just to get an extra portion of food." I realized that the daily food ration we were getting from the American soldiers was not enough to satisfy Sigmund's hunger. I felt guilty.

I'd used cigarettes and coffee to buy any food my heart desired from the German civilians while he, Sigmund, lived on allocated food. I excused myself and walked out of the office. I lit up one cigarette after the other. I waited for Stanislav to return and give me work to do, but he never showed up that day.

I had difficulties falling asleep that night. Everything that happened in the office rehashed in my mind. What in the world gave me the right to lecture Sigmund? Was it lecturing or concern for someone I felt connected with? I tried to figure out when that connection happened. Of course! It happened when he stood up and gave me a mock salute as Stanislav introduced us. I recall feeling a special pang to which I paid no attention. This connection intensified when I realized that the both of us had the thirst for knowledge. He was the hero of my dreams!

Still, this warranted a more accurate explanation, I thought. I started all over. I recalled step by step what had happened in the office. When I got to the scene in which Stanislav humiliated Sigmund, I stopped. I reflected about my emotional state. I recalled being truly angry. Why angry and not embarrassed like in any other insulting cases I ever witnessed before? Had cupid done his work? It seemed so because the next morning it was, "Move over Ferenz, here comes Sigmund!" We apologized to each other and a strong bond was born, a bond that eventually developed into a blissful sixty years of an unimaginable life of love.

Now I wanted to know everything about his past. I found out that he was in the Red Army for five years, that he was decorated twice and that he was discharged from the army with the rank of a full lieutenant.

I loosened up as well. I mentioned that my mother was gassed in Auschwitz, holding my sister Rose's two and a half year old son in her arms. I also told him that Rose saved my life and the lives of dozens of other inmates in the camps. I asked him to speak to me about his family. He became almost agitated; he moved his head from side to side as if in disbelief of what he had just heard. "I am sorry for bringing up painful memories," I said. "We all have them, but each of us copes with them differently." I went to my desk and busied myself with my work for the rest of the day.

Friday morning was pay day. I found out that we would be paid in food. Sigmund seemed to come alive; he opened up to me. His only sister and brother had survived the war, he said, and were now somewhere in Canada. I asked him whether he wanted to join his siblings. He hoped the Zionist organization that brought him here would do just that. The news that he intended to join his surviving family saddened me. Is it true that love is selfish? I better stop thinking about it or I'm bound to commit the biggest blunder. I began talking about my family. I said that my father immigrated to America in 1938, and that my sister Rose and I intended to join him in the near future.

"Yes, I recall you saying your father sends you cigarettes."

"And coffee," I added.

"I wasn't aware about the coffee."

"Do you know what I plan do in America?"

"Get married."

"Noooo! Not before I continue with my studies. I intend to go all the way to getting a doctorate."

"A doctorate in what?"

"As of now, I don't know in what." Sigmund got lost in his thoughts. I felt like smoking a cigarette, but decided against it.

"Funny," he suddenly replied, "My father studied at the University of St. Louis, in America in his youth." He then led me into an amazing story. His grandfather, from his father's side, Yoshua Krancberg, was a rich banker in Shepetovka, Czarist Russia. At the turn of the century, it was customary among the rich European Jews to send their sons to Germany or Switzerland to study. These countries were racially non-discriminatory. The Krancbergs of Shepetovka, trying to outdo their Jewish rich friends, sent their son, Boruch, Sigmund's father, to America to study. About six years later, Boruch received a disturbing letter from his mother. Her health was failing, she noted. She saw no other cause but for the fact that she was missing her son more than words could say.

As the devoted son he was, Boruch took the next ocean liner home, arriving in Shepetovka just as World War I broke out. He was conscripted into the army; fought on the front; sustained multiple wounds and survived it all in a German prisoner of war camp. He escaped from the camp in 1918. He learned that the Bolsheviks had entered Shepetovka in 1917. He wondered what had happened to his rich parents. According to the Bolsheviks, rich citizens were the enemy of the people.

He remembered that his parents owned property in Koretz, Ukraine. When he arrived in Koretz, he found his father, Yoshua and Yoshua's younger brother, Yankel there. His mother, in her mistaken belief that the Bolsheviks landed in Shepetovka only temporarily, remained there to guard her confiscated fortune. Boruch's baby sister, Yitka was torn between fleeing with her father to Koretz and remaining in Shepetovka to take care of her aging mother; she decided for the latter.

As the saying goes, "Life spins its wheels." Yoshua died in Koretz of a broken heart waiting for his wife, Tzurtl, who together with her daughter Yitka, died of starvation in Shepetovka while waiting for the Bolsheviks to leave. Yankel, Boruch's uncle, married and had one daughter who died in World War II. Boruch, Sigmund's father married a beautiful 19-year-old amateur actress, named Hana Rudnick. The couple had three children: Sigmund, Alex and Sally. Boruch, Sigmund's father, worked in Warsaw as a manager at an American ocean liner company, called Cunard Red Star and White Star; he'd come home only on the holidays.

In 1928, Boruch's company moved to Rovna, Poland. He moved his family to Rovna as well. In 1932, the Polish Government closed the offices of the American ocean liner company and established a Polish traveling agency instead. Boruch had to make a choice, either he convert to Catholicism, or lose his job. He lost his job.

The Krancbergs lived through very hard times. To add to their hardships, the bank in which they had their savings declared bankruptcy.

The war of 1939 caught the Krancbergs in all their misery. Sigmund, their first-born son, had set his heart on studying at a pedagogical institute in Lemberg, now under the Soviet Union occupation. With his parents' blessing, but no financial help, he went to Lemberg. He was exempt from paying tuition, in that the educational system in the Soviet Union was free. He also became the charity case of the Institute for the Blind in Lemberg. He received a military cot to sleep on among the blind people free of charge. He used his suitcase as a pillow. What did he do for board? He tutored students and, with the money earned, bought horse salami, which turned into a daily diet.

The next spring, Sigmund returned to his family with mononucleosis, a severe viral condition, exacerbated by malnutrition. His mother worked very hard and nursed him back to health. She assumed he would not return to Lemberg the next fall. But he returned against her better judgment. Before he had a chance to register in school, the Soviets inducted him into the Red Army.

Back to Salzburg, Austria, where I was talking to Sigmund in the office. While mentioning his parents during the recounting of his life story, Sigmund transfixed his eyes on me, but seemed to be somewhere else. I felt like snapping my fingers and saying, "Sigmund, where are you?"

Suddenly, he uttered, "Now do you see why I couldn't talk to you about my parents the other day?"

"No, I don't see," I said.

"I was not at their side when they needed me; I was in the Red Army."

I sensed his guilt. "Sigmund, my sister Toby, my sister Rose and I were right at my mother's side when she needed us. Still, we could not prevent her from being gassed," I said.

He fell silent for a moment as though lost in thought. Then, he began talking about his parents again. After the war, he found out that in 1942, the Germans started slaughtering Jews indiscriminately around Rovna where his parents then resided. The young and the healthy elderly Jews fled the region in groups, mainly by foot. His father having had problems with his legs refused to join the fleeing people. If only he had been there, he could have done something about it, he said. "What could you have done, Sigmund?" I asked. "Carry my father on my back."

"For how long, Sigmund?"

"I don't know!"

I took out a pack of cigarettes from my handbag and offered Sigmund one.

"Livia, do you know the value of cigarettes?" He looked at me.

"How many times do I have to tell you, Sigmund," I said. "I don't care about the value of cigarettes; I'll have plenty in America. I spoke from the mythical, European belief that the streets in America were paved with gold and that all people in America were rich.

In the end, he understood that my father was supplying me with enough cigarettes to feed my habit, to give to friends and to buy fresh food from the German people in town. I finished two cigarettes while he was still on his first. I felt totally relaxed. Sigmund was worried about catching up with his work.

At the end of the day, Stanislav, our office manager came into the office with our pay. It consisted of canned goods and chocolate. I offered my pay to Sigmund. He thanked me but refused.

"Remember, Sigmund? My sister and I are buying fresh food from the German people for cigarettes and coffee. If you don't take it, I'll give it to someone else." He then changed his mind.

Two weeks later, Stanislav asked me on a date. I wanted to discuss it with my sister. "I'll give you an answer tomorrow," I told Stanislav.

"Whose permission do you want, your mother's?" he said cruelly. It was as if he plunged a knife into my heart; he knew my mother was gassed in Auschwitz. But the thought that I might have a chance to expose him to the authorities held me back from slapping him in his face. The next day, I gave him a "yes" answer. He picked me up in front of my barrack. I carried a blanket with me.

"What's that blanket for?" he asked.

"To sit on a patch of grass behind my barrack."

"Preposterous!" He stamped his feet.

"Then take me to a restaurant in town; make your choice!" He debated with himself then agreed to my terms. We sat down on the blanket. He looked like an overgrown boy. He was perhaps five feet four inches tall and skinny like a rail. He didn't realize that the patch of grass we sat on was about four yards behind the window of the room I shared with my sister, Rose. My sister was to watch from behind a curtained window every move Stanislav made and come to my aid when necessary.

During the two, maybe three minutes we spoke, I told him that I had a father in America and that he sends me cigarettes and coffee on a regular basis. He asked me whether I knew what I could buy for cigarettes. "I could buy you," I smiled. "I have plenty of cigarettes from my friends, the American soldiers! I buy my dates with them!" He looked at me as if saying, 'Ha! Ha'!

He seemed to have had enough of talking. He forced his lips on mine, while trying to take hold of one of my breasts.

I jumped to my feet and called out, "Pig!" Before I could utter another word, Rose was next to me waving a broom at Stanislav.

"Who are you?" He asked in dismay.

"My mother came back from the gas chamber to protect me!" I looked at him with contempt. "Crazy, provincial woman!" He raised his voice and left.

I stopped working in the office. Now I had time to do acrobatic gymnastics on the abandoned equipment on the grounds. Sometimes, I'd see Sigmund watching me from behind a barrack.

One day, Sigmund broke the news to me. The camp was closing and we would be taken to different displaced persons' camps in Germany. There would be five transports, each several months apart. He, Sigmund, would be in the first transport, and Rose and I would be in the last.

So Stanislav is avenging my budged up date with him by putting me in the last transport? I'll outsmart him! I'll be in the first transport! I'll find a way! And a way I found. If cigarettes can buy diamonds, why can't they buy my way into the first transport?

Two packs of cigarettes did the job. The smugglers staged a brawl in the front of the train. As Stanislav and his helpers rushed to the front to see what happened, the smugglers whisked Rose and me into the last car of the train.

The night before the first transport was to depart for Germany, I said good-bye to Sigmund. I pretended I was patiently waiting for the last transport I was assigned to. I offered him two packs of cigarettes to have on his trip. He refused my offer. I convinced him I had enough cigarettes to last me three months. He still wouldn't hear of it. I then thought of a Yiddish saying, "Mountains don't meet; people do!"

Suddenly, it was as if he woke up. He looked at me; his eyes glazed. I knew he wanted me. Another minute and I would have screamed. I fell on his neck and gave him a passionate kiss. It was the kiss I held back from Ferenz for 13 years. I turned around and started running. Suddenly, I realized I still had the cigarettes I'd offered him. I stopped and looked back. Sigmund stood put. I ran toward him. I held out the cigarettes and said, "I have a feeling we'll meet again, Sigmund! Take the cigarettes and promise to pay me double someday!"

Sigmund took the cigarettes. He seemed to be choked up. He lifted his right hand into the air. I could've sworn I heard the wind whispering his wishful thinking, 'I swear I'll never stop paying you or loving you'! And pay me he did, for 60 glorious years of love, devotion and understanding.

I don't recall how long we traveled from Salzburg to Germany. I do remember when we arrived at Wetzlar where there was a displaced persons' camp run by the American soldiers.

Around 7:00 p.m., passengers from three cars of the train starting, with the last car, were loaded into trucks and taken into the camp. When Rose and I wanted to ascend one of the trucks, Stanislav said, "You tricked me! You stay! No truck for you! Walk to the camp!"

"This is preposterous! You can't do this to us!"

"Watch me!" he said, ascending the train that would take the rest of the transport, including himself, to another destination in Germany.

"You're a scoundrel; the American soldiers are going to hear about you," I uttered. "Yeah? I could've left you in any town in Austria when I found out you were on the train! I'm a gentleman after all!"

Rose embraced me; I leaned my head on her shoulder. "Don't worry, we have our ammunition," she said.

We went into the waiting room and sat on a bench huddled together. A man walked in, went to the ticket window and talked to a clerk. "Why don't I talk to the clerk and offer him cigarettes for taking us into the camp in the morning?" I said to Rose. The clerk was not surprised at my proposal, but he wanted to consult with his superior. Ten minutes later, he gave me an answer. For three packs of cigarettes, he'd take us into the camp in the morning. He also promised to keep an eye on us during the night.

We arrived at Wetzlar Displaced Persons' Camp. We complained about Stanislav to the American soldiers in charge. Our complaints fell on deaf ears. My sister and I figured it all out: Stanislav could not be touched; he was a black-marketeer! He had accomplices here!

I contacted Father and gave him our new address. Cigarettes and coffee began arriving regularly. Two months later, I thought I'd had enough of socializing, and decided to look for work. I entered the camp's employment office. Behind an impressive wooden carved desk there sat Sigmund. We locked eyes. We were meant for each other! I saw myself jumping up and down; wrapping my arms around his neck; suffocating him with my kisses, when reality set in.

"Mountains don't meet, Livia, people do!" Sigmund said as his face lit up.

I regained my posture. "I'm here for a job." I lowered my head to control my emotions. He smiled. Was he guessing my turmoil and maybe combining it with his?

"I don't have a job for a translator; I have a job for public relations," he said. I accepted the job.

We developed an inseparable relationship. He'd walk me home from my office on a daily basis. He talked about the circumstances that brought him to Wetzlar. He began with Salzburg. Stanislav, together with three American officers, were in charge of the transport to Germany. They had decided to route the people from the front four cars of the first transport to the Displaced Persons' Camp in Munich, Germany. In Munich, Sigmund befriended a Jewish-American officer. He told him he had attended a pedagogical institute in Lemberg, and would the officer advise him what to do about continuing his studies here.

His friend gave him a list of five displaced persons' camps with names of universities outside those camps. Sigmund picked Wetzlar. "With a name like Wetzlar," he said to me, "only something good could happen." And something good has happened; we met again!" I took his words, "We met again," as a declaration of love.

I love you, too, my mind repeated. I asked him how long he was in Wetzlar before we met again.

"Four weeks! Four wasted weeks!" Sigmund said.

What a way of reinforcing his declaration of love to me. I was in seventh heaven. I convinced him to eat fresh food a few times a week with us. He enjoyed my sister Rose's cooking.

Then, the unexpected happened. One day, Stanislav walked into Sigmund's office in Wetzlar and found us talking.

"What is she doing here?" he pointed at me in contempt.

"She's working in public relations."

Stanislav was infuriated. "She must go!"

"I was put in charge of this office by an America captain; he's my boss, not you," Sigmund told Stanislav. Soon, both of us got fired. We realized that Stanislav would visit this camp quite often and throw his weight around. He'd sometimes hire no-good idlers to beat Sigmund up. I remember one time these hooligans were standing under the window of the room Rose and I lived in, waiting for Sigmund to show up. Rose immediately got into action; she took a pot with hot water and threw it out the window. Those hoodlums never showed up again.

Sigmund wanted to register at Phillips University, but had no means. German money had no value. So I asked him what the registration fee would be in cigarettes. He said, "Two cartons." And so it was: Two cartons of cigarettes every semester for two years. From time to time, I'd go to the university with Sigmund. He introduced me to the young woman he had sexual relations with.

For the puritans in the United States. In Europe, women were brought up to bring innocence to their weddings. For the convenience of men's sexual needs, prostitution was legalized. Prostitutes in Europe were examined by State doctors every week for venereal diseases in order to prevent transmission. Young women like myself who were in steady relationships, actually encouraged their boyfriends to visit these prostitutes. Thus, they could remain virgins. Moreover, young men of means would seek sexual favors from widows and divorcees who were desperate for money to raise

Wedding day. Livia and Sigmund with Rose and her husband Mendel.

their families. I was grateful to the young woman at the university and to show my gratitude, from time to time, I'd buy gifts for her.

Life was a dream for Sigmund and me. We never missed a Saturday night dance. There was no alcohol allowed at these dances. We didn't miss alcohol; we were drunk with love. One Saturday evening, we arrived at the dance just to find out that someone smuggled in a few cases of beer. Temptation took hold of me and I drank a few cans.

Sunday passed and Monday passed and Sigmund hadn't shown up. I rushed to my best friend Ruth's house and found Sigmund in a corner, his hands covering his face. I asked Ruth whether he was in an accident that deformed his face. I said, he didn't have to worry; I'll be at his side for the rest of my life no matter how he looked!"

"Don't you remember?" Ruth said.

"Remember what?"

"You broke up with him Saturday at the dance!"

I began laughing; I didn't remember a thing. Then it dawned on me; I must've been drunk and talking nonsense!

Within the next week, we moved to Bamberg, Germany; we stayed with Rose who had married Mendel Kahn a few months earlier. I told Rose I was ready to marry Sigmund.

Rose was overwhelmed with happiness. She had not only saved the life of her sister, Libelah, in the concentration camps, now she would see her get married. No matter what type of marriage, she must give Libelah a religious wedding.

I took no part in the organizing of my own wedding. I was basking in the splendor of love with my soon to be husband, Sigmund Krancberg.

Sigmund and I were legally married on March 9, 1948 in Marburg, Germany. Three months later, we had our religious wedding ceremony in Bamburg, Germany. It was a beautiful day in June, 1948. The canopy under which the ceremony took place was built outdoors. It was to be officiated by the Rabbi of Bamberg. I stood under the canopy wearing a white blouse, a short blue skirt and a white wedding veil I personally rented from a German woman for one pack of cigarettes. I looked at the strange faces of people holding lit candles completing the circle in which Sigmund and I appeared overwhelmed and tense.

According to the ritual, we were circling. The woman in back of me tripped, her candle touched my veil. Aaah! My veil caught fire. Rose, my savior once more, jumped out from the circle and cupped my face in her hands, threw me down to the ground and covered my body with hers. None of us sustained burns.

The year 1949 was a turning point in our lives. Thanks to the DP Act sponsored by President Truman, Sigmund and I arrived in the United States of America in April, on the Ocean Liner SS Hershey. I was pregnant with our first daughter, Shelly. Rose had arrived in the United States at the same time by airplane with twin boys, Julius and Michael. Mazel Tov!